BALLISTS,
DEAD BEATS,
AND MUFFINS

To ML,
who rescued me
from countless disasters
of my own making and
is a great, trusted &
treasured friend —
with great affection!
Rob Sampson
4-15-2023

BALLISTS, DEAD BEATS, AND MUFFINS

Inside Early Baseball in Illinois

ROBERT D. SAMPSON

UNIVERSITY OF
ILLINOIS PRESS
Urbana, Chicago, and Springfield

Publication supported by a grant from the
Winton U. Solberg US History Subvention Fund.

Library of Congress Cataloging-in-Publication Data
Names: Sampson, Robert, 1949– author.
Title: Ballists, dead beats, and muffins : inside
    early baseball in Illinois / Robert D. Sampson.
Description: Urbana : University of Illinois Press,
    [2023] | Includes bibliographical references and
    index.
Identifiers: LCCN 2022045146 (print) | LCCN
    2022045147 (ebook) | ISBN 9780252045059
    (cloth) | ISBN 9780252087189 (paperback) |
    ISBN 9780252054341 (ebook)
Subjects: LCSH: Baseball—Illinois—History—
    19th century.
Classification: LCC GV875.I3 S26 2023 (print) |
    LCC GV875.I3 (ebook) | DDC 796.35709773—
    dc23/eng/20220930
LC record available at https://lccn.loc.gov/2022045146
LC ebook record available at https://lccn.loc.gov/2022045147

To Christine L. Sipula, whose love, patience, and support made this and all things possible; to my parents, the late Charles F. and Floretta Weber Sampson; and to the memory of those who first played the game on the fields of Illinois.

CONTENTS

ACKNOWLEDGMENTS

Individual achievement does not exist in historical research and writing. Behind every page, every footnote, and every choice lies a network of individuals without whom the book would have floundered on its decade-long path.

The late Bill Kreuger, a retired English professor from Millikin University in Decatur, Illinois, set the trap that ensnared me. In the late 1980s, scavaging 1860s-era newspapers to reconstruct daily life tidbits for living history program volunteers, Kreuger found a few articles about a baseball team. Among these was an intriguing reference to the Grand Base Ball Tournament of the Western States, which nearly collapsed amid controversy and hard feelings. Like Kreuger, I was part of the Macon County Conservation District's Prairie Heritage Volunteer Program, united around the Trobaugh-Good House, an 1850s-era log cabin now on the National Register of Historic Places. Leading the program was R. Lee Slider, the district's cultural interpreter, a genius in attracting enthusiastic people and letting them develop previously unknown talents. Kreuger went on to write programs drawn from mid-nineteenth-century letters and his research into old newspapers.

Kreuger's tantalizing nugget, the Grand Base Ball Tournament of the Western States, remained half-buried in my mind until about 2010. Looking for a new research project, I remembered the tournament and its controversies. Envisioning a one-and-done journal article, I plunged into the thicket. A decade later, I emerged with a complicated story involving community rivalries, hopes and disappointments, gambling, at least one free-for-all, racial discrimination, humor, and a game evolving from two words "base ball" to one, and transformed from a "gentleman's game" to a contest emphasizing winning above all. "'The Spirit of Discord Arose': The Birth Pangs of Base Ball in Central Illinois, 1866–1868" (*Journal of Illinois History* 15 (Winter 2012) was the first result. But as a great newspaper editor, Fran Reidelberger, used to say of my copy, it "raised more questions than it answered." Examples from mentors in the University of Illinois history department—Robert W. Johannsen, James R. Barrett, Walter L. Arnstein, and John M. Hoffmann— prodded me deeper into the thicket. Were the difficulties of teams in Decatur, Bloomington, Springfield, and Pana unique or did other Illinois ball clubs have problems finding and retaining playing fields or did any endure disputes over rules and gambling, and did their community support fluctuate between boosterism and condemnation?

Answers to these brought more questions. Drawn deeper into those times, patterns slowly emerged. Images of players and events obscured by 150 years came into focus. During days and nights peering into a microfilm viewer, their enthusiasm became palpable to me. Their quarrels and shouts, laughter and fun echoed across time.

Jan Perone, then head of the Abraham Lincoln Presidential Library and Museum's Newspaper Microfilm Library, and her assistant, Debbie Ross, opened my window to the past by making available every extant Illinois newspaper between 1865 and 1870. They provided tips, insights, and guidance at critical times. Not the least was their willingness to ship the reels to Millikin University's library, allowing me to check them out for use at home. Jan Perone found a large, old-fashioned microfilm reader (an endangered species these days). Its purchase made possible my working from home on days free from my classes at Millikin and on other days before and after class. Those two things—a microfilm reader and easy access to the reels—accelerated this book. Millikin's director of interlibrary loans at the time, Ruth Nihiser, signed off on the plan and facilitated my requests for new reels. Not long after I finished the microfilm work, the executive director of the Abraham Lincoln Presidential Library and Museum stopped loaning newspaper microfilms to other libraries. Had this individual arrived sooner or my research taken longer, you would not be reading these words.

Others on the museum's staff lent important assistance. Teri Barnett, Jan Perone's successor at the Newspaper Microfilm Library, helped me tie up loose ends after microfilm circulation ended. Meghan Harmon, a reference librarian, dug out various files, census reports, and city directories and had them ready at the library's reading room. Lincoln Museum historians Christian McWhirter and Jake Friefeld and former Abraham Lincoln Collection Curator James Cornelius offered encouragement and help. Roberta

Fairburn, a Lincoln Museum technical assistant, located, scanned, and sent several photographs.

Additional assistance with illustrations was provided by Lisa R. Marine, image production and licensing manager at the Wisconsin Historical Society; Jim Orr, image services specialist at the Henry Ford Museum; John Horne, coordinator of rights and reproductions at the National Baseball Hall of Fame; and Jenny Marie Johnson at the University of Illinois's Map and Geography Library. Eric Edwards and Joe Natale of the Illinois State Library in Springfield tracked down the source of an important illustration.

Brent Wielt, Slider's successor as cultural interpreter at the Macon County Conservation District, provided tips about sources, especially an illustration of the Grand Base Ball Tournament of the Western States site.

Decades ago, I learned that librarians are the historian's best friend. The good ones anticipate materials useful in your research and find connections to more. John M. Hoffmann, the retired director of the University of Illinois's Illinois History and Lincoln Collections, knows more about Illinois history—of all types—than anyone in the state. His aid and especially his friendship made my job less stressful. The University of Illinois's Geography Library, an incredible resource for maps, provided an 1867 Illinois map displaying its burgeoning railroad network. This map, when overlaid with baseball club locations, illustrates the connection between transportation and the spread of the game.

My research led to local libraries. All were helpful. Standing out are Merredith Peterson, president of the Rock Island County Historical Society, who oversees a wonderfully organized and accessible collection; Rici Dale of Ottawa's Reddick Public Library, who steered me through local maps and city directories to find the location of the city's first baseball field and provided information on the city's history; and Becky Damptz, director of the Local History Room at Decatur's public library. Curtis Mann, head of Springfield's Lincoln Library Sangamon Valley Collections, and his staff consistently met my requests and, again, pointed me in new directions during the project's early days.

A trip to Cairo, Illinois, a once-thriving Illinois community ravaged by a changing economy, population loss, and difficult, sometimes violent, race relations, included a visit to its beautifully maintained library. Like most things in Cairo, volunteers run the library. Preston Ewing, who also doubles as a volunteer city government official, greeted me and revived the mid-1960s for me, a time when, as leader of the local NAACP branch, he visited the campus of Eastern Illinois University in Charleston where I was a student.

We shared memories of those days and common friends as he offered rich insights into Cairo's colorful past. He too helped me locate an early ball field.

Research is demanding and sometimes dull. As with Preston Ewing in Cairo, people enlivened the journey. Lee Slider, a good friend, was my companion on occasional excursions. In Decatur, we tromped through weeds covering rough ground lying at the intersection of two railroads, using vague descriptions to find the city's first ball field. Later, he tagged along to Centralia, where we explored its library's collections and met a local historian, Steve Loomis. Loomis wrote an outstanding history of the game's start and early years in Centralia. We spent hours with him, including time at the Centralia Area Historical Society's Museum, trying to find old photos, tying up dangling threads of information, and gaining a greater understanding of why Centralia's Egyptian Base Ball Club was important in its time. Loomis also helped later when questions arose.

Dan Monroe, as chair of Millikin University's Department of History and Political Science, encouraged me to develop a baseball history course and, as the author of three books himself, provided sound advice.

Since the initial research focused on the Decatur tournament and a Bloomington club's divisive role there, an early stop was the McLean County Historical Society's library led by Bill Kemp. Kemp, whose quiet manner overlays deep knowledge and insights into Illinois history, led me through the library's holdings and answered repeated questions about local Sunday blue laws and neighborhood composition. On short notice, he located, scanned, and sent magnified map sections and other illustrations. He and volunteer Terri Clemens tracked down the post-baseball life of several Black players.

To all these individuals and others unnamed, I offer my deepest thanks.

This project might have failed without the support of the University of Illinois Press. Its editor-in-chief when I made my book proposal, Willis G. Regier, embraced the project and kept up his kind encouragement until he retired. His successor, James Engelhardt, never flagged in enthusiasm for the book he inherited, though there was little to it at first beyond a journal article and vague outlines. James offered key ideas and suggestions as the work took shape. After Engelhardt's departure in the summer of 2020, Alison Syring and then Daniel Nasset kept the flame burning while the press struggled with understaffing and COVID-related challenges. Martha Bayne joined the press in late summer 2021 and brought the project home. Her critiques of the manuscript vastly improved it and made me a better writer. Mariah Mendes Schaefer, assistant acquisitions editor, oversaw the book's production, dealing patiently with a disorganized author's foibles. Other press staffers adding their talents to this work are Heather Garrett, publicity manager; Michael Roux, marketing director; senior editor Tad Ringo; Kevin Cunningham, copywriter; and Kristina Stonehill, social media manager.

The late famed historian, Arthur M. Schlesinger Jr., reportedly could "write to galley," meaning the work he handed in to publishers need not be copyedited. Not blessed with such talent, many including myself rely on the sharp eyes and quick minds of copy editors. Geof Garvey, a freelance copy editor for the press, cleaned up my mangled prose, correcting grammatical and stylistic mistakes with patience and good humor. Every change he recommended made this book better. Freelancer Judy Davis skillfully produced the index. I am indebted to both.

Thanks goes to the two anonymous readers whose criticisms and recommendations made the manuscript better.

The only person to write a similar state history of early baseball, Peter Morris, demonstrated how to translate solid research into interesting writing in *Baseball Fever: Early Baseball in Michigan* and, later, in *But Didn't We Have Fun? An Informal History of Baseball's Pioneer Era, 1843–1870*. If one wants to understand the early game and how and why it evolved and at what costs, Morris's books are the place to start. Morris was always available for counsel and assistance.

One day in the summer of 1992, Lee Slider answered his phone and said "yes" to taking a group to Columbus, Ohio, for something called "vintage base ball." I was one of those making the trip and playing. Thirty years later, I'm still playing. Though approaching the topic as a historian, playing without gloves to cushion a hard baseball's impact while wearing hot uniforms in humid midwestern weather gave me an appreciation for the players who did the same between 1865 and 1870. My vintage base ball friends in New York, Ohio, Indiana, Michigan, Minnesota, Missouri, and Illinois offered encouraging words. I hope this provides them and others playing the game with mid-19th century rules greater understanding of the era they recreate.

When she met me in late 2004, Christine L. Sipula did not realize what she was getting herself into, things such as politics, vintage base ball, and the travails of historical research and writing. Nevertheless, she married me and, during the past fifteen years, has sat patiently through innumerable long, hot, sometimes rainy afternoons watching old men pretend they are young on roughhewn playing fields or putting up with my absences to scroll newspaper microfilm or to write or to simply get lost in thought over an unresolved question leaving me absent while present. Without her love and support, this project would have ended with the first journal article. Appreciation extends as well to my sons [Darrell Joseph and Ryan McClenahan Sampson] and son-in-law [Joshua Israel] who respectfully listened to my old baseball stories and to my two grandsons [Charles Robert Sampson and Frederick Paul Israel-Sampson] who will hopefully one day find the product interesting.

My deep appreciation goes to all mentioned above and those who were not but also played a role as simple as a kind word at the right time. All are responsible for the good things in this book. Any errors or misinterpretations belong to me.

A DYING EMBER

Americans of all ages, all stations in life, and all types
of dispositions are forever forming associations.
—Alexis de Tocqueville, *Democracy in America*[1]

Early afternoon on October 13, 1869, lines of people stream onto the
Quincy, Illinois, fairgrounds to see the talk of the sporting world—the
Cincinnati Red Stockings Base Ball Club, returning from tours through the
East and Midwest and games in San Francisco, California, with an unblem-
ished record. They and the hometown Occidental Senior Base Ball Club await
the contest between the founding ideals of "base ball" (then spelled as two
words) and the new reality of professionalism.[2]

The Ohio club is the finest in the land. Its players, dashingly attired in white
knickers and red stockings, have been lured to Cincinnati from throughout
the country by dollars. Only one is a Cincinnati resident. Baseball tradi-
tionalists find the club's existence and success troubling.[3] Paid players raise
disturbing implications for a self-proclaimed gentlemen's game, undermin-
ing the amateur nature of a sport that for the past four years swept through
nearly every village, town, or hamlet in Illinois large enough to field a team
of nine. If players are harvested far and wide and compete for money rather
than exercise, sportsmanship, and the prestige of their community, what
happens to the amateur game?

James Shoaff, from his editorial chair at Decatur's *Magnet*, answered, "Base
ball is being killed by the growing custom of employing professionals to do
the hard work and play the matches." But people paid to see the best players.[4]

Even before the Red Stockings arrived in Quincy, the game's transforma-
tion was under way. By its third year, Quincy's Occidental Senior Base Ball
Club slipped behind its auxiliary, the Occidental Juniors. Once Quincy's
most successful team, the senior club's critics now diagnosed its failings. A
victory that summer over a St. Louis club left a local newspaper disappointed

because the Occidental Seniors failed to dominate their foe, demonstrating the team's unfitness to compete with the state's leading clubs. The reason, the editor charged, was simple: "want of practice." The club admitted inferior players who refused to practice, undercutting its potential.

Responding in a letter to the editor, an anonymous player shifted the blame to local citizens and the press who failed to support the club. "Let them encourage us by their presence at practice as well as match games both home and abroad. Let them aid us by donating a few dollars every year for the support of the club." Financial support could aid with travel and other expenses, relieving the players' pockets. Moreover, because the club had lost but one game, the editor's complaint made no sense. Unconvinced, the editor replied in the next edition, repeating his main point: "No man should be excused from practice games unless he has attained such perfection or skill as the club aims at." If a player didn't have time to practice, he should yield his position to one who would.[5]

Ignored alike by critics and defenders was the main reason for the Occidental Senior's disappointments—lack of athletic skill. Endless practice could never overcome inferior talent. A Quincy editor renamed the senior club "the Accidentals," after whimsically describing its players missing catches or being hit by errant balls, only gaining for their trouble "sore heads, black eyes and broken fingers, sprained ankles, . . . swelled knees, skinned shins, torn clothes." As they took the field at the fairgrounds that October day, the talented Red Stockings left nothing to chance. They were professionals.[6]

The failings of the Occidental Seniors and the consequent dissatisfaction of the press were not unique to Quincy. Similar editorial grumbles could be heard across the state because, as the game took root, ball clubs became symbols of civic pride. A team's performance reflected not only on its nine players but on the whole community.

Struggles like those of the Occidental Seniors occurred throughout adult baseball clubs as the 1860s ended. Among the challenges were junior clubs, players usually between sixteen and eighteen years of age, whose performance eclipsed their parent, adult team. Earlier in 1869, the *Quincy Herald* editor, reviewing the state of the game nationally, described enthusiasm for baseball as surging. But now, he added, local senior clubs were yielding to the juniors.[7] For 1869, the Occidental Seniors planned an abbreviated schedule. Beginning by hosting top teams from St. Louis and Rockford, the club's season would culminate with the Red Stockings in October. July 5's opener against the St. Louis Olympics reinforced critics' complaints: the Quincy Senior club fell 45 to 16. To compete in a new environment with more professional clubs, a newspaper harped, demanded systematic and faithful practice. Illustrating the generational shift, the Occidental Juniors came closer to the St. Louis club the next day, losing by a 31–20 margin. A newspaper editor noted the youngsters' superiority against the seniors. Not by coincidence, the senior club soon added junior players to its roster.[8]

Besides athletic skills, financial demands increased pressures on the senior club. The Occidentals moved to a new playing field to host Rockford's Forest City Base Ball Club, the state's best team, including future Hall of Famer Albert Goodwill Spalding.

At the fairgrounds, admission could be charged. It was needed to cover the Forest City Club's appearance fee. The fifty-cent ticket charge drew even more grumbling than the 43 to 7 shellacking administered by the Forest City Club. Signing himself "I. C. A. Schwindle," a spectator complained to the *Quincy Whig and Republican*. He had no objection to letting the home club earn some money, but he bridled at dividing the money among refreshment concessionaires, the ground's managers, hotels, and "foreign ball clubs." Although he wanted the Occidental Club to succeed, "Schwindle" urged reducing admission by half or raising private subscriptions and returning to the old—and free—home field, a reference to Alstyne's Prairie, an open space within Quincy's city limits.[9]

A bigger price tag came with the Red Stockings—the Cincinnati club demanded $250 plus expenses for the game. (Adjusting for the rate of inflation, that charge equals $5,314.50 in 2022.[10]) Playing up the professional club's stature, newspapers promoted the game as a chance to see "the fearful and remarkable batting and fielding of the red-legged nine . . . who, not satisfied with beating the world, propose to beat Quincy." The newspaper's next issue reminded readers that the chance to see the country's finest players should draw a large crowd. Left unsaid was the need for strong ticket sales with the Occidental Club obligated to meet the guarantee.[11]

Observing the traditions of the old game, some Quincy players met the Red Stockings at the depot and escorted them to a local hotel. Later, ten carriages carried the visitors to view Quincy's sights.

By 2 p.m., both clubs and many spectators were on the playing grounds. The game unfolded as promised—at least on the Red Stockings' part—as they awed the crowd with their fielding and batting. Cincinnati line drives sizzled into all fields, striking two people in the crowd. A woman watching from a carriage was knocked senseless by a ball while another drive jolted a boy lying in the grass. "The only wonder is that no one was badly hurt as the batting of the Red Stockings was at times terrific and foul balls occasionally went crashing into the crowd, causing a momentary stampede," a reporter noted. There was also a stampede of Red Stockings players across home plate, as their team prevailed 51 to 7.[12]

Spectators indeed had witnessed baseball's future, a new game requiring superlative skill and ensuring competitive demand for the best players wherever they resided. The old game, the "gentleman's game," died that day on Quincy's fairgrounds. So too did the Occidental Senior Base Ball Club. It never played again.[13]

A Pivotal Moment

This snapshot of a long-forgotten baseball game captures both the sport's past and its future. October 13, 1869, was a pivotal moment in the baseball craze that swept Illinois from 1865 through 1870. For five years, Illinoisans enthusiastically embraced baseball, creating some 690 organized clubs playing the game between 1865 and 1869. An estimated 380 more were added in 1870 for a total of well over 1,000. Nearly all these clubs featured constitutions, by-laws, committees, and regular meetings. Men came together, following formal procedures, organizing for fun, exercise, and comradeship. Most of these clubs were outside Chicago, the state's largest city, teams sprouting in remote places now vanished from the map. (See appendix A.)[14]

Popping up, thriving, and then floundering, the Illinois baseball clubs may appear as single trees, solitary sentinels of local phenomena unrelated to other clubs. But close examination of the game, how it was played and by whom, its underlying principles and its struggles to maintain those ideals, reveals a forest, a big picture blanketing the state with the game and its conflicts. Competition occurred not only on the playing field but eventually among communities, some of whom came to see the game as a source of pride, publicity, and advantage.

Baseball's arrival in Illinois communities was more a social phenomenon than a sporting activity, especially with the early emphasis on fun and inclusion. Though important (and sometimes the source of hot dispute), baseball's rules were augmented with unwritten customs and rituals. The rituals served to tamp down competition and ensure friendly feelings and fellowship among clubs.[15]

On and off the field, the game proved an exciting pastime, generating levels of enthusiasm akin to a contagion infecting both participants and spectators alike. But, as time passed, the emphasis on winning increased as small towns and cities jockeyed for commercial, economic, or social superiority. A winning ball club was a feather that many communities wanted in their cap.

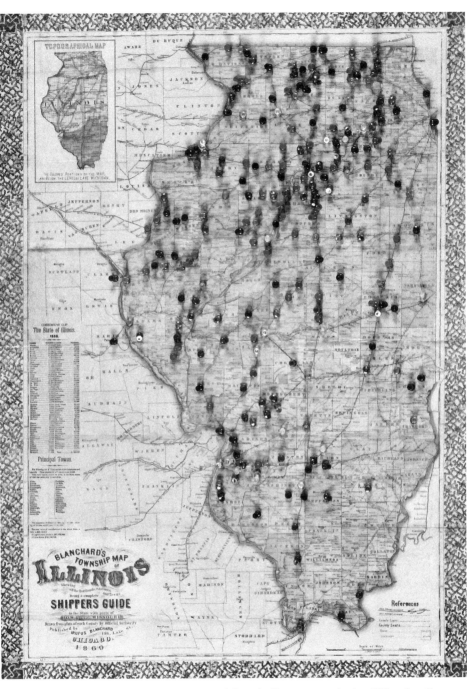

Colored pins noting communities with baseball teams overlaying "Blanchard's Township Map of Illinois . . . and Shipper's Guide," 1869. It illustrates how the game spread along railroad lines and rivers, each providing transportation for baseball clubs traveling to other communities. Base map courtesy of the Map Library at the University of Illinois at Urbana–Champaign.

The competitive spirit brought with it unforeseen problems—rule disputes, difficulties between umpires and spectators, players imported from other teams to provide an edge, failures to observe the unwritten customs and rituals. The early euphoria, then, soured as the nature of the competition changed.

Furthermore, baseball did not exist in a social vacuum. It reflected the prejudices of the time, especially about Blacks and women, notably when those groups sought to join in the fun. Denied the opportunity to play on or against white teams, Black players used their own agency to compete against each other and, on rare occasions, against white teams. In doing so, these pioneers faced discrimination and condescension, especially in press coverage. Attempts by women to play the game were mocked by the press.

Outside the organized club structure, games between white and black players or mixed teams or women likely occurred. Unorganized baseball was precisely that—no clubs, no formalities, but instead largely impromptu games that were, at times, disruptive. Newspapers did not cover the informal meetings, and the record, save for when players interfered with traffic or a neighborhood's peace, is blank.

Between 1865 and 1870, baseball's popularity grew and spread unevenly. Some towns and villages were early adapters; others came late to the game. Local enthusiasm sputtered in one community as it kindled in another. Setbacks from concerns over gambling and disappointed expectations, for example, came earlier in some places than in others. And baseball fever, having passed over a community, suddenly could erupt there.

Baseball in this period cut across social, class, and economic lines. Players sprang from a variety of occupational and social backgrounds, and athletic skill was not necessarily required. Over time, clubs with sufficient members created "first nines," teams featuring the best players with other players relegated to the "second nine" or the "muffin nine," the latter the poorest athletes. Important to note is that clubs existed to *play* baseball, and the vast majority of play occurred within a club and not through match games against other clubs.

By the 1869 and 1870 seasons, however, the momentum toward competitive games increased, forcing clubs to contend with a new set of expectations. Most of the adult clubs composed of men in their late teens and early to mid-twenties responded by simply dropping out.

The experience of the Quincy Occidental Senior Club in playing the professional Red Stockings vividly illustrates this new era, one dominated by athletic talent. No amount of practice, determination, or community support could overcome deficiencies of skill or give the part-time Occidental Seniors a victory against men who played the game for a living.

As a result, by 1870, the old game, the one that had arrived between 1865 and 1867, was dead as an organized activity for amateur adult men. The new game, the competitive game, was left to junior clubs and professional teams like the Forest City Club of Rockford and Chicago's White Stockings. Now, for some top junior club games and all contests involving professionals, spectators had to buy tickets.

That October game in 1869 between the Occidental Seniors and the Red Stockings represents a dying ember of the fiery enthusiasm for baseball in Illinois that manifested with its arrival in 1865. While by 1870 professionalism and the importance of winning extinguished the old game, baseball did not go away. Adults still played informally (and later more formally on town teams) and left no accounts of their games. But then, why would they? The new game, while shaped by its casual birthing years, was more competitive, exclusive, and exciting. The inclusive ideals and rituals of the old game were irrelevant. Now what mattered most was who won.

Baseball's Birth and Evolution

Baseball did not spring, like Athena, full-grown from someone's brain. Neither Abner Doubleday nor Alexander Cartwright played a role. For more than 150 years, the game's roots were obscured by deliberate distortion and lack of serious scholarly interest. That changed in the last decades of the twentieth century when careful research found baseball's true origins. But those historians looked largely at the New York City area, providing no insights into how and why Illinoisans passionately embraced baseball in the post–Civil War years.

The game we know as baseball emerged from playing fields in and around Manhattan in the 1830s and 1840s. Resembling a multitude of other bat-and-ball games going back to ancient Egypt, the New York game, today's baseball, evolved from specific circumstances, needs, and uses that allowed it to sweep aside competitors like the Massachusetts game and "town ball" in the post–Civil War years. Even before the Civil War, the game gained a foothold in the old Northwest. As early as 1856, the Union Club of Chicago organized and played. In succeeding years, a small number of short-lived clubs rose in a few Illinois towns and cities, including Downers Grove, Waukegan, Bloomington, Pekin, Jacksonville, Byron, and Rockford.[16]

By 1858, two Alton clubs drew the attention of the leading sports periodical of the day, *Porter's Spirit of the Times*, published in New York City. At the northern edge of the state, Freeport, too, earned a baseball reputation before the post–Civil War boom. "Our city has been noted for the number and excellence of its ball clubs and ball players," bragged the *Freeport Bulletin*. Later, Freeport earned its own footnote in the game's history when an 1865 game between its club and the visiting Empire Club of St. Louis was among the first played with the "fly rule" in the West, bringing Illinois in line with the latest rule changes. Adopted in 1864 by the National Association of Base Ball Players, the fly rule eliminated the option of retiring a batter by catching fair and eventually foul balls on the first bound. Beginning in 1865, fielders had to take fair fly balls in the air and could no longer protect their fingers from hard-hit balls by letting the ground absorb the first impact. (For a few subsequent years, foul balls caught on the bound continued to be outs.) This was the game—without fielder's gloves or other protective equipment—played in Illinois.[17]

In describing the growth of baseball in Illinois, my reference point is organized clubs, not the spontaneous, disorganized, and sometimes disruptive play likely predating the 1865–69 period, raging throughout it, and continuing into the twentieth century. Americans invariably organize things, in pursuits as diverse as reading, dog agility, stamp and coin collecting, and stock investments. In short, about any activity or cause attracting like-minded people has been organized.

Three decades before the Civil War, Alexis de Tocqueville traveled through the United States, absorbing, comparing, and translating for his fellow Frenchmen the mysteries of a democratic society. He perceived the "associative principle" at the core of the young republic, describing a "thousand different types" of associations manifested everywhere he looked. Baseball players in the Prairie State followed familiar formalities, creating clubs with constitutions, by-laws, committees, regular meetings, and social activities, all to lend them purpose and legitimacy. While Illinois baseball clubs came together primarily for fun and exercise, there were other goals, not the least being character development. Governed by a set of expectations—how to treat and interact with opponents and how you should be treated in return—the organized baseball clubs played within a framework designed to *restrain* competition.[18]

Baseball, a subject that de Tocqueville sadly (for us) missed, offered many things to strike his fancy—its sudden adoption and growth in Illinois along transportation lines of railroads and rivers, the public's fascination with the game, its unique rules and language, uniforms and team names, the sheer number of places it reached, and its failure to disappear after the public's gradual cooling of attention.

To steal a phrase from John Thorn, the official historian of major league baseball, the 1860s Illinois game was a cauldron of fun, rituals, moral purpose, and civic pride, determining whose play is worthy of attention and whose is not—all recounted in newspaper commentary that boiled and simmered before turning tepid toward the end of the decade.[19]

As the game moved through Illinois, tracking along rivers and railroads, new clubs became identified with community images. The conjunction of a sport with civic self-image was new to Illinois and, during this period, baseball is better described as a social enthusiasm, one enlivening conversations on courthouse squares and merchants' emporiums from Cairo to Galena, and Danville to Quincy. The curious filled carriages and horse railway cars or just walked to see the game played or simply practiced.

Examining extant copies of the era's newspapers reveals the complex relationship between sport, economics, politics, and social activities that flourished, briefly, during baseball's embrace by Illinoisans. And so, like de Tocqueville in the 1830s, we begin our travels through an unfamiliar place.

Illinois's economy roared through four years of war, its population booming so that by 1865 its 2,100,000 residents ranked it fourth among the states. At war's end, the late historian John H. Keiser notes, Illinois was poised for "phenomenal growth." An overwhelmingly rural population orbited around the state's only metropolis, Chicago, with its railroads, warehouses, and mercantile suppliers. Fewer than one-half of the state's residents at the time were born in Illinois, more than one-fifth having taken up residence within the preceding five years. Seventy-six percent of Illinoisans relied on remote farm trading centers now reached, or hoping to be reached, by the burgeoning network of steel rails transforming the state.[20]

Post–Civil War Illinois was a place of contention, optimism, confrontation, competition, worry, and hope. Communities scrambled for an edge, be it a state university or a railroad connection or a winning baseball club. Alongside brief baseball reports, editors filled their columns with all sorts of matter, such as a eulogy for Tom, Quincy's town cat, who was found dead. "Alas, poor Thomas! It is sad, in the prime of life, when the days of your usefulness was just approaching, to be cut down as the spears of grass and torn from the festive scenes of earth." Municipal problems included wandering dogs, cattle, and hogs, the latter from Belleville to Joliet but especially bedeviling Danville, which suffered a hog stampede through its downtown streets. Racist language was the norm and editorial kindliness for humans, especially those considered outside "polite" society, did not match that shown the late feline, Tom. For instance, a woman derisively given a man's name, "Frank Douglas," was described by a Cairo editor as, "a lady whose virtue is easier than an old shoe." Illinois was still close enough to its frontier past that a public offering of bear steaks procured locally could be announced matter-of-factly.[21]

Into this world, brimming with confident spirits, came the Fairfield Snails, the Marshall One Gallows, the Mount Zion Sum Punkins, Rock Island's Lively Turtles, the Shakespeare Club of Bunker Hill, the Du Quoin Wallapus Club, and the intriguingly named Ashley Dead Beat Base Ball Club. Their stories and those of the other clubs tell us much not only about baseball but the times when they played the game enthusiastically until sun set over the prairie.

BASEBALL FEVER
AND PIONEERS

It attacks old and young alike.
—*Pike County Democrat,*
September 6, 1866[1]

Fresh from a September 1866 trip to the state capital at Springfield, the editor of Pittsfield's *Pike County Democrat* reported to his readers that "there is no cholera there." Yet, he cautioned, running rampant was another malady unknown in medical texts. "We suppose it may be called 'base ball on the brain,'" infecting "old and young alike—from the hoary headed veteran to the youngest child."

The malady transcended class and political affiliation. "Uncle Jesse has got it," he wrote, referring to former state auditor and Republican powerhouse Jesse Dubois. "And Starne has got it—Hatch slightly"—references to Democrat Alexander Starne and Ozias Mather Hatch, a leading Republican, both former elected state officials. Another prominent Illinois Republican, attorney Milton Hay, once thought immune to the fever, displayed symptoms after watching a game. Baseball paralyzed the capital city. "On the occasion of a match game, most of the business houses are closed and the city seems quite deserted," the editor continued. "In business hours on the street, go where you will and you hear the professional terms of the game flying in all directions. . . . We are satisfied that it is an epidemic needing no adventitious aid to cause it [*sic*] spread in all our cities. It is the *fashion* to have it and that insures its raging."[2]

Rage it did in postwar Illinois, seizing the attention of young men, boys, editors, young ladies, and others. "It is spreading like an epidemic," the *Chicago Tribune* observed. At Peoria, ballclubs sprouted everywhere. To the west, along the banks of the Mississippi, the *Quincy Herald* urged local young men to adopt the game. In northwestern Illinois, the *Sterling Gazette* pronounced the game "all the rage here—everybody's got it on the brain." And down where the Ohio and Mississippi rivers meet at Cairo, the craze crested. "Everybody is batting balls and running to bases—young, middle-aged and old."[3]

Alton produced clubs in the 1850s, but the game floundered and then revived in 1867. The *Alton Weekly Telegraph* ran a story copied from another paper, recounting a church deacon's prayer: "Oh, Lord, as we start for a home run to glory, don't let us by the devil be caught out on the fly!" Back in Springfield, the *Illinois State Journal* tracked the game's progress: "Last year we heard of 'the base ball mania.' What will it be called this year intensified as the 'mania' will be?" And places without clubs campaigned for them. The *Lee County Journal* wished for a club to demonstrate its superiority over neighboring communities. "We think we could outshine Dixon in the way of material."[4] Baseball fever spread beyond the playing fields. The editor of the *Pana Gazette*, about thirty miles south of Springfield, described a local businessman placing an advertisement: "He looks excited—something is evidently the matter. (Base ball on the brain, we guess)."[5]

Some resisted the fever. Near the Wisconsin border, a Galena editor scanned the exchange newspapers on his desk, their columns filled with stories about baseball. "But we don't see as these games have very much to do with the salvation of the country or the high price of butter," he wrote. Fed up with a constant barrage of game results, a Belleville editor grumbled, "We don't know as anyone has any objections to our young people playing base ball to their heart's content, but we do not think the general public quite so deeply interested in it as the players themselves. Indeed, the game has fast become a national nuisance and we do not feel disposed to add much fuel to the flame." A frustrated Springfield citizen voiced a complaint, requesting that the *Illinois State Journal* establish a "'Department' of your paper for the special purpose of giving intelligence respecting the 'national game' and to give an order that all telegrams and items relating thereto shall be place therein. We can then read our papers without annoyance."[6] And disgust was one editor's reaction to the whimsical story of the preacher who prayed before his congregation for "a home run for glory" uninterrupted by the devil catching them "out on a fly." "The game is being run too far and fast," and as to the baseball prayer, "If this is a fact the preacher ought to be caught out on a foul; if not, the editor who perpetuated the story."[7]

Such naysayers resisted more than the fervid embrace of a novelty. Entwined with the game was a prescription for a better America.[8] The *Chicago Times* echoed such sentiments, pronouncing the city's ballplayers to be noble young men, representing "the best blood of their respective communities."[9] "For the young men confined in stores or offices, a few hours playing at ball now and then . . . would be off [*sic*] great benefit," a Peoria editor observed, and "W. K. Beans," who wrote a school column for an Aurora newspaper, agreed. "One game of 'American Base' actively played would do more good than the most carefully prepared prescription that could be given."[10] The *Sterling Gazette* sounded the same theme, the editor envisioning an American people degenerating physically at a rapid pace since 1776. Now, he hoped, his countrymen were finally aroused by the new game, which promised a nation's regeneration. Baseball was the "national game."[11]

As the national pastime, baseball benefited from lack of serious competition. Cricket's tenuous foothold in some communities crumbled despite editorial endorsement. In Springfield and a few other places, editors tried to push cricket but, as baseball surged, cricket clubs faded.[12] Walking races generated minor enthusiasm, despite a Jacksonville editor's prediction they might supersede baseball. Neither was croquet taken seriously.[13] The "velocipedes" surge, an early version of bicycling, peaked by 1869. But that summer's hot weather spiked that fad's wheels in Peoria, while in Princeton the "velocipede fever" disappeared when city fathers proclaimed Main Street off limits for races.[14]

Baseball Pioneers

Like any contagion, baseball needed carriers, individuals transforming dreams into team nines. Who brought the national game to Illinois's cities, towns, villages, and crossroads? Who were its founders, the advance agents for its health, moral, and spiritual benefits?

In the summer of 1866, William Corwin Johns came home to Decatur on break from his studies at the University of Michigan. Earlier introduced to baseball at what today is Illinois State University in Normal, the left-handed Johns now pitched for the University of Michigan's team. Deciding to introduce his hometown to the game sweeping the Midwest, Johns borrowed a set of surveying instruments and engaged a bookkeeper and a high school student as helpers to lay out a field near the intersection of two railroads a short distance east of downtown Decatur. The future circuit court judge never claimed to be the father of the game in Decatur, but a local newspaper judged him to be just that forty-three years later. Later that summer, Johns and others organized the town's first club, the McPherson, named after Union General James "Birdseye" McPherson.[15]

Born into an elite Ohio family who came to Decatur in 1849 and befriended Abraham Lincoln, Johns was named for his father's friend, Ohio

Judge W. C. Johns, the father of baseball in Decatur, in his later years. Courtesy of the Abraham Lincoln Presidential Library and Museum.

politician Thomas Corwin, who served as governor of Ohio, as US secretary of the treasury, and in both Houses of Congress. When Corwin visited Decatur in 1861, his namesake delivered a speech, written by his mother, Jane. Years later, W. C. Johns recalled it as a "cracking good effort." Looming equally large in his memories of that event was a conversation with Thomas Corwin. During his early years in the House of Representatives, Corwin, a

Whig, earned notoriety for "spirited and witty debate." An example of his stinging rhetoric came on February 14, 1840, when he rose in the House to reply to a Michigan militia general's attack on his party's candidate for president, William Henry Harrison, for deficient military skill. Corwin called up a vision of the leadership required by a militia general, his troops armed with "umbrella, hoe, axe handles, and other like deadly instruments of war." Driving home his point, Corwin pictured the militia general leading his troops mounted on "crop-eared mare, with bushy-tail and sickle-ham," a sight sure to "literally frighten off the battlefield a hundred Alexanders." The speech gave Corwin a national reputation—and cost him the presidency. At least that is what Thomas Corwin shared with his namesake in that evening's conversation. "Never be a clown," he warned, adding that save for that and similar speeches, leading voters outside Ohio to dismiss him as simply a humorous platform politician, he could have been president. As historian Peter Morris notes, during a long legal career culminating in his election to the bench, W. C. Johns was never accused of an excess of levity.[16]

Johns fits the typical picture of players in his era—young men with the occupation, money, or time to be available in the early afternoon. In childhood, Johns discovered the fun of striking a ball with a piece of wood when he and his companions played early ball games. As the preferred flat plank for batting was not readily available, the boys used whatever was at hand. "I was accustomed to swinging at a small rubber ball with a hickory club and had a fairly good eye for the game."[17]

Johns recalled learning what may have been the New York game (as opposed to town ball or round ball—other ball and bat games competing with baseball in this period) from a "Mr. Pillsbury" at the Normal school, who brought his knowledge of the game from Harvard. Although later known for his pitching, Johns gained Pillsbury's attention by his prowess with a round bat.[18] The judge's memories not only reveal the types of early baseball equipment, but one path followed in the game's spread—in this case from Normal, Illinois, to Ann Arbor, Michigan, to Decatur.

Aside from Judge Johns, identifying the pioneer who brought baseball to any community is a challenging task, as accounts of club organizational meetings fail to name the instigator. Johns's actions on that summer day in 1866 provide the only example of a recovered birth moment. Without newspaper stories decades later, we'd know nothing of Johns's role. And we know that only because a newspaperman became interested and started asking questions, importantly while the judge and some of his teammates were still alive. Without such interest and survivors, the stories are lost. Still, we can find people influential in growing the game even if they did not plant the seed.

Writing to the *Peoria National Democrat* on June 15, 1866, "M.A.S." recommended baseball. "The clerk at his counter, the book-keeper at his desk, the mechanic at his lathe, go to their work better fitted mentally and physically for the exercise of the duties devolving upon them after a few hours [*sic*] chase after the ball, and the utter weariness and lassitude which characterizes their daily succession of labor is dissipated as if by magic." The writer was Captain M. A. Stearns of the Eighteenth US Infantry, who was serving as recruiter in Peoria. He reappears in print on July 17, 1866, as one of several men calling a meeting to reorganize the Olympic Base Ball Club, which faded after the 1865 season. The meeting's attendees elected Stearns club president.[19]

Practicing on grounds between Jefferson and Madison streets, the new Olympic Club hosted an August 4 intraclub game. Picked nines of the club—one led by Stearns, the other by a player named Rugg—attracted many spectators, some on the ground, others watching from carriages. Playing was "scientific," the newspaper noted, using the favorite description for a well-played game, and lasted between three and four hours. Rugg's team emerged the victor.[20]

A few weeks later, the Olympics fell 53 to 35 to the Celestial Club of Pekin, from across the Illinois River. Stearns pitched for the Olympics. He remained at the position during his club's two games with Bloomington—the first at Peoria, a 76 (or 79) to 28 loss, and another defeat at Bloomington by a 49–33 margin.[21]

Stearns's final game for the Olympics was in October, against the Celestials, a rival from Peoria's September tournament. Stearn's pitched and again lost, and the captain's baseball career had ended, as he subsequently had to report to his new post at Fort Reno, Montana Territory. Stearns's role in pioneering Peoria baseball consisted of his letter promoting the game, his leadership in reorganization of the Olympics, and his service both as club president and as an active player.[22]

To a regular army officer assigned to a sleepy post in a peaceful country, baseball offered a release for energy and organizational skills. As he wrote to the *Peoria National Democrat*, "no reason exists why Peoria, the second city in the State, should be behind in the establishment of an institution which would result in so much benefit to her young men as a class." In the time he had, he did his part.[23]

A pioneer did not have to be a player.

"The base ball Mania is raging in all the cities of the country. It has reached Cairo," a newspaper in the deep southern Illinois city reported in August 1866—on the same page as a story tracking the progress of cholera. While difficult to assign the role of founder there, one name—Sol S. Silver—appears frequently—not as a player but as a club officer, scorer, promoter, and local businessman.[24]

Silver was present when Cairo's first baseball club, the Egyptians, was organized in July 1866. Attendees elected him a club director and to the committee to draft a constitution and by-laws. Described as an "eloquent auctioneer," Silver's business interests aside from auctioneering included selling books, newspapers, stationery, fine cigars, steamboat tickets, and various goods. A colorful character, his name appears frequently in newspaper briefs, commenting on his potential candidacy for local office, a fishing trip, and his efforts as a theatrical entrepreneur.[25]

A high profile in a small community ensures attention for someone like Silver. With wide-ranging interests and a flair for publicity, he was exactly the type of person to whip up and maintain enthusiasm for baseball. Silver is best termed a friend of the game, providing support off the playing field. In that role, he resembles Hiram Hungerford Waldo, president of Rockford's famous Forest City Club in the mid-1860s.

Described as Albert Goodwill Spalding's mentor by historian Peter Morris, Waldo remembered watching town ball in Rockford as early as 1846. Waldo is credited with spotting Spalding's potential when Spalding was a teenaged pitcher for the nearby Byron Club. In 1855, Waldo opened a bookshop in Rockford, remaining in that business past the end of the century. By the 1860s, he was president of the Forest City Club, guiding its recruitment of players, his success crowned by Rockford's upset victory in 1867 over the touring Washington Nationals, who were in effect a professional team. It was Waldo to whom Spalding, that game's winning pitcher, went for advice after the Chicago Excelsiors, in return for his playing services, arranged Spalding's employment in a local business with hours that allowed for practice and travel to games. Although his departure would harm his club, Waldo advised Spalding that the opportunity was too good to pass up. Waldo continued to be a leader of the Forest City Club through the club's first openly professional year and was a fan for the rest of his long life. He was, Spalding recalled, "one of the noblest, purest, most unselfish men I ever have known."[26]

Another pioneer combined the roles of player, team official, umpire, and statewide promoter of the game.

Sixteen-year-old George W. Lackey moved to Bloomington in 1858 from his Indiana birthplace. Later city directories show several Lackeys in the McLean County seat, but it is not clear whether he joined relatives already there. He worked for a druggist and, in his spare time, perhaps joined in informal baseball playing. Baseball had arrived—or at least had become noticed by a local newspaper—in 1857. "The base ball club was out last night in good force. . . . This fine game is becoming popular among the young men of our town. Amen!" noted the *Bloomington Pantagraph*. Later, to the editor's chagrin, enthusiasm for the game faded. Competition from a cricket club led the initial baseball craze to pass quickly. Not deterred, the editor called on young men to take up the game again and practice a couple of times a week. Cricket, he sniffed, "is hardly equal in the way of excitement to our national game."[27]

While no one accepted the challenge of organizing a formal club, it is reasonable to assume that impromptu, unorganized play continued intermittently. In 1861, a larger event—the outbreak of the Civil War—attracted Lackey's attention. Nineteen-year-old Lackey was elected a major in the Sixty-Eighth Illinois Volunteer Infantry, a unit enlisted for a three-month term of service. Lackey's original volunteer company was a Zouave unit, known for their colorful uniforms and skill in drilling. His later career makes it clear that Lackey was skilled in teaching and leading intricate drills. After the Sixty-Eighth's term expired, Lackey returned to Bloomington and reenlisted as a colonel in the 145th Illinois Volunteer Infantry. His election as an officer in two units demonstrated his popularity. Neither unit saw combat during Lackey's service and, at war's end, he went back to Bloomington and opened a drugstore.[28]

Lackey was often referred to as "Colonel," an incongruous rank for the operator of a modest drug and tobacco shop on Bloomington's courthouse square. The shop on the busy square's northwest corner placed Lackey at the center of the community's business. People strolled in and out, passing the time in conversation and, perhaps, one day talk turned to the earlier challenge to Bloomington's young men to organize a baseball club. If that was how it happened, Lackey was one who responded.[29]

The status of those attending the organizing meeting on May 22, 1865, is indicated by the location—the McLean County courthouse. The twenty-three-year-old Lackey and three others had clearly met earlier, because their committee reported on a constitution and by-laws that night. They recommended adopting those of the National Association of Base Ball Players. A name was chosen—the Bloomington Base Ball Club—and officers were elected, among them Lackey as treasurer. And the first practice was scheduled for three days later at the Fifth Ward School grounds.[30]

Surviving box scores show that Lackey usually played catcher, a position described by New York sportswriter and early promoter and teacher of the game Henry Chadwick as central to any team's success. Among the skills needed by a catcher were the ability to throw quickly "a line ball at a distance of fifty yards" as well as stopping "swiftly-pitched balls" and fielding grounders. Lackey and his fellows at the position played without gloves or protective gear, providing context to Chadwick's admonition that they have "the nerve to face sharply-tipped balls direct from the bat." A good catcher should also work out strategies with the pitcher for handling batters. And the catcher should be team captain because he had the best view of the field.[31]

Lackey collected dues for his club. And, in at least one instance, he arranged a match with a touring team. Lackey's energy and organizing skills soon allowed him to transcend Bloomington's baseball environment. The 1867 convention of the Illinois State Base Ball Association elected him president.[32] Umpiring also took him away from Bloomington, filling the role in games throughout the state, including one, as we will see later, marred by controversy.

Scattered and incomplete records complicate comparing Lackey to his peers in the state's burgeoning baseball community. Others may well have been as active as Lackey, but their names are lost. Energized by youth, ambition, and enthusiasm, Lackey excelled as a player, promoter, and umpire.

Johns, Silver, Stearns, Lackey, and countless others were young men on the make—vigorously embracing the game, committed to making a mark for themselves and their communities. In the few years they spent planting and nurturing baseball before moving on to new roles, their contributions spread baseball in Illinois.

ORGANIZING CLUBS, FUNDING, TRAVEL, AND THE GAME'S RITUALS

Don't elect bad tempered men in your club, no matter how noted as players they may be. Leave them out, for they will eventually do more injury to a club than benefit.

—Henry Chadwick, *Haney's Base Ball Book of Reference*, 1867[1]

Baseball clubs did not spontaneously appear on the Illinois prairie. Each used existing models to shape its passion for the game, goals, hopes, and practices.

Organize was a key word for Illinois baseball enthusiasts. Conditioned by the American spirit of association, young men who organized clubs were led in absentia by Brooklyn sportswriter Henry Chadwick. Though the English immigrant had little experience as a player, it is difficult to exaggerate his impact on the game and Illinois's clubs.

According to his biographer, Andrew J. Schiff, Chadwick served as "baseball's moral conscience. He advocated fairness, truth and honest play." Baseball historian Jules Tygiel credits Chadwick with doing more than any other to create the game passed down through generations, molded by his "vision, innovation and reforming passion." Chadwick denounced gamblers and their influence on the game, developed standards of play for each position, created a forerunner of the scoring system used today, introduced the batting average, and lobbied incessantly for the fly rule—which meant fair balls caught on the bound would no longer constitute an out. Adopted at the end of the 1864 season, the rule now required players to catch fair balls on the fly to retire the batter. Although he wrote for New York area newspapers, Chadwick's influence reached deep into the US interior with his annual guides, begin-

Sometimes referred to as the father of baseball, New York sports reporter Henry Chadwick did not invent the game but exerted tremendous influence on its growth through his various publications, including rules, interpretations, and guidelines. He traveled to Illinois in 1867 with the touring Washington National club and witnessed its upset by the Forest City Club of Rockford. Courtesy of the National Baseball Hall of Fame, Cooperstown, NY.

ning with 1860's *Beadle's Dime Base Ball Player*. This and subsequent yearly publications, such as *Haney's Base Ball Book of Reference*, were small enough to fit into a pocket, belying the wealth of information packed inside. *Haney's* contained the latest rules adopted by the National Association of Base Ball Players along with Chadwick's commentary on them, detailed instructions

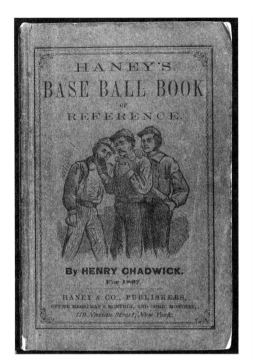
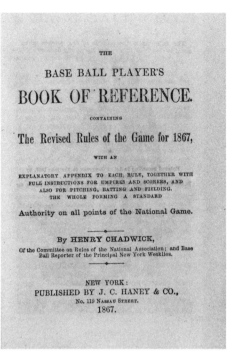

Chadwick's 1867 edition of *Haney's Base Ball Book* contained not only rules but his recommendations on how the game should be played and, notably, how players should conduct themselves. Courtesy The Henry Ford Museum.

on how to organize a club, the proper spirit of the game, how to play each position, and the ideal type of player for each. True to his reforming nature, Chadwick also included a section on the moral behavior expected of every player, including abstaining from foul language, preserving self-control, never taking "ungenerous advantage" of opponents, and practicing the Golden Rule. Time revealed those to be challenging guidelines.[2]

Gathering to organize clubs, Illinoisans brought with them Chadwick's ideals. If they merely wanted exercise and entertainment, why bother holding evening meetings, writing constitutions and by-laws, electing officers? Through formal organization, they conformed to American notions of association, creating an infrastructure to achieve the game's larger purposes.

The players and enthusiasts were not idlers. Lawyers birthed Springfield's first club, meeting in the state supreme court's offices in the capitol building, establishing committees for playing spaces, and selecting team names and uniforms. In Cairo, a local newspaper welcomed a similar effort: "Every city, town and village is organizing a Base Ball Club and why should not Cairo follow the good example set her?" asked the *Cairo Democrat*. Far to the north, in Aurora, a preliminary meeting in a lawyer's office to organize a club elected the local agent for the Family Sewing Machine, O. B. Knickerbocker, as chairman and proceeded to set up committees to draft a constitution and create a temporary finance committee and committees on playing grounds and equipment procurement.[3]

Parodying such formalities, the *Aurora Beacon*, tongue firmly in cheek, revealed another club entering the lists, the "Light Weights." Describing its ample-bodied members as "well incorporated men . . . they will strike well— the only difficulty will be with the fielders." Compensating for their bulk, each player came equipped with a mule to aid in chasing balls.[4]

As baseball clubs sprouted, newspapers in towns left behind sounded editorial alarm. "Is there not enough energy about the young men of Maroa to organize a Base Ball Club?" complained the *Maroa Times*. "Every town surrounding us, even to Forsyth [a town a few miles to the south], has a Club. Who will be the first to put this thing in operation?" The next week, it happily reported the new Grand Prairie Club. Promotion for the organization of clubs, as seen in Maroa, was common. Jacksonville's *Journal* anticipated a meeting of more than forty local men who signed its call, pronouncing the gathering vital to ensuring the "health, amusement and physical development of our young men, especially for those whose profession or business is necessarily confining." The meeting in the Morgan County courthouse elected George M. McConnel, a local lawyer and son of leading citizen Murray McConnel, president of the new club. As elsewhere, committees were appointed to choose a name (Hardin Base Ball Club) and other details. Members paid a one-dollar initiation fee and the club pledged itself to follow the rules of the National Base Ball Players Association.[5]

Such formal structures invited satire. In north central Illinois, the *Bureau County Patriot* announced a new club with rules banning players weighing over three hundred pounds; "express wagons will be on hand to carry the players from base to base"; any player taking longer than fifteen minutes to get from one base to another would be called out; players were allowed to stop for refreshments at each base; hogs and cattle were prohibited on the field during games; and participants must carry their own refreshments "to avoid the necessity of going in for a drink." It surprised no one that no accounts of any games or other club activities followed.[6]

Establishing new clubs followed similar patterns because they used the same source, courtesy of Henry Chadwick. As noted earlier, the National Association of Base Ball Players' rules and Chadwick's interpretations provided direct connections between the East Coast and the interior, nurturing and guiding the game, setting standards that, as we will see, sometimes were difficult to maintain. But why were by-laws especially needed? Historian Peter Morris explains that, because club members were "so intent on having fun," by-laws were essential for transacting any business in the meetings.[7]

A Club's Primary Symbol

Organized clubs needed more than the formal framework erected by Chadwick and the National Association of Base Ball Players. The uniform, notes Peter Morris, created a club's primary symbol. Club initials or names could appear on shirts, a belt, or armbands.[8] Early players gloried in their team's attire; an 1867 newspaper clip provided a varied and vibrant picture. A rich tableau of colors accompanied clubs arriving in Decatur that year for the Grand Base Ball Tournament of the Western States. "On every side blue, red, pink, and green caps, shoes and coats denote the devotees of the manly art," marveled a correspondent for Springfield's *Illinois State Journal.*[9]

No peer exceeded the specifics detailed by a Waukegan editor. "Now let us suggest to the boys that each of the clubs select some suitable uniform, appropriate for such organizations." Cautioning against costly uniforms, he urged, "a neat inexpensive shirt or blouse of colored or striped flannel, with loose flannel pants of some modest color contrasting the blouse and appropriate light cap and canvass belt." And don't forget shoes, he added, custom dictated canvas shoes. Careful attention to the uniform was worth it. "All this outfit need cost but a few dollars to each member and would give a much better appearance to members of the club when engaged in play," he wrote, noting the newspaper's office was open to any wishing to see illustrations of uniform styles.[10]

Little is known about meeting uniforms' cost, though, in one case, club supporters picked up the tab, as shown by thanks from members of Amboy's Pastime Base Ball Club to citizens who bought the team's uniforms. Playing the game took a toll on the colorful regalia. Shirts worn by Peoria's Olympic Club's split down the back during a game, "making each clubber look like a seventeen-year locust just sprouting." The *Peoria Transcript* noted, however, that the team's headwear remained intact. "The cap is white background with a top like . . . the lone Star of Texas, worked in colors," praising the hat's maker, George Gilbert of Gilbert Brothers Hat Store, for making better and cheaper hats than those found in Chicago or New York.[11]

Four photographs of Illinois uniformed baseball players in this era have been found to flesh out the print descriptions. Three capture full teams—the 1865 Liberty Base Ball Club of Centralia, Harvard's Lazy Nine Base Ball Club, date uncertain, and the 1869 Forest City Club of Rockford. The fourth is a studio portrait, circa 1867–68, of the Egyptian Club's James Cunningham holding a bat and ball. In the team photos, all players wear a white shirt. The Liberty Club players wear a tie or scarf, but no shield, an identifying emblem often buttoned or sewn on the shirt front. The players sport dark pants and a boxlike cap. Cunningham's shirt features an embroidered shield, lighter pants, and a belt. His pants flare out at the ends just above a canvas shoe or slipper. He is hatless.

Period illustrations and photographs reveal East Coast clubs wearing similar uniforms with a greater variety in hat style. Written descriptions of team uniforms worn in Illinois that exist for the immediate post–Civil War years, though lacking the detail of a photograph, do provide a general idea of the panorama on the ball fields of Decatur in September 1867.

When the Mutual Club of Warsaw traveled to Carthage for a match, a critic deemed their appearance inferior for its paucity of "ornamentation . . . running mostly to cap, while our fellows were inexpressibly gorgeous in red breeches," the *Carthage Gazette* recounted. Jacksonville's two clubs, the Hardins and the Hercules, met in May 1866, and members of both first nines, "in their new uniforms, formed arm and arm and marched down from the square to the [playing] grounds," according to a Springfield correspondent. "The uniforms of each club are neat and tasty; that of the Hardin club consisting of a scarlet cap, white flannel shirt trimmed with blue, and blue pants. The Hercules' boys have a slate-colored cap, trimmed with red, white shirts and red pants." An earlier description of the Hercules Club indicated a Zouave-style outfit, complete with "blue Turkish hats," indicating a style change. Aurora's *Argus* termed "neat" the Aurora Base Ball Club's uniform, consisting of "black pants, lettered belts and white shirts." When two junior clubs, Jacksonville's Grants and Springfield's Mystics, played, red, white, and blue was the theme for the day. "The Mystics were uniformed in white caps, blue shirts, and red pants; the costume of the Grants was equally patriotic, blue caps, white shirts, and red pants." Rock Island's Wapello Club players turned out in blue "torkish [sic] pants" with white linen shirts and blue caps trimmed in red, topped by a white button.[12]

A meeting between two Springfield clubs on an extremely warm day inspired a reporter for the *Illinois State Register* to write "About two o'clock the thermometer in the neighborhood of Sixth and Monroe streets [site of the game] suddenly went up nearly three degrees, owing to the heat emanating from several gentlemen clad in red pantaloons of that cool material, flannel, and adorned as to the upper man with blue coats. The crowd was interspersed with other gentlemen in white flannel unmentionables with blue coats and the whole assemblage looked as gay as a flock of tropical birds." The red

The Liberty Base Ball Club of Centralia assembles in 1865. Though it collapsed after one season, many of its players joined the Egyptian Base Ball Club that played into 1870. Courtesy of the Centralia Area Historical Society and Museum.

pantaloons belonged to Springfield's Capital Base Ball Club, whose uniform was later—and more clearly—described as "red pantaloons, deep blue shirts, and white skull caps."[13]

For a match between the Ristori Base Ball Club of Henry and the City Base Ball Club of nearby Lacon, a thousand spectators turned out to see Lacon Citys take the field wearing red pants and caps, white shirts, and canvas shoes. The Ristoris countered with blue pants and caps, white shirts, and white shoes, according to the *Marshall County Republican*. Expectations and standards were high enough that Ottawa's Shabbona Club drew a mild editorial reprimand for its appearance in a game with its rivals from Peru, the Live Oak Base Ball Club. The Live Oaks were "fine looking fellows in good condition and a gay uniform," but the Shabbonas came up short, "each of whom was uniformly dressed different from any other."[14]

Even teams organized with clearly humorous intent had to have uniforms. The clerks of Amboy organized a club, the Counterjumpers. Their uniform

CELEBRATED LAZY NINE
J.McGahan S.S. C.M. Johnson F.B. F.Elwood L.F. C.Hanna R.F. G.Goodell 2.B.
C.W. Swenk P. T.Kelly 3.B. E.Dunn C.F. C.Weld C.
Of Harvard, Ill.

This team from Harvard, Illinois, may not have been, as inscribed on the photo, the Lazy Nine, as no surviving records indicate a club by that name. The uniform pants and shirts are correct, however, for a team in the 1865–70 era. Courtesy of the Abraham Lincoln Presidential Library and Museum.

consisted of "red knee breeches, slate colored stocking, canvass shoes, white shield with blue sailor collars and red caps." An interesting combination to envision.[15]

Uniforms, balls, bats, travel, and food for visiting clubs required money. No account books of Illinois clubs have emerged, but hints about fund-raising exist.

Paying the Bills

Promoting a new club, an editor of the *Grand Prairie Review* of Onarga, a small central Illinois town, attended a Muffer Base Ball Club practice and editorially linked the team's fortunes to the community's. Soon, Onarga citizens stepped up, funding a banquet for visiting clubs, one man printing and donating badges and "Prof. C. L. Smith and lady" providing musical entertainment.[16] Like a new hotel building or a railroad depot, a baseball team signified progress.

Even with such identification, however, pleas for community support were not always successful. After Mendota's paper urged citizens to give money to the local club for uniforms and equipment, the neighboring *Ottawa Republican* grumbled. "Upon what precise ground the people of Mendota" should pay for a club's uniforms, "we would like very much to know." Noting that LaSalle County religious groups, public improvement schemes, and other causes were begging for cash, the Ottawa editor complained, "just how a base ball club, fitted out at the expense of the public could be a material or moral benefit" to Mendota was unfathomable.[17] Others had no problem with such support; the *Jacksonville Journal* encouraged its readers to financially support a Bloomington trip of the city's Hardin Club for a tournament.[18]

Avoiding such direct appeals, most clubs found other ways to meet expenses, often staging social activities to lure cash from the pockets of friends and neighbors.

Dances, referred to as balls, and picnics were the most common fund raisers, as Peter Morris found in other states during the game's early years. In November 1866, the Elfin Base Ball Club of East St. Louis hosted a ball praised by attendees. With its ball, the Elfin Club simply followed the lead of the city's St. Clair Base Ball Club, which hosted a ball the previous January.[19]

From DeKalb in the north to Cairo down south, some Illinois baseball clubs danced through the off seasons. Cairo's Egyptian Base Ball Club hosted its first ball at a local hotel in early December 1866 and the city's Independent Club followed with a "grand calico dress ball and sociable" on New Year's Eve. DeKalb's baseball players hosted a dance in late May 1868 and, in Nashville, a town east of East St. Louis, the Sucker Base Ball Club hosted a "Cotillion Party" at the county fair. Farther north in Lincoln, attendees were promised good times at the local club's ball with skilled musicians working to "guarantee to the devotees of the Terpischorean [*sic*] art a good time generally."[20]

Dances became a regular—and popular—fund-raising vehicle for Centralia's Egyptian Base Ball Club. To stoke enthusiasm for the coming season and raise funds, the Egyptians promised a festive dance, giving their neighbors relief from "the monotonous apathy of the long, cold, damp, disagreeable, disgusting spring." Four months later, the Egyptians hosted another ball and, within thirty days, the club was at it again, hosting a ball termed "one of the most brilliant and pleasant affairs of the season." The frequency and success of the balls did not surprise a local newspaper, its reporter describing Centralia's players as always noted for their "'style,' good looks and gentlemanly deportment." In the ballroom, the Egyptians displayed a silver cup and two rosewood balls mounted in gold taken from other clubs in Illinois. Centralia's Egyptians kept on playing and dancing into 1868, the dance at the end of the 1868 season cementing their reputation as champions of southern Illinois on the field and in the ballroom. Still waltzing in 1869, a local newspaper proclaimed the Egyptians "champions in all kinds of BALL games."[21]

Picnics and ice-cream socials proved popular fund raisers. The Olive Branch Base Ball Club of East St. Louis ensured easy access to its first picnic by locating it near the junction of a railroad track and a plank road. And if St. Louisans wanted to attend, they needed only to ferry across the Mississippi, walk less than a mile to the grounds, and pay a dollar (equivalent to $19.75 in 2022 dollars). An 1867 indoor festival for the Freeport Empire Base Ball Club raised $150 ($2,962.50 in 2022 dollars). And East St. Louis's St. Clair Base Ball Club charged $2 admission (equal to $39.50 in 2022 dollars) for its picnic on an August Sunday. Nearby in Alma Mines (today's Centreville), the Lone Star Base Ball Club hosted a basket picnic after its game with the Atlantic Club of St. Louis. Belleville's White Star Club promised dancing and refreshments at its festival following a game with the East St. Louis Base Ball Club. Opting for an indoor venue, Vermilion Base Ball Club of Danville staged an ice cream social, proceeds applied to securing a playing ground. And temporarily abandoning dancing, the Egyptians of Centralia plunged into the craze with a picnic in the middle of the 1869 season.[22]

Getting There

With bats, balls, a field, uniforms, and equipment funded, travel costs posed a remaining challenge for teams wanting to play out-of-town opponents. To get to these games, most teams utilized Illinois's already extensive railroad system. Placing teams on an 1867 railroad map of Illinois vividly demonstrates the link between transportation and the game. With few exceptions, teams were in cities, towns, and villages served by Illinois' growing railroad network, one that by 1870 would be the largest in the United States. "Everybody wanted to be close to a railroad," historian John H. Keiser writes of Illinois communities in this era.[23] For baseball, rail connections were essential for interteam play. Teams located on the Illinois, Mississippi, and Ohio Rivers could, and often did, use steamboats. By contrast, only a few teams took the state's muddy, unpaved roads to reach their destinations.

Illinois's railroads led, eventually, to Chicago. When Chicago's Excelsior Base Ball Club hosted the touring Washington National Club in July 1867, the Chicago and Northwestern Railway Company offered reduced fares from July 23 to August 1, luring spectators from "the country"; other railroads soon following its example.[24]

Local newspapers often included transportation information in promoting out-of-town contests. When two Rock Island clubs—the Wapello and the Lively Turtles—arranged July 4, 1867, games with the Scott Club of Davenport, Iowa, supporters arrived at the railroad depot for a 7:20 a.m. train. The round-trip fare was $1.50 ($29.62 in 2022 dollars). Before the Wapellos' match at Geneseo, the club reserved rail cars for the trip. For an important match with Quincy's Occidental Junior Club, the Springfield Liberty Club chartered a special car to carry the team and its backers to Quincy, the round trip costing $3 ($59.25 in 2022 dollars). Embarking to Quincy, the Clipper Base Ball Club of Monmouth and its friends occupied two passenger cars and would, a newspaper projected, pick up additional supporters to occupy the whole train by the time it reached its destination.[25]

These Monmouth and Quincy matchups generated crowds. In 1868, supporters gathered in Monmouth to fund a rail excursion to Macomb, a neutral site, to play Quincy's Occidentals. On game day, Monmouth baseball backers packed the town's railroad station with the largest crowd ever seen in the depot. Monmouth citizens, "old and young, middle-aged, married and single, lovers and sweethearts, beaux and belles, all caught the infection, and in their minds no spot on the map of this hemisphere appeared so large and prominent as Macomb."[26]

Sometimes other excursionists shared trains. Peoria's Excelsior Club agreed to play Galesburg at Maquon at the same time a Universalist Church picnic occurred near the playing field. Passengers for either event could go round trip for half fare. A much-anticipated match between the Aurora Base Ball Club and Elgin's Young America Club prompted a railroad to offer a round trip at 60 cents for adults and 30 cents for children. (On June 9, 2022, the tickets would cost $11.85 and $5.90, respectively.) Those taking advantage of the offer could enjoy a "basket pic-nic and view of the play."[27]

Peoria's location both on the Illinois River and at a crossing of rail lines gave its clubs options. The Fort Clark Base Ball Club and supporters boarded a special car attached to a train for a match with Chillicothe to the north. A year earlier, Peoria's club took the *Peoria City* steamboat up the Illinois River to Lacon, promising passengers multiple recreation activities on board and on land. Quincy, on the Mississippi, often traveled easiest by water. The Occidental Junior Club booked the *Gray Eagle* steamboat for games in Keokuk, Iowa, and Warsaw, Illinois. The St. Louis Olympic Club came upriver to Quincy by the steamboat *Andy Johnson* for its 1869 game with the Occidental Senior Club.[28]

Again, as at Peoria, such riverboat trips offered something for everyone. A steamboat leaving Quincy in May 1869 for Keokuk, first booked by Quincy College, had space for baseball players and interested spectators. Those putting up the $1 ($21.49 in 2022 dollars) round-trip fare looked forward to "music, Gallup's ice cream," and omnibuses to and from the boat at half-fare. Also included were special accommodations for the ladies, with all passengers promised "a general delightful excursion by daylight and moonlight." Relying on riverboats did have its disadvantages. A return match at Quincy between the Occidental Juniors and Keokuk's Hawkeye Junior Club ended after five innings because one team's boat was scheduled to depart.[29]

Important games, as seen at Chicago in 1867, attracted crowds from beyond the contesting towns. A steam tug brought Mound City residents to Cairo to watch the ballyhooed match between the latter's Cairo's Independents and a Paducah, Kentucky, club.[30]

The pressures for playing space (detailed in another chapter) created a new transportation issue. Playing fields located farther from town centers meant spectators needed transportation to the games, prompting a Quincy man to offer an omnibus route from downtown to the playing field. The Jacksonville Alert Club shifted its game with an unnamed Jerseyville club to the fairgrounds and another entrepreneur offered transport from town to the playing field—"No charge for the ride, but ten cents will be collected from each and all prior to *exeunt omnes.*"[31]

Some clubs took to the rough roads. The Jacksonville Union Base Ball Club departed at 8 a.m. in a bandwagon for a game in Winchester. Three hours later, the team arrived at its destination. To the north, Aurora hosted a match with a St. Charles team that traveled in a four-horse carriage, "neatly trimmed in the stars and stripes." Its colorful arrival was a harbinger of a successful day. A newspaper account terming it "worthy of note, not a single oath was heard during the progress of the game."[32]

Without the equivalent of modern spring training, how did the enthusiastic ballists keep active between winter and late spring? Baseball historians Warren Goldstein and Peter Morris find evidence that ball clubs often socialized together, "sometimes to raise much-needed funds but often just for the enjoyment of renewing friendship."[33]

Despite playing fields covered with snow, Illinois winters offered chances to burn off inactivity and maintain club spirit.

After its first season, the Vermilion Base Ball Club of Danville organized a volunteer fire company, "for the winter service and to open out the base ball exercise with the return of Spring." Within a month, the club made good on its promise, billing itself as the "Hook and Ladder Company." It turned out, however, that, as fire laddies, the players had trouble getting to first base.

When a fire broke out late one Saturday evening and the "terror-stricken community" scrambled to extinguish the blaze, a local newspaper noted a prominent absence. "Where the Hook and Ladder Company? Echo answers, where?"[34]

The Spirit of the Game

Aside from members, a name, a place to play, balls, bats, and a source of funding, Illinois clubs had yet another challenge—upholding the spirit of the game. In *Haney's Guide*, Chadwick devotes considerable space to player conduct and recommendations, easily outnumbering pages occupied by the rules. Chadwick admonished clubs to exercise care in selecting members: "Don't elect bad tempered men in your club, no matter how noted as players they may be. Leave them out, for they will eventually do more injury to a club than benefit." A successful club needed the right kind of members, those ensuring good relations within the club and with other teams and who would uphold baseball's ideals. Acknowledging rituals' importance, an Onarga editor warned his town's new team to do "nothing that will mar or effect the interest of their opponents but what is legitimate and right, and then, although there may be a large amount of partisan zeal during the game, you'll feel like a band of brothers as soon as the play is closed."[35]

Encapsulated in the editor's advice is the game's essence—an activity that, while expecting competition, relied on safeguards. Not only rules, but also expectations grounded early baseball in Illinois, expressed through orderly behavior, standards, and rituals. Winning was nice, but how one played the game and treated opponents, umpires, and fellow players was paramount. Failure to meet these ideals reflected on a community as well as its team.

Taking an early train from Jacksonville, the Hardin Base Ball Club arrived in Springfield at 8:30 a.m., September 10, 1866, and was greeted by players from the city's Capital Base Ball Club. The Hardin Club was traveling to Bloomington for a tournament, and they opted to spend a day in the state capital before catching a later train to their final destination. The delegation of Springfield ballists escorted the visitors to a local hotel for breakfast. Then the Hardins and their hosts moved to the Illinois Supreme Court rooms in the capitol building, joined by more members of the Capital Base Ball Club. After the groups joined in song, former Illinois state auditor and prominent Republican businessman Jesse K. Dubois officially welcomed the visitors with a speech. But the address was only the day's midpoint. Next came lunch at a hotel before transport by Dubois's street railway to the Capital Club's playing grounds and a three-inning game. At its conclusion, escorted back to town and the depot by their hosts, the visitors boarded a train to Bloomington "delighted with their stay . . . and expressing the liveliest satisfaction with the hospitality extended to them by the Capital [Base Ball Club]."[36]

Note that all this—breakfast, lunch, singing and speeches, greetings from prominent citizens in the rooms of the state's highest court—was arranged for a three-inning exhibition. Such hospitality reinforces the importance of ritual in early Illinois baseball. There were expectations, and teams like the Capital Club strove to exceed them.

A month later, another Jacksonville team came to Springfield, this time for a full game. The Morgan Base Ball Club took the same train from Jacksonville, arriving at 8:30 a.m. and being met again by a delegation of Capitals, who escorted them to a hotel. Joining the Morgans there were the governor of Illinois, a judge, a future US senator, and civic leaders. At noon, all moved to the Avenue House for lunch, and by 1 p.m. both clubs were on the playing grounds. The visitors repaid the hospitality by defeating their hosts 32–22, a loss termed by a local newspaper an honorable defeat. Rather than the game's result, the writer focused on baseball's ideals, describing both clubs as "composed of young gentlemen worthy of all praise for their many sterling qualities. Success to the winners of this match, and may the next game display a different result, if can be, if not, all right." Instead of dividing players between winners and losers, the early game experience unified young men around the behaviors, treatment, and ideals represented in the rituals.[37]

Scholars of baseball's earliest years point to the centrality of these rituals even as they diminished on the East Coast by the 1860s with the game's increasing competitiveness. In Illinois, these rituals flowered most during the years of explosive growth. Why were such values as hospitality, gentlemanly behavior, courtesy, and honors so paramount in the early days?

"Early baseball . . . was more than anything else about having fun," explains Peter Morris. Rules could structure the game and provide guidelines for play on the field but, he added, only rituals could regulate fun. Rituals too played a significant role in mitigating the inevitable bruised egos and hard feelings spawned by competition, providing a framework to contain competitiveness and ensure inclusivity and shared reference for baseball's ideals. As Warren Goldstein notes, rituals began with the written invitation or challenge to play and continued with a welcoming escort for the visitors, meals, entertainment, and, at the end of a game, the presentation of a ball by the losing club to the winners. Often accompanying the awarding of the ball were brief remarks by the vanquished and a response by the winning club.[38]

Certainly, clubs wanted to win games, but *only* within a gentlemanly framework. The observance of the rituals reveals determination to keep the final score in context. Winning was a goal, Morris notes, but "losing with honor was infinitely better than behaving in a way that discredited one's club."[39]

Surviving clippings from Illinois's newspapers reveal just how important rituals were to the enjoyment of the game by players and spectators alike.[40]

As the emerging Illinois clubs strove to follow Henry Chadwick's guidelines in organizing, so, too, did they practice his recommended etiquette for interclub matches. Typical is an 1866 match between two Quincy clubs—the Quincy Base Ball Club and the Occidentals. A local paper reprinted both the challenge from the Quincy Club and the Occidental response with the formal—and expected—language of the time: "For the purpose of creating greater interest in Base Ball and also to establish better social relations between the clubs of our city, I challenge you to a friendly match game, best two in three," wrote E. C. Selleck, captain of the Quincys. Accepting the invitation, Occidental second nine captain Frank Bradly deferred to the challenger's choice of time and place of the first game, as well as the choice of umpire.[41]

In writing game accounts, editors paid close attention to ritual and the perceived standards of the game. Eschewing a lead paragraph giving the score and leading plays or players, as is the case in modern baseball coverage, these 1860s stories focus more on pageant and spirit than game details. Newspaper accounts of games in Lee County, Jacksonville, Freeport, and Harvard began similarly with a team's arrival, who met them, where they ate, who delivered speeches to them, what bands played, and how the uniforms looked. Readers had to wait a paragraph or more to learn the final score. The game—its preliminaries, play and postplay rituals—and *not* its result, were paramount.[42]

While the focus on travel, uniforms, and off-field activities frustrates modern readers seeking details of play, these often long, sometimes even poetic, accounts do reveal the obsession with spectacle, ritual and good spirits stamping the game a social phenomenon rather than a simple athletic contest. And, as we shall see later, when winning increased in importance, interest in the pageantry of the game and the game itself faded in newspaper columns and among readers.

A game at Cairo generated a story that would mercifully expire today on the copy desk. After describing the arrival of a Paducah, Kentucky, team by steamboat, the editor waxed eloquent on their uniforms of red, noting citizens congregated on the city's levee, staring at the visitors "as if they were something more or less than ordinary men." Following the usual pre-game rituals and festivities, the game began, prompting an outburst of poetry from the editor:

The game was oped [*sic*],
the play grounds being cleared,
Hundreds on hundreds there are seated round
Long ere the Umpire's cry of "time" is heard.[43]

Continuing, the poem again reviews the visitors' uniforms—"jolly red pants and their pretty red hats/Looked nice in the sun as they handled their bats." Only at poem's end does the reader learn in a roundabout way that the Cairo Independents won. "For the might of the Cairenes, unsmote by the bats/Best the Jolly red pants and their pretty red hats."[44]

Less florid but still colorful is an account of a match between an Elgin club (likely the Young Americas) and the Aurora Base Ball Club, ending with attention to the expected rituals. "At the close the Auroras gave the Elgins three cheers. Elgin reciprocated, and a series of combined cheers were given for the umpire, scorers, ladies, etc." Then the umpire, George W. Lackey of Bloomington, presented the game ball to the winning Aurora club "in a neat speech." Escorted to a local hotel and fed, the Elgin players then returned home by train. "The deportment of the members of either club was in the highest degree commendatory, and their obedience to discipline most excellent." Weeks later, when Elgin won a rematch, readers learned the losers had the "comforting reflection that they had been beat by *gentlemen*." Moreover, the Elgin club awarded Aurora's best player "an elegantly colored photograph of himself in full costume, either in ink or water colors, worth $12" ($450 in 2022 dollars).[45]

Tensions raised in a close game between the Black Hawk Base Ball Club of Camden Mills (later Milan) and the Athlete Club of Coal Valley quickly dissipated at game's end when both clubs cheered each other, the umpire, and the scorers and "formed in line and marched to the Camden House" to a banquet, then "parting in mutual goodwill." Likewise, following the Marengo Star Base Ball Club's pounding of the Harvard Base Ball Club 58 to 39, the victorious players and the Marengo Brass Band accompanying them to Harvard dined for free at a local hotel. There, the Harvard Cornet Band played and, as the evening went on, the two bands combined and performed on the hotel's balcony. As the players drifted away, "they departed with the best feelings towards each other." Another contest with potential to create hard feelings was Kankakee's Grove City Base Ball Club's defeat of Wilmington's Tempest Club, 95–40. According to one account, the losers "owned it up like men and acted like men about it." The Grove City players "are loud in their praises of the entire friendliness and manful deportment" of the Tempest team who, in turn, hosted a grand ball with entertainment for its guests, continuing late into the evening and leaving the Kankakee team "anxious to reciprocate."[46]

After the victory of the Amateur Club of Princeton over Sheffield's Olympic Base Ball Club, the winners "were presented with bouquets by some of our ladies." In the immediate post–Civil War years, game accounts typically ended with phrases like "the best of feelings prevailed among the members of the two clubs," players leaving the field "like a band of brothers," or "throughout the game, good feeling and harmony prevailed." A team's conduct drew careful notice. The Warsaw Mutual Base Ball Club thanked the visiting club from Keokuk, Iowa, for its "friendly and gentlemanly conduct" in a game. Although a club from Morrison, playing its first game, could not best the Sterling Base Ball Club, the latter praised their gallant behavior. And after Springfield's Capitals beat their fellow townsmen of the National Club, 50–17, "the vanquished took their defeat like true heroes—good naturedly; and the best feeling prevailed throughout the game."[47]

Hosting teams treated visiting clubs as honored guests. The Dead Beat Club of Ashley traveled to nearby Centralia to play its Union Club and lost. Their hospitable treatment eased the sting. And the Centralia Union Club gained praise for its accommodations for female spectators, which included a large shed with an ice-cream stand. Any sting from a narrow defeat suffered by the Wapello Club of Rock Island at Geneseo against its Pioneer Club faded amid the postgame rituals, including a dinner, music, and a stroll around the town. Geneseo residents welcomed the visitors with friendly treatment. "Fact is," the Rock Island Argus allowed, "the Wapellos have a decided liking for that Geneseo club—they are all gentlemen—'spect that's the reason." And, in the political partisanship endemic in newspapers of the time, the Argus pointed to the Geneseo voters' support for a Democratic judicial candidate in the previous election, which "showed her good sense; good intelligence of her people, and all Rock Islanders ought to like her."[48]

A Rock Island–Geneseo rematch later, in June 1867, demonstrated that the gentlemanly expectations extended to spectators. "There was frequent applause during the playing when some fine catch or run was made—and it was just as hearty for one side as for the other," and at the end of the game, there was no applause, which the correspondent judged to be "in very good taste." Simply let the clubs, as they did, cheer each other, celebrating the sport's brotherhood. An account of another Capital–National match in Springfield described the crowd around the playing ground. Spectators joked, laughed, and enjoyed each other's company. It was, the newspaper recounted, a group marked by "respectable character," adding that the "entire absence of betting other than good natured bets of lager beer, as are made by mutual friends" tempered the potential for serious disagreement.[49]

Illustrating the power and pervasiveness of ritual in the early Illinois game are the rare occasions when a team failed to observe them. After Downers Grove (now a suburb of Chicago) players ignored such obligations in 1867, both Aurora players and the city's newspaper chastised the offenders. Arriving in the village, the Aurora Base Ball Club found no one to greet them. Nor did the Downers Grove Club players appear at the pregame picnic. Though the contest was to be a friendly game and not a match contest, the Aurora club expected their hosts to offer the ordinary courtesies that "are always as a matter of course between gentlemen." Downers Grove players lacked baseball manners, believing that "by becoming Base Ballists they have ceased to be gentlemen." If receiving shabby treatment was not enough, the Aurora team lost the game. Three years later, in 1870, when the once-treasured rituals were all but gone, a match between the Magnolia Base Ball Club of Edwardsville and the Alton Wide Awakes ended in a 50–34 defeat of the latter. There was no reconciliation at game's end or unity in celebrating the brotherhood of baseball. Alton was "so mortified at being beaten, that with but one exception they could not treat their opponents with common politeness."[50]

Most clubs strove to maintain a reputation for gentlemanly behavior in a game that was as much social as athletic. This mixture of sport and courtesy sparked sheer joy in players and spectators alike and attracted hundreds of teams and spectators to rough-hewn playing fields carved out of empty lots or open spaces.

PLAYING FIELDS, GAMBLING, AND INJURIES

. . . a criminal offense to take a little free and healthful exercise within the corporate limits.
—Letter to the Editor, *Bloomington Pantagraph*, May 29, 1867[1]

As August 1867's summer simmered, a Bloomington baseball player angrily addressed the local newspaper. At stake after the city council's recent action was not only the future of his baseball club but, he insisted, that of the community as well.

Protesting the Bloomington City Council's ban on baseball playing, the anonymous letter writer deployed images of classical Greece to drive home his point. "Athens was no less renowned for her Gymnasium than for her Academy; no less famous for her soldiers than her scholars." Yet "we cannot but feel ashamed of the discouragement we receive of our physical education." In fact, the city had "prohibited the playing of base ball within the city limits; have made it a criminal offense to take a little free and healthful exercise within the corporate limits of the city," he continued. Players were left with a choice: "go out into the country" for recreation "or frequent a saloon."[2]

Banning baseball games in a city with one of the state's most successful teams demonstrates in the extreme the potential difficulties teams faced finding a place to play during the post–Civil War era and reveals the tensions between competing groups over public space.

Competition in Illinois for space and the resulting field conditions mirrored developments years earlier in the East. High land values in New York City and Brooklyn, for example, limited open space. And teams using playing fields in or near residential neighborhoods heard citizens' complaints about noise, crowds, and foul language. Early baseball historian Peter Morris concludes, "Base ball clubs didn't make good neighbors." Moreover, what land was available could offer uneven playing space. One field in New York was a triangle-shaped tract surrounded by a railroad embankment, forcing outfielders pursuing balls to run uphill.[3]

Carving out playing fields on the prairie, vacant lots, or school grounds was not always easy. Space was valuable and contested. The idea of a park was unknown. People at the time associated the word with a sometimes-fenced-in grassy area around a county courthouse. Parks and playing fields funded and maintained by the public were far in the future, and baseball created new and potentially controversial demands for space. From Harvard in the northeast corner to Cairo at Illinois's southern tip, the need to find playing space spawned various solutions.

And answers proved far from ideal. For a multistate, multiteam tourney in 1866, the Forest City Club of Rockford chose space on the infield of the county fairgrounds racetrack. But the tree-filled playing field offered challenges. "The umpire could not see a foul unless it was hit back of the plate or a few feet on either side of the base lines," one man recalled. "At the edge of the outfield was a deep gutter that drained a nearly quarter-mile race track. Only Providence's protection kept more players from breaking legs in that trap." Sixty years later, memory of that field prompted a quip from a local historian of the game, "that Fair Grounds diamond had more hazards than any respectable golf course."[4] Racecourse infields also provided potential playing spaces in Danville, Waukegan, and Woodstock, among others.

Rockford's fairgrounds field was not a unique ball-playing situation, in part because competition for open spaces in communities often pushed baseball players to the outskirts, sometimes onto rough surfaces. When Kankakee's Grove City Club lost a game at Rockville, a newspaper compared the playing surface to a "plowed field." Clubs from Elgin and Aurora played the deciding game of their series at neutral Turner Junction. But upon arrival, they found a field sprouting "wheat stubs, well filled with clover," complicating the fielding of ground balls.[5]

Illinois clubs addressed their need for playing space in a variety of ways. Aurora's club played near a local college. In Belleville, teams played near a railroad depot, and Cairo's teams took over a Civil War fort's abandoned parade grounds. Eureka's club took an empty lot near a hotel, and the Defiance Club of East St. Louis tested its skills in "Gallagher's pasture." Freeport's junior clubs found a home when one woman donated the lot at the rear of her home. Living up to its New England antecedents, Harvard's clubs scampered on the village green.[6]

Where most Illinois clubs played remains unknown. Surviving newspaper accounts simply refer to the club grounds, indicating that readers already knew where the team played, not unusual in small communities. In only a handful of cases do surviving newspaper accounts or later interviews with early players provide a full picture of the first fields.

Alstyne's Prairie, a quarter-section of land in Quincy, long termed a civic embarrassment, became a prime location for baseball in the western Illinois city, used by the Occidentals and other clubs. With limited seating at the prairie, important games moved to the fairgrounds, just as in Rockford and Decatur.[7]

More details are available on the McPherson Base Ball Club of Decatur and its first playing field. It was laid out by future Macon County Judge William Corwin Johns northwest of the intersection of the city's two main railroad lines. Eventually, a small grandstand rose around those grounds, but when the club hosted a multiteam tournament in September 1867, play moved to the fairgrounds west of the city (today's Fairview Park), to facilitate charging for admission.[8]

Although the McPherson Club never received criticism about noise—only about its terrible record—Decatur's city council banned baseball, specifically the unorganized play in the streets that plagued many Illinois communities. Decatur's leaders prohibited the game in the business district, where, the local newspaper reported, "noisy urchins who have infected our most public streets for the past months" played "'the National Game.'" Baseball enthusiasm transcended organized clubs. For example, consider Jacksonville, where, as 96-degree temperatures sizzled its streets, a newspaper editor glanced out his window, spying "a gay party of young gentlemen" playing ball. The editor observed that "for some time, the whizzing ball was made to cleave the frying air, while shouts and burned hands, and other familiar base ball pleasantries, constituted an agreeable episode in the 'long and weary day.'" The next year, however, baseball playing was not necessarily a pleasant distraction on a hot day in Jacksonville. First, Sunday ball playing earned an editorial rebuke after a group of boys broke Sabbath restrictions. "It will be well for parents to discover in what occupations their boys are engaged Sundays, and it will also be commendable if the police will put a stop to such proceedings hereafter." Three weeks later, a downtown sight once called welcome on a hot day by an editor became a "downright nuisance." Boys playing catch in the streets slowed commercial traffic. Wagon drivers feared a ball striking a horse, leading to a runaway. Boys and young men were guilty, the editor conceded, more from carelessness than malignant intent, though warning "those hard, heavy balls are frequently thrown with a swiftness that might do serious injury to the unwitting passer by who should without malice aforethought catch one of them in his eye."[9]

Concerns about ball playing in the streets frequently overlapped with outrage about Sunday games. Jesse Stout, a Clinton man in his seventies, was injured when struck by a baseball while crossing the town's square. At fault were young men playing "toss and catch. Mr. Stout very injudiciously stood in the way of a skyscraper." The editor warned elderly men and women to avoid the town square in the early evenings when young men were playing the game.[10]

A Peoria newspaper reported "certain boys and young men" were playing ball on Sunday in various parts of town "to the great annoyance of the neighbors in the vicinity." Once, three loud young men tossed a ball outside a room where a Sunday school class met. Initially, one Peoria editor tolerated ball playing on the city's courthouse square, noting that boys were there simply for fun. Within weeks, the view changed, at least for those doing business in the square. While boys were throwing a ball over the spire atop the courthouse, "a couple of little girls, drawing a baby's buggy, come along and the ball, falling from a height as far as the thrower could project it, struck close by the side of them." Had it hit either girl, the editor predicted, the result might have been serious injury or death.[11]

And rowdy Peoria ballplayers damaged the square's young shade trees. Carrollton and Danville papers reported similar problems. In Quincy, a neighbor complained to the newspaper about boys playing baseball near his home and using loud and "indecent language." Observing young men tossing a ball around in the streets, a Quincy editor warned of potential dangers: "We have seen several horses badly frightened by these gentlemen," creating risk of serious injury or death. On another occasion, "a gentleman seated in a buggy, an entirely disinterested party," was struck by a ball "on the top of his head. Incidents of this kind are of daily occurrence and are calculated to cause a man to 'fly' into a passion."[12]

Cairo's city leaders moved quickly to control the unorganized game. During the Civil War, a simple snowball fight on the streets could "lead to a shooting scrape." With baseballs zipping up and down the river city's avenues, the City Council passed an ordinance against "snow balling or a game of base ball in the streets," its goal being "to protect the heads of pedestrians, the windows of houses, to prevent the scaring of horses, etcetera and so-forth." A local editor thought the ordinance needed broader scope. Even throwing baseballs in city streets should be outlawed. "The balls used are generally of the size and weight of grape shot, and, when vigorously flung, have nearly the same effect upon the object that arrests their progress." Enforcing similar laws could be costly. According to a report in the *Chicago Tribune*, the mayor of Shelbyville, Indiana, fined boys for playing ball in the town's square, only to be "impeached before the City Council by the boys, charged with 'willful neglect of the duties of his office, also with adultery and association with prostitutes.'"[13]

All these issues—ball playing or tossing balls on crowded city streets, Sunday games, noise, and obscene language—came to a head in Bloomington.

Trouble at the Fifth Ward School

The 1867 baseball season's opening found the Bloomington Base Ball Club, one of the state's best, competitive with the Chicago Excelsiors and the Forest Citys of Rockford and a source of community pride. Yet, by early April, complaints rumbled, indicating that not all the city's residents were happy with the baseball craze or with baseballists. The McLean County Agricultural Society placed a notice in the *Pantagraph*, warning that anyone found playing ball on its grounds just west of the city limits on Sundays faced prosecution. The game's troubles in Bloomington spilled into other days of the week. A *Pantagraph* editor denounced ball playing on the courthouse square as "an unendurable nuisance. Too many windows are broken in the sport, and if not stopped voluntarily, measures will be taken to make it cease." He continued, criticizing the game in general. "A person might think listening to some of our base ball clubs while playing that *swearing* was necessary to the play," leaving families near the ball ground "excessively annoyed by the vulgarity and profanity of the players." City residents felt an urgent need to stop such behavior.[14]

Complaints eventually focused on the Fifth Ward School grounds, a block bounded on the north by Empire Street and on the south by Walnut. Its eastern and western boundaries, respectively, were West Street and Lee. The school occupied the southern portion of the large block, leaving the north open for baseball—played there by organized teams like the Bloomington Base Ball Club and unorganized teams in impromptu, sometimes rowdy, games.[15] In 1867, the site was a square surrounded by residences. A city directory in 1868 indicates that most of them were occupied by working-class families, whose breadwinners held occupations such as fireman, machinist, brakeman, or engineer, which is not surprising considering the proximity of a railroad yard and shops to the west. Others not associated with wage labor lived there, among them the McLean County clerk, the county's sheriff, a lumber dealer, a homeopathic physician, and a real-estate agent.[16]

Neighbors may have pressured elected city officials to eliminate the noise and profanity rising from ball playing on the Fifth Ward School grounds. That might explain why within a week of the newspaper's complaints, the

Fifth Ward School Grounds, Bloomington, a battleground in the use of public space for baseball. Home to the Bloomington Base Ball Club and other teams, the school grounds' neighbors successfully lobbied the city council to ban the game within the city limits. Detail of the "Bird's Eye View of the City of Bloomington McLean County Ill. 1873," drawn by Augustus Koch and published by Chicago Lithographing. Courtesy of the McLean County Museum of History, Bloomington, Illinois.

Bloomington Base Ball Club was seeking a new and permanent field. Two days later, the city council made it clear that baseball—organized clubs and unorganized players alike—was the target. Upon a request from citizens living near the Fifth Ward School, a motion reached the council instructing preparation of an ordinance banning baseball playing on and around the school's grounds. An amendment to include all the city's school grounds plus "commons" within a mile of town failed. Passage of the motion would signal the end of the Bloomington Club's home grounds in the city.[17]

Giving the complainants their wish, the council reconvened six days later to vote on the ordinance now prohibiting ball playing on all the city's school grounds except by school pupils during school hours. Furthermore, it termed baseball a "nuisance," with violators facing fines from $1 to $10 ($19.75 to $197.50 in 2022). No legal distinction existed between groups of unruly boys and the city's organized clubs. But the Bloomington Base Ball Club was not without political and social standing itself. Among its members were courthouse square merchant George W. Lackey; Henry A. Ewing, then a law student and later elected sheriff; Charter S. Roe, son of the clerk of the circuit court, and the city's mayor, R. H. Rood, who ironically signed the ordinance.[18]

Responding quickly, the club met in the courthouse. There, in a reaction to the council's action, club members expressed their surprise and pointed to at least ten "separate and distinct clubs" in the city but only two organized ones—the Bloomington Base Ball Club and its junior affiliate. Conducted in an "orderly manner," the practices and games of these two clubs usually had ladies present, ensuring gentlemanly behavior and language. Club members sought only "physical development" not "profit," perhaps a swipe at the suspected professionalism of their great rival, the Chicago Excelsiors. Rather than the two organized clubs, they asserted, the problems stemmed from "juvenile ragamuffins, who play in the Court House yard, break windows, swear, throw stones, chew navy tobacco, etc."[19]

Why, the club asked, must all organizations suffer punishment? Instead, handle problem ballists individually. Was it not unfair to "deprive from seventy-five to one hundred young men of the privilege of playing ball" because of the irresponsible actions of others? Instead of dealing with the real problem—rowdy, unorganized players—the ordinance penalized the Bloomington Base Ball Club's members, who were busy in their offices and stores and didn't have time to walk outside the city limits to practice and play.[20]

"We wish to ask the public generally which of the two is best, playing Base Ball, or to spend our leisure time in saloons, standing on the street corners, etc.?" The ballists' reference to saloons indicated familiarity with their community, which barely tolerated liquor and eventually banned most Sunday activities. Club members further resolved that the current ordinance had "gone beyond all precedent as furnished by neighboring cities." After adopting its formal complaint, the club voted to move to a site outside the city limits.[21]

Although not one of the "first nine," Mayor Rood resented the affront to his club. At the next council meeting, he yielded the chair and argued for amending the baseball ban. Terming the council's previous action an injustice to regularly organized clubs "whose rules for order and sobriety are as strict as [those of] any society" in the city, Rood moved to exempt organized clubs from the ban outside of school hours. After an alderman seconded his motion, another city council member defended the ban, noting that the petitions sparking the ordinance came from "a large number of highly respectable citizens." If Rood's motion passed, he argued, "every club of boys will declare themselves regularly organized," evading the council's intention to end rowdiness, foul language, and property damage. The votes showed Rood's amendment failing by a decisive 2–7 margin.[22]

For a time, newspaper comment ceased, only to reignite in August when a letter writer identified as "a Member of the Bloomington Base Ball Club" attempted to set the debate in historical context. After invoking the earlier mentioned classical allusions, he contended that the game benefited everyone, just not players. Chicago, Rockford, Jacksonville, and "every city in the northwest" acknowledged the benefits by taking "an interest in encouraging the game." Concluding, he asked citizens who recognized that the Bloomington Club contained "the best young men in the city" to force "some radical measure" to end the ban. Another player on an unnamed club answered, pointing out that the new practice-ground location was not more than a "rod farther" from the center of town than the Fifth Ward School site. The new location, removed from neighborhoods, ensured no disturbances by "lawless boys. . . . No injury has been done the club [Bloomington Base Ball Club], and the citizens who asked for a change of base are relieved."[23]

Subsequent reports indicated that the Bloomington Base Ball Club moved to a new "Driving Park" on the city's southeast edge, but there is no evidence it ever played a game there, despite promises of a large amphitheater for spectators. Instead, the club relocated to the fairgrounds, just past Bloomington's western boundaries. Naturally, the ordinance did not relieve the problem of unruly youths. A year later, a citizen complained to the *Pantagraph* of "base bawlers" disrupting "quiet, piously-disposed people" on Sunday afternoons. His neighborhood centered at the corner of Douglas Avenue (now Low Street) and Olive Street, several blocks to the south and west of downtown. The writer and his neighbors, who lived adjacent to a railroad track and streets regularly traveled by delivery wagons, tolerated everyday noises but did not appreciate their once-peaceful Sabbaths interrupted by "your hallooing, shouting and screaming." He reported three windowpanes broken by errant baseballs at a repair cost of 75 cents ($14.81 in 2022). Behind those broken panes lay a sick child and the writer's wife, the latter with a "crick in the neck" caused by "sitting near the broken window." To the offending ballists, he warned, referring to a frog slowly boiled in water, "It may be fun for you but, as the frog said, 'it is death to us.'"[24]

Bloomington baseballists needed look no farther than Springfield to see a very different public reception to the game and its playing fields. If Bloomington represented the reaction of cranky neighbors and strict Sabbatarians to the new game, Springfield revealed prominent people and entrepreneurs embracing the game for enjoyment and profit.

Clout and Baseball

Leading citizens of Illinois's capital welcomed the game by providing playing space for the city's clubs. Foremost among them were two businessmen—Jesse K. Dubois and Alexander Starne—both former state officeholders, the first a Republican, the other a Democrat. Each enjoyed economic and political power. A native of Lawrence County in southeastern Illinois, Dubois rose rapidly through politics after his election to the state's House of Representatives at the age of twenty-two, becoming an intimate friend of fellow legislator Abraham Lincoln. After serving as a judge in his home county, state voters gave Dubois the state auditor job in 1856, reelecting him in 1860. Losing the Republican Party's nomination for governor in 1864, he left politics, bought property west of Springfield's city limit, and in 1865 organized the Capital Horse Railway Company.[25]

The new street railway's superintendent was Alexander Starne. Starne, a Philadelphia native, settled first in Alton, later moving to Pike County. As a county commissioner there, he won a seat in the Illinois House of Representatives and later became clerk of the circuit court in Pike. Elected Illinois Secretary of State in 1852, he moved to Springfield but after one term left politics temporarily to head the Hannibal and Naples Railway. He was a delegate to Illinois' 1861 constitutional convention and in 1862 won the race for state treasurer. His business interests included coal mines. In politics, he remained a Democrat, the partnership with Dubois ensuring the pair had all the political bases covered.[26]

As might be expected in a state capital, political and economic influence aligned with baseball in Springfield from the start. At their organizational meeting, members of the Capital Base Ball Club, one of Springfield's first two clubs, selected as its playing grounds "five acres of enclosed pasture owned by the Hon. J. K. Dubois." Dubois had purchased the property in 1865, which was near the terminus of the Capital Horse Railway.[27]

Dubois and Starne were ahead of their time joining public transportation with baseball. Such connections between the needs of transportation enterprises and baseball would flower in the early twentieth century as ballparks rose near railroad and streetcar lines. Owners of trains and trolleys

Jesse K. Dubois, powerful political and business leader in Springfield, played a key role in providing a baseball field for the Springfield Capital Base Ball Club, whose name partially matched that of
the Capital Horse Railway Company, owned by the former state
auditor. Courtesy of the Abraham Lincoln Presidential Library and
Museum.

and ballclubs alike recognized a commonality of interests in locating ballparks. Springfield capitalists perceived the same in 1866 just outside the city's
boundaries. The Capital Club's grounds served the horse railway in at least
two ways. First, it provided an attractive destination at the end of the line,
presenting another opportunity to make money through sales of refreshments and fares for long trips to and from the other end of the line. Second,
the team's name was no accident—putting the company's brand on the club,
effectively advertising the horse railway every time it appeared in print.

Dubois and Starne quickly reaped benefits from the decision. Scores, if not
hundreds, of spectators rode the cars to the Capitals' first game. And Railway
Park, as the playing ground was known, got more good news when the city's

The Capital Horse Railway's superintendent, Alexander Starne. The Democrat was a former state officeholder who, like his Republican partner, Dubois, left politics for business ventures. Both Starne and Dubois had sons playing for Springfield teams. Courtesy of the Abraham Lincoln Presidential Library and Museum.

second club—the Olympics—decided to temporarily locate there, a precursor to shared ballparks of the twentieth century such as the Polo Grounds, home to New York's Giants and Yankees, and St. Louis's Sportsman's Park, home to the Cardinals and Browns. Two other clubs also occupied the Capital Railway grounds—the Pioneer Fire Company Club formed by members of a volunteer fire company of the same name and the city's National Base Ball Club. The field's location beyond the city boundaries encouraged many spectators to ride the Capital Railway to watch all four.[28]

A visiting editor of Pittsfield's *Pike County Democrat* diagnosed Springfield as afflicted with "base ball on the brain" that summer, naming Dubois and Starne among its sufferers, and noting the game's connection to the pair's enterprise. "Gentlemen not yet attached [to the game] insinuate that the spread of the disease is very much encouraged by those interested in the pecuniary fortunes of street railways, but we consider this a slander." Dubois and Starnes, the political odd couple, did not limit Railway Park to baseball games. This nineteenth-century private park offered something for everyone by hosting rallies in support of beleaguered President Andrew Johnson and pigeon-shooting contests. To cover the off-season of baseball and picnics, the park leased three acres for an ice-skating rink.[29]

Crowd-pleasing baseball put passengers in the seats of the horse-drawn railcars. A July 1 match with Jacksonville's Hardin Club attracted "one thousand to two thousand" spectators," packing the "streets, field and fencing adjoining the grounds." Publicizing the club's matches while advertising the railway reaped success on July 4, 1867, when a tourney with teams from Jacksonville, Bloomington, St. Louis, and Springfield occupied the grounds. Urging people to attend the all-day event, a local newspaper noted that to rapidly deliver spectators to Railway Park, "the cars on the Capital Railway will be run at shorter intervals than usual." The article promised spectators relief from hot weather through "an abundant supply of ice water" and "the deep shade about the ball grounds." Attendees could bring their own picnic lunches or partake, for a price, of refreshments sold at the park. And for the nonbaseball spectators, there was music for dancing.[30]

On the Fourth, such editorial drumbeating proved effective, the crowds exceeding even the promoters' expectations. Despite sending cars to Railway Park every twenty minutes, demand overwhelmed the horse railway. An "immense crowd, larger indeed than could be comfortably transported" showed up. By 9 a.m., when the first game started, Railway Park "contained all the people who could be accommodated." Dubois and Starne had good reason to congratulate themselves for investing in the game.[31]

Dubois and Starne were not unique in such support. Other prominent Springfield citizens stepped forward. The city's second club, the Olympics, soon moved to its own grounds a few blocks east of Railway Park on land was donated by Springfield alderman James Brown. The Capital Railway Company still benefited, as its line ran right by the new playing grounds. A local newspaper reminded spectators that they still could travel to the field on the horse railway.[32]

Explosive club growth soon overloaded the city's two playing grounds. After playing its first few games at Railway Park, the National Base Ball Club moved to a field south of the downtown district, a pasture opposite the Home for the Friendless, an orphanage on South Sixth Street. Local bank vice president Major Elijah Iles made the site available. Two junior clubs—the Eagle and the Star—shared another field on the city's northern edge, at the northeast corner of North Seventh Street and Enos Avenue. The lot's owner, Pascal P. Enos, was the clerk of the United States Circuit Court.[33]

Both Dubois and Starne had sons who were active players, adding pride and parental support to profit as their motives. Brown, Iles, and Enos appear to have had no direct connections to the game but did encourage healthy activities for young men. These Springfield men present stark contrasts with its neighbor to the northeast, Bloomington, in community acceptance and support for the game. While members of the Bloomington Base Ball Club may have had political connections, theirs paled in comparison with the political power behind the game in Springfield, accounting for the different outcomes in the contest for playing space.[34]

Political connections and influence could, as we have seen, provide a decisive edge in resolving baseball's playing field challenges. Yet other difficulties did not fit easily into that model. Most commonly, these arose from human nature.

Gambling, the Serpent in Eden

Not all baseball's problems occurred between the foul lines. Off the field, a member of the Sucker Base Ball Club of Nashville may have been involved in a "disgraceful affair," according to the town's newspaper. A group of Nashville's young men accosted members of a traveling theatrical troupe as they were returning to their hotel after a performance. One "performed the 'valorous' deed of STRIKING A WOMAN—one of the ladies belonging to the troupe." The injured party received a painful wound above her eye. The Nashville editor fumed that this was only the latest in a series of incidents on the town's streets involving young men who were making it "almost an impossibility for a stranger to travel our streets after dark without being insulted and perhaps knocked down." Young men such as these, "making pretensions of respectability" but still "pride[d] themselves in being the authors of such transactions." No action followed, the editor complained. No one seemed to wish the laws enforced. The guilty party only had to leave town for a few days until "the community relapses into a state of lethargy."[35]

Editorial scolding jolted the authorities out of lethargy, and, within two weeks, two men were arrested, one of them possibly a player on the Sucker Base Ball Club. That individual, Thomas J. Vernor, was charged with insulting one of the ladies of the troupe. Thomas Stoker, his associate, stood accused of striking the injured woman. The release of both men under low bail caused indignation to swell and, when rearrested, Stoker went back to jail on $5,000 bond and Vernor on $2,000 bond. (In 2022, those amounts would be $102,900 and $41,160, respectively.) Again they made bail, and no further action followed, defeating, according to the newspaper, "the ends of justice." Complaints to the newspaper about its coverage led a senior editor, who had been absent when the story of the arrests appeared, to endorse the offending article—"every word of it."[36]

Spectators too could tarnish the game. The intense rivalry associated with the 1869 series for the state's junior championship between the Occidental Juniors of Quincy and Springfield's Liberty Club, also a junior team, attracted people, at least from Quincy, who continued celebrating their victory long after the teams left the field. A Quincy editor preparing the next day's edition for publication wrote of "sweet strains of delightful music . . . stealing" through his open window. The source—"an immense band wagon . . . discoursing music to the denizens of our fair city." A competing newspaper's editor perceived the racket in a different light, noting "considerable rejoicing and much noise during the night" that not only was "annoying to the police, bringing no good result" but likely "a source of regret to some of them [the noisemakers]" the next day. "There is no fun in these night carnivals; not a bit," he concluded. Quincy police did their duty that night, arresting four residents on charges ranging from disturbing the peace to drunkenness.[37]

But worse than rowdy celebrations was gambling, which bedeviled and damaged the emerging game. It was endemic. Often, wagering lay at the root of crowd behavior problems, fueled by betting during games in progress.

"Scarcely a game is played now-a-days in Ottawa and surrounding towns except their [sic] is some betting on it," complained the *Ottawa Republican* in 1867. "This low business for men, low business for boy and ladies—it is despicable." Earlier that year, the National Association of Base Ball Players' convention barred two New York City players for throwing a game two years earlier. In truth, gambling was already linked irrevocably with baseball at its emergence two decades earlier in New York City.[38]

Rather than "a latter-day pestilence brought upon a pure and innocent game," gambling, contends historian John Thorn, was "the vital spark that in the beginning made it worthy of adult attention and press coverage." He persuasively punctures the game's pious founding myths, locating baseball's rise in New York City's Jacksonian-era culture, one marked by class conflict. The "sporting class" playing a key role in the metropolis's political and social life: players and "sporting men alike loved to gamble, so in this they were united and from this union a national pastime could grow." Baseball was not played exclusively by genteel young men like the Knickerbockers, but rather, was equally enjoyed by "blue-collar clubs for [seeking] bragging rights and gambling spoils." Moreover, gambling whetted public interest by creating demands for statistics and styles of reporting—each providing information sporting men needed. Thorn identifies gambling as one of the three factors that turned baseball into a national pastime. "Adults must care about the outcome, and their willingness to place a wager is a reasonable measure of their interest," Thorn wrote. The other two factors—statistics and publicity—stem from gambling interest. Ironically, Henry Chadwick, who detested gambling and its influence, was responsible for several early rule changes, statistics, and establishing the style of reporting familiar in the twenty-first century—each providing information useful to bettors. Thorn argues that Chadwick nurtured what he most hated—betting. It should come as no surprise, then, that wagering having attached itself to the game on the Elysian Fields of Hoboken, New Jersey, migrated with it to Illinois.[39]

Gambling worried Illinoisans. In March 1868, the *Cairo Democrat* printed a letter from a New York City resident, who reviewed the upcoming baseball season in Manhattan. "It is hoped that fewer games will be jockeyed and sold this year than last," he wrote, referring to what later generations termed "throwing" contests. The writer believed clubs should self-discipline and "leave 'corners' and 'selling short' to Wall street," referring to the 1867 charges that troubled the 1868 National Association of Base Ball Players convention. During the prior season, problem clubs "appeared to have its exclusive gang of 'roughs,' who made it their business to swindle outsiders. . . . Games were sold with the most open indecency."[40]

Not outdone by the East Coast ruffians, Illinois boasted homegrown roughs. In a Springfield newspaper's columns, a member of the Sheridan Base Ball Club of nearby Chatham complained about his club's mistreatment by the capital city's Active Club. During the game, "a lot of Springfield 'roughs'" pressured Chatham's "honest old farmers" to make sideline bets. To the south, a game deciding the winner in a three-game 1868 series between Centralia and Mount Vernon featured heavy betting, with each team bringing their own roughs to settle disputes with fists.[41]

As noted by Thorn, gambling enhanced excitement around important games even when held on neutral sites. The Clipper Club of Monmouth and the Quincy Occidentals selected Macomb for a deciding game between them. By game time, more than the hot weather was overheating spectators. "Excitement had reached such a pitch that 'betting' became a lively business," the *Macomb Eagle* recounted. Macomb citizens' wagers were equally divided between the contending clubs, and the newspaper blamed gamblers for the crowd's excitement, including vocal complaints about the umpire. A series of games in 1869 between the Liberty Junior Base Ball Club of Springfield and the Occidental Juniors of Quincy featured sideline wagering. "Considerable money changed hands," and when the Occidental Club emerged victorious after the final game, "the pockets of the Springfield crowd were again emptied."[42]

Gambling losses suffered by their foes provided opportunities for newspapers in winning towns to chide rival towns. After its Shabbona Club decisively defeated a Springfield club, the editor of the *Ottawa Free Trader* shared that an Ottawan visiting Springfield before the game had telegraphed a friend in town to "Bet your money on the Libertys: the Shabbonas can't touch 'em on base ball—*tell father*." After the game ended, the telegram's recipient wired his friend, "The Shabbonas have beaten the club you wanted me to bet my money on, at the rate of 15 to 8. I have *told your father*."[43]

Illinois's premier baseball event in 1867 was the touring Washington Nationals' surprising defeat of the Chicago Excelsior Club—the city's best team—a day after the DC team lost to the upstart Forest City Club of Rockford led by seventeen-year-old Albert Goodwill Spaulding Jr. Rumors swirled of gambling and possible fixing of both games. The *Chicago Tribune* first attributed the gambling to players on the touring Nationals, who supposedly lay down for the Rockford club, thereby becoming underdogs against the Excelsiors and creating a chance for major gambling profits. But the Tribune later retracted the charge. "We are satisfied that it was an entire mistake." Acknowledging a large amount of gambling on the games in Dexter Park, the *Tribune* was satisfied that those placing large bets on the Nationals were "parties who came hither of their own volition from St. Louis, and others who live in Chicago." Washington's players, it added, were known to be opponents of gambling.[44]

To one Illinois newspaper, the results of the National-Excelsior contest provided a timely warning: if the stakes were high enough, a game could be fixed. "But unfortunately, there is a disposition to pervert games designed only for amusement, recreation and physical culture into the means of speculation and gambling," the editor stated. Noting some $50,000 changed hands at the game [the Washington Nationals vs. Chicago Excelsiors], he admonished that it was "an illustration of this unfortunate tendency. So far as the loss of money staked is concerned, it was probably a good thing." Anyone who wagered on the game and lost deserved no sympathy. The larger question for baseball was "how anything designed to be only beneficial should be cursed so soon with this prevailing tendency to corruption and gambling." A year later, things had not improved. "The American national game of base ball is likely to soon cease being the national game if it is not free from the American vice of betting," predicted the *Woodstock Sentinel*, going on to name gambling and professionalization as making the game a farce, warning that "If this beautiful game is to be popularized and rendered really the national game, betting must be tabooed." A good first step would be abolishment of championship matches, which were open to exploitation by gamblers.[45]

The *Ottawa Republican*, one of the first to fret about baseball gambling, had its own dire prediction. "Soon our ladies who *gamble*—that is the name for it—will want bull *fights* gotten up in regular Spanish style for their edification." Or worse, demand that boxers "come to Ottawa and fight for their amusement!"[46]

Though these editorial jeremiads resulted from crystal-ball gazing, slightly more than a half century later, modern baseball's worst gambling scandal— the Chicago "Black Sox" and the 1919 World Series—occurred when professional gamblers bent odds in their favor after bribing enough Chicago players to sabotage their team's efforts.[47]

Battered and Bruised

Troubling as gambling was, however, notices of broken bones and bandages were more common than lamentations over betting. From Rock Island to Danville and Waukegan to Cairo, Illinois suffered an epidemic of baseball-related injuries during the 1865 to 1870 period. "Base balls are becoming almost as dangerous as cannon balls," warned the *Illinois State Register* in reprinting a report of an Ohio game that left dislocated fingers, sprained ankles, and bleeding hands in its wake. While conceding baseball to be a great game, the *Peoria Transcript* enumerated its drawbacks. Aside from the practice time necessary to master it and the subsequent neglect of business, baseball carried risks of serious injury. For evidence, the writer described a lad working on a local railroad. During a game, a bat hit him in the head, the blow opening a three-inch tear in his scalp and knocking him senseless. With a shake of the editorial head, the editor added, "It is a wonder to us that a game which calls for so many broken heads and fingers, sprained ankles, and a such a great amount of time, should be so highly popular and have so long a run. . . . There is such a thing as running even a good sport into the ground." Besides, it took too much time. A Rock Island newspaper offered a solution to that—a faster way to break bones. "An unappreciated editor announces that a machine has been invented for breaking fingers and stiffening joints as effectively as base ball."[48]

Injuries marred the game when Ottawa's Shabbona and O.K. clubs met on the east bank of the Fox River. One of the pitchers caught separate line drives in each eye, "which when he left the field were beautifully variegated by different colors." A third baseman, trying to stop a ball, dislocated his finger. "Dr. Hathaway reduced it, after which he played the base with his usual vim." To the west, near Rock Island, Dr. Antis, a catcher for Geneseo's Pioneer Base Club, suffered a severe blow from a ball—catchers in those days wore no protective equipment—"which disabled him in such a manner that he had to withdraw from the field." During Elgin's 1869 season opener, one of its players broke his leg. James Munn, an attorney pitching for teams in Cairo, broke his collarbone. Another pitcher, this time for the Egyptian Club of Centralia, suffered the same injury during game two in a best-of-three series with the Mount Vernon Stars. A batter for the Stars—as was the rule at the time—called his pitch, indicating he desired the delivery to be shoulder high. "It was delivered . . . and batted with tremendous force," striking the pitcher near his right shoulder. Though the Centralia hurler "was seen to stagger and clasp his shoulder" he managed to throw his opponent out at first. Another catcher, this time with the Harvest Club of Carlinville, left a game after he took a foul ball to the eye.[49]

It is hardly surprising that a hard ball colliding with gloveless hands led to innumerable finger injuries. In practice, Tom Beasley of Champaign's Empire Base Ball Club attempted to catch a speeding sphere. The ball struck on the end of his finger, "which was thereby disjointed, the flesh badly cut on the inside of the joint, and some of the tendons broken." L. H. Allis, a member of the Bloomington Base Ball Club, broke his thumb, "the bone penetrating through the flesh," while catching another "hot" ball. First baseman George Solander of the Wapello Base Ball Club in Rock Island tried to catch a ball but took it "between the third and fourth fingers of his right hand, tearing the flesh and splitting the little finger down into the palm of the hand."[50]

Most players shrugged at these dangers, either going back into the game, as we have seen, or to the sidelines to recuperate. A humorous exchange printed and reprinted in Illinois newspapers revealed the spirit of the game to its players and adherents:

> Base Ball—The following which we find in an exchange, illustrates aptly the mania for base ball playing which is so prevalent in our midst.

"What is the matter with your finger?"

"Struck with a ball and drove up, but it is a noble game," was the reply.

"Precisely—and your thumb is useless is it not?"

"Yes, struck with a ball and broken."

"That finger joint?"

"A ball struck it. No better game to improve a man's physical condition—strengthens one's sinews."

"You walk lame; that foot, isn't it?"

"No. It the—the-the—well, a bat flew out of a player's hand and it hit my kneepan. He had the innings."

"One of your front teeth is gone?"

"Knocked out by a ball—an accident."

"Your right hand and your nose have been peeled—how's that?"

"Slipped down at a second base—only a mere scratch."

"And you like this kind of fun?"

"Glory in it, sir. It is the healthiest game in the world, sir."[51]

Straying close to a baseball contest or even a simple game of catch posed a risk. A Charleston store clerk stepped outside to the sidewalk and engaged in an impromptu game of catch with other young men. He requested that his companions "pass them in 'hot.'" Per his instructions, the ball came back to the clerk "harder than he expected, slipped through his hands, hit his nose and broke the bone." Watching the 1869 match between the professional Cincinnati Red Stockings and the Occidental Senior Club of Quincy, Mrs. J. P. Bert was struck by a ball off the bat of a Red Stocking, hitting her forehead and leaving her momentarily stunned. "The print of the ball was quite visible where it struck and a portion of the skin denuded." But, like a game baseballist, Mrs. Bert remained to see the contest out.[52]

Some were not as lucky as Mrs. Bert. By 1870, Illinois newspapers were tallying fatalities. "Base ball," the *Woodstock Sentinel* claimed, "has killed twenty-five persons during the past season." The *Bloomington Pantagraph* carried accounts of two fatalities that season—one in Ohio, the other in Chicago. "It was bad enough before the ball was purposely divested of all elasticity, and made solid as a cannon ball, and almost as dangerous," the *Pantagraph* explained. Another Illinois fatality may have occurred in Clinton, where a five-year-old boy supposedly died after a ball struck his stomach. And the same year, the *Chicago Tribune* informed its readers that a Dover, New Hampshire, youth died when a ball hit his head.[53]

Three years before the dangerous 1870 season, Illinois suffered two baseball-related fatalities. In August 1867, eleven-year-old James O'Donnell of Chicago died when struck by a bat that slipped from another player's hands.

"It flew a distance of twenty feet and struck O'Donnell in the lower part of the stomach, causing him to fall senseless to the ground." Later, it was determined the blow ruptured his lower intestine. That October, fourteen-year-old Henry Gondolf of Ottawa hit a pitch over the outfielder's head. As he was running the bases, the fielder retrieved the ball and attempted to throw him out. The ball struck Gondolf in the groin but he was able to score. Caught in the game's excitement, the lad did not notice his injury. But later that evening, pains began, overcoming him as he tried to exercise at a gymnasium. Two days later, Gondolf displayed symptoms "indicating an internal rupture of a blood vessel" and lingered a few hours before dying. The death of the "quiet, intelligent, noble-hearted boy" saddened the whole community.[54]

Still, few of Henry Gondolf's companions quit the game. Baseball proved irresistible, as a poem printed in two Illinois newspapers acknowledged. "Base Ball" recounts the story of a young man "with hat on high" amid a hard-fought game. Bruised by balls bounding off his head, his "eye was black" and his coat "torn off his back." Yet "like a tattered bugle run / The accent of that blistered tongue, / Base ball!"[55]

A young woman pleads with him to leave the game. He refuses and again is hit, this time in the eye by the ball. "And still he answered with a sigh, / Base ball!" Finally, "used up, he sinks upon the ground / While pitying comrades gather round / And in the awful throes of death / He murmurs with his latest breath / 'Base ball!'" The youth's lifeless body remains on the playing field. "There on the cold earth, drear and gray / To perfect jelly smashed he lay; / While o'er the autumn fields afar / Was heard the victor's fond huzzah, 'Base ball!'"[56]

For Mount Vernon's Joseph L. Bogan, death came not from baseball but a hunting accident. The Washington, DC, native was the younger brother of J. S. Bogan, clerk of the circuit court of Jefferson County. In September 1867, Bogan distinguished himself in a game with Richview, playing catcher and scoring ten runs. One of them was a home run, one of four for the Mount Vernon Stars in a 100–56 victory.[57]

Slightly more than a month later, however, Bogan, a great favorite of Mount Vernon's young men, was dead, killed in a tragic accident and much of his body consumed by the wild hogs he and his companions were hunting. As later reconstructed, Bogan and the hunting party separated. Hours later, his companions assumed he was hunting on his own, only becoming worried a day or two later. Retracing their steps, Bogan's comrades found his body "horribly mangled by hogs which were at that very moment holding a carnival" over the remains. Nearby evidence indicated his double-barreled shotgun discharged accidentally, killing Bogan.[58]

News of the tragedy reached Mount Vernon and the Star Base Ball Club assembled at the courthouse. Declaring his death "an irreparable loss," Bogan's teammates vowed to remember his "manly virtues and tenderly cherish his memory as a generous hearted companion." The club's resolutions expressed members' loss of a "worthy member" whose funeral was attended by the Star Club "in body." All wore mourning symbols for the next thirty days.[59]

Injury, the rare death, clubs driven from their fields by government action, gamblers hovering around the game creating potential corruption and overexcited spectators—all these things challenged early baseball in Illinois. Smaller challenges from cricket, croquet, and velocipedes did not smother the sport in the crib. The game's attractions transcended its faults.

What kept men—and women—playing? Who were these players, their economic and social backgrounds? And what were the results for inexperienced players with no protective equipment?

THE GAME AND ITS PLAYERS

Fielding is the most attractive feature of a base ball match, and of all the requisites for a first nine player skill in fielding should be the primary qualifications demanded. "Muffins" can bat well, in a majority of cases, and occasionally we find one of this class who can pitch a pretty effective ball. Their lack of fielding skill, alone gives them the title of "muffins."

—Henry Chadwick, *Haney's Base Ball Book of Reference for 1867*[1]

A twenty-first-century time traveler coming upon a baseball game in post–Civil War Illinois would be thoroughly perplexed by much of what transpires on the field. The diamond, while featuring the familiar ninety-foot basepaths, a home plate, and perhaps foul poles, would seem primitive, its surface marred by trees or ditches and unmowed infields and outfields. Players might appear less skilled, even clumsy.

Our traveler is experiencing a work in progress; baseball's players are learning its nuances on the field, dropping fly balls and fumbling grounders. Erratic baserunning abounds. The traveler's search for explanations in game accounts the next day yields little detail or clarity. Our perplexed traveler might fall back on Casey Stengel's question about his forlorn 1962 New York Mets, "Can't anybody here play this game?"[2]

Henry Chadwick, quoted in this chapter's epigraph, states something that was obvious in the 1860s—good fielding usually beats good hitting. As a starting point for understanding the game played in Illinois, Chadwick's observation is hard to beat.

Even players of lesser ability, known as "muffins," could hit. But in a glove-less era, most players struggled to catch and hold a hard-hit ball, field it cleanly, and toss it to a baseman for the out. Those who did so with ease and regularity held the advantage. In this bare-handed game, Chadwick explained, success required courage.

"Among the requisites of a first-class fielder, are first, the moral qualifications of courage, nerve, control of temper, and coolness of judgment in emergencies, together with perseverance in the face of difficulties and in contending manfully against large odds," Chadwick wrote in his 1867 guide. "The physical ability necessary, consists of the strength to throw a ball a hundred yards; the agility to catch a flying ball close to the ground, or two or three feet above your head; the activity to pick up a ball while running; the quickness of the eye to judge the fall of a high ball, or the rebound of a foul one, and the endurance to stand the fatigue of a long game."[3]

Fielding earns less attention in the modern era dominated by power hitting and basket-style gloves. Contemporary accounts of Illinois's mid-1860s games seem vague on fielding's importance—until you look closely. Nearly all game reports between 1865 and 1870 are frustratingly brief—usually only a line or two giving the final score. Where more detail appears, it is often extraneous matter—modes of travel, observance of rituals, how many "ladies" were among the spectators, and for whom they cheered.

At first glance, the double-digit, frequently lopsided, scores of the time indicate offense was king. Yet carefully examining the few inning-by-inning accounts show just the opposite, though hidden within sentences obscuring as much as they reveal. For instance, players cross home plate with no information how they got on base. Game stories with simple and clear explanations of every player's performance didn't exist in this era, leaving a reader baffled as he or she slowly navigates through complex and misleading accounts by reporters who themselves had limited understanding of the game playing out before them.

Disappointment awaits those seeking straightforward evidence of superior performance or reliable statistical measures or even simply what happened when Centralia played Pana.

Such was the case for a Jacksonville reporter in late November 1866. Despite the cold and the rays of the sun blotted out by "heavy snow clouds," which occasionally let loose a flake or two, the game between two city clubs—the Hardins and the Morgans—went on. "Reporting the tournament was *delightful*," the scribe observed. "Bundled in overcoat and gloves with our knees or a friendly back for a table and our boots for a chair, we penciled and scrawled, shook and scribbled, until, to our joy, at the close of the seventh inning, the umpire called the match."[4]

The result of his uncomfortable work on a frigid afternoon confounds a modern reader. For example, the first inning: "The Hardins had the ins and

McConnel to the bat, making his first base on the first ball. Rutledge made his three strokes and reached his second. Cassell got to his first. King and Ten Eyck followed; the latter put out by a foul caught by Frank Edgar on the first. Broadwell followed suit. Newman and J. Smith left on bases by W. Smith, who was put out on foul bound. Four tallies for the Morgans went in. Edgar, Allen and Jones were put out in quick succession. W. Smith caught Allen out by a splendid fly. Thus, the side was whitewashed."[5]

What happened? McConnel, lead-off batter, hit the first pitch safely. Did Ruggles hit his double after two strikes or was the "three strikes" reference merely another term for batting? The next two batters—Cassell and King—hit safely and Ten Eyck made the first out, hitting a foul ball caught by Frank Edgar at first base. Broadwell made an out, perhaps a foul to Edgar. (It is important to note that foul balls caught on the fly *or* the first bound made an out.) Two more Hardins hit safely before W. Smith was out on another foul bound. "Four tallies for the Morgans," who were in the field, is probably a misprint, instead referring to the four runs scored by McConnel, Rutledge, Cassell, and King. For the Morgans, three players were retired quickly, leaving the club with no runs or, in the parlance of the time, "whitewashed."

And so, it goes until the seventh inning, when the umpire, earning the chilled reporter's everlasting gratitude, calls the game. Along the way, there are examples of good fielding. "W. Smith caught Allen out by a splendid fly"; "Jo King put the side out by beautifully catching W. Smith's ball"; the Morgan second baseman, Dunn, retired three Hardin batters in succession in the third and caught another fly ball worthy of notice in the fifth. But, despite Dunn's efforts and "fighting against such odds," the Morgan club fell, 29 to 18. Players B. Brown and N. Newman made the best catches of the day. Ed McConnel hit the ball "farthest from the striking base [home plate]." No box or line score exists to impose order on this jumble.[6]

While the Hardin-Morgan game account recognized batting, fine fielding enjoyed equal, if not greater, attention. Such was the case in other games and places. A player in a game between Aurora's Black Hawk Club and Earlville was "praised by his comrades for some excellent playing, especially the taking single handed of a ball sent from the bat well to the center field." Two fielders received credit for contributions to a decisive 89–39 victory by Greenville's Sucker Base Ball Club over the rival Okaw Club of Carlyle. Called out were catcher Larrabee for his "agility and skill," and outfielder Ezra Sprague, judged "first in 'taking in flies,' he holds them even when they come like the falcon's flight, 'swift down the storm's advancing line.'"[7]

Ottawa editors demonstrated familiarity with baseball by 1868. Unlike the Jacksonville game, the match between the hometown Shabbonas and the Pioneer Club of Geneseo came in pleasant weather. The newspaper account, though not up to later reporting standards, incorporates contemporary baseball slang and colorful descriptions. Ottawa's center fielder Howe "took first premium" and left fielder Blake broke open the game with "a skyscraper out of the corporation which secured him a home run." And the Shabbona's pitcher, Newkirk, redeemed himself after failing five times at the plate with a "lightning shot into the breadbasket of the Pioneer pitcher, Steward." The reporter judged first baseman Shaw "nonpareil . . . and stands up like a stonewall" to fielders' hard throws "and his gyrations around his base are no snail's bait for one of his weight, even if he does take a little spare time in making bases." Third baseman Stone "stopped all balls that come within several square yards of him." Brief sentences absent detail explain the play. "Shabbonas went first to bat and made one tally, Pioneers succeeded in scoring two." The game turned just past the midway point when "On the 6th inning the Ottawa nine scored 8 and the Geneseo boys were whitewashed." In the final inning, "the 'Warhoppers' [the Shabbonas] did some tall batting and skeedaddled around the bases 10 times, while the Forest Harvesters trapped five saplings and threw up the sponge." Final score: Shabbona 33, Pioneers, 22.[8]

An account of an 1866 Bloomington Base Ball Club versus Peoria Olympics game is opaque. Stevison of the Olympics "sent the ball into center field but was put out on first base," but we don't know how the out was made. Was it a short hit intercepted by the second baseman, who then fired the ball to first, or did the center fielder charge, sweep up the ball on the bound, and throw it to first before Stevison arrived? Interrupting the game's progress at the end of the third inning, "a fat Englishman in the crowd persisted in getting in the way, and at this stage of the game created some disturbance." Again, the reader wants more than that the offender "was finally quieted." In the fourth, Peoria's Hayne was "put out on second base." How did he get there? Story was "caught out by the catcher." (Foul tip or fly?) Bunn scored—again, where did he come from? "While Wheeler was at the bat Stevison was put out on second base"—though we don't know he got on first base. Bloomington comes to bat and McCart flies out to Stevens. Lee Cheney and G. W. Lackey score and two more Bloomington runners tally before Roe is retired by the catcher. The third out is made later with two Bloomington players on base yet with no explanation of how they arrived. And in the fifth inning, another incident. "A female goose came on the ground and waddled towards the short stop as if to take [his] place, but a ball from Stearns [Olympics] drove her from the field."[9]

This mixture of information and unanswered questions continues until the ninth inning "when it became too dark to play and the game was broke up [sic]." Final score: Bloomington 79, Olympics, 28. The Peoria writer was unsurprised. Bloomington's players, then at their peak after the Rockford tourney earlier that summer, "displayed the highest skill in pitching, running, stopping, and catching." Bloomington outfielder Lee Cheney "seemed to be as active as a cat and never let a ball pass him." Emphasizing defense's importance, the box score included not only a category for "fly catches made," but "fly catches missed." Peoria's Stearns took dubious honors in the latter with three. Bloomington's Cheney contributed two.[10]

Even a correspondent for the *Chicago Times*, a newspaper regularly covering baseball, reported only marginally better on a match between Bloomington's Star Club and Jacksonville's Hardins at the 1866 Bloomington Tourney. "Third Innings—Cris [of the Stars] to bat scored. Taylor found the second base man ready for him—Reeve sent a foul to the catcher. Selbird could not make first base. Side out. D. Smith of the Hardins went to bat, run out getting home. Rutledge out on first base. W. Smith out on a foul bound. The Hardins now retired, having scored eight. At this time game stood . . . eighteen to three on even innings. The Stars felt bad." Fielding played a crucial role in the seventh inning. The Star's leadoff batter scored, possibly on a home run, but his successors could not generate another run. In the Hardin's half, the Star's defense fell apart, for example its shortstop lost a fly ball when the second and third basemen got in his way. This and other miscues allowed the Jacksonville club to tally eight times, on its way to a 43–30 victory.[11]

Better description marks a lengthy account of a game between the Red Jacket Club of Paxton and the Empires of Champaign in 1867.

"First Inning—Taft of the Red Jackets was sent to the bat and on his first strike knocked a foul ball which Arnold caught. DaLee then took the stick and after making two passes he struck on the third and made his first base. Clark batted a foul ball on his first strike but it went uncaught; on his third pass he popped it up over Jefferson's head who caught it easily and then passed it to third base to which DaLee was running and failed to make. Side out. The Empires then took the side with Hurlick at the bat, who knocked a sky-scraper upon which he made three bases. Jefferson after knocking a foul ball which was missed, sent one away off in the centre [*sic*] field, upon which Hurlick came home and Jefferson made a home run. Seger then made a good strike, but the ball was well fielded and he only made first base. Pierce made first base on his strike, Seger passing to the second. Arnold struck well and made two bases, Seger coming home. Scott after knocking a foul, sent the ball starting up and made the first base. Smith put the ball straight up again and made two bases, Dodd muffing both high sent balls. Guy batted well and made second base. Grabill the same and made third base, the others all coming in. Hurlick sent her with a vim into the right field and got two bases.

Jefferson then gave it a hoist into left field, but good fielding only let him to first, while Hurlick came home. Seger batted a nice airy ball and made the second. . . . Pierce did the same, but Jefferson was forced from his base and put out while making the next." And it went on until the third out by which point the Empires had tallied sixteen runs.[12]

In more modern terms: For the Paxton team, their catcher, Taft, hit a foul ball caught by his Empire counterpart, Arnold. With two strikes, the next batter, DaLee, hit safely, reaching first base. Clark struck foul, the ball eluding the fielder, and on his last strike he popped up to the Empire pitcher, Jefferson, who then threw to third base, retiring DaLee.

How were Empire's sixteen runs made? In their first inning, captain and first baseman Hurlick hit a triple. Jefferson, after another near-miss foul, hit to deep center field, bringing home Hurlick and himself; two runs. Seger, the club's center fielder, hit the ball sharply but it was cleanly fielded, holding him to a single. When the next batter, second baseman Pierce, singled, Seger went to second. Catcher Arnold's double scored Seger and advanced Pierce; four runs. Scott, the third baseman, hit a fly bungled by the Red Jackets' pitcher, Dodd, allowing Scott to reach on an error. Smith repeated Scott's example—and Dodd his own, and Smith ended up on first. Left fielder Guy hit a double and shortstop Grabill slammed a triple, clearing the bases, bringing up Hurlick again; seven runs. The captain hit a double to right field and Jefferson held to a single by "good fielding" in left, though Hurlick scored; eight runs. As the result of a "nice airy ball" Seger ended up on second base. Eventually, in attempting to advance, he was out at second base. And so, the account continued until the last out.

A Work in Progress

The reporting indicates baseball was a work in progress for both players and newspaper writers. Clumsily played and erratically reported, baseball appears a mishmash of running, throwing, hitting, and confusion. Frustratingly silent on key points, these reports nonetheless provide a window into the game's early years in Illinois.

Sharper detail reveals hard hitting neutralized or erased by good fielding. And the reverse was true—poor fielding led to trouble. As the *Quincy Whig and Republican* concluded while praising the Occidental Junior Club's outfielders, "High fly catches cannot be beaten by any club, not excepting the 'Crimson Hose'" [a reference to the professional Cincinnati Red Stockings Club].[13]

Hitting balls required timing and accuracy, but stopping them demanded courage. The adoption of fielding gloves lay years in the future. All fielders made catches bare-handed. Even though slightly softer than modern baseballs, the spheres used in the 1860s could sting or, worse, break hands and fingers. The collision of soft tissue and hard baseballs explains many of the injuries peppering game accounts during this time. Add to this the fact that most players were learning the game and unaccustomed to catching the ball, especially high flies in the outfield or spinning infield pop-ups. Mastering the art of fielding provided a competitive advantage.

Moreover, players were not specialists at assigned positions with the possible exceptions of pitcher and catcher. "If a man could hit, throw, catch and run he could play baseball and it was not considered necessary to tie him down to one position," explained a writer in 1918 looking back on the early game. An inescapable reality lay in the game's heart—fielders had to catch fly balls and line drives, bare-handed. Failures to do so help explain the high scores.[14]

In the late 1860s, the "fly rule," forcing fielders to offer bare hands to a speeding baseball, still was a recent addition. Adopted by the National Association of Base Ball Players at their 1864 convention as a trial for the 1865 season, it followed years of lobbying by Chadwick and baseball pioneer Henry Lucius "Doc" Adams. The trial extends to the present day. Before the fly rule, players could be retired on fly balls caught on the first bound. The same was and remained true for foul balls into the 1880s.[15]

Illinois quickly adopted fly rule for what the *Sporting News* later termed "the first fly match played in the west." Baseball historian Jeffrey Kittle describes St. Louis's Empire Club and Freeport's club of the same name negotiating an 1865 Fourth of July match in the Illinois community. Freeport's club began practicing with the new fly rule hoping to gain advantage over the visitors. As the game progressed, however, the Freeport club found their opponents "just doted on fly balls when they came along," aiding St. Louis's 27–20 victory.[16]

Between 1865 and 1870, extant accounts indicate all organized Illinois games played under the fly rule, again explaining the frequent double-digit game scores. Skilled clubs aspired to a higher standard. Good fielding was expected and recognized. When the *Bloomington Pantagraph* learned by telegram of the Bloomington Base Ball Club's victory over the famed Forest City Club of Rockford, which only weeks before defeated the touring Washington (DC) Nationals, earning headlines and praise, the newspaper qualified the win. The 67 to 41 margin in Bloomington's favor was "too heavy a score for a sharp game, indicting [*sic*] slow pitching and heavy batting." And, unstated, poor fielding.[17]

Base stealing goes largely unmentioned in game stories but can be inferred from the high scores. Lacking protective equipment, catchers usually stood well back of the batter. Such positioning allowed the catcher to snare more foul balls on the bound but at the same time it offered base runners greater opportunity to dash to the next base. "Under these circumstances, any body [*sic*] moderately fleet of foot could steal second base," one early player reflected sixty years later. "It was expected that when a batter got to first, he would steal second." He vividly recalled one catcher who upended assumptions by standing right behind home plate. "With this shortened distance he shot the ball to second like a bullet." After a six of his teammates were retired stealing and others picked off base by taking too large a lead, the player's team gave up any attempts to steal. "In fact, with any thing short of a two base hit they were helpless."[18]

The Decatur McPherson Club receiving this lesson was unfamiliar with Centralia's twist on positioning the catcher. Even Henry Chadwick recommended against it in his rules and guidebook for the 1867 season. "The objection to the custom," he wrote, lies "in the fact that it cramps the movements of the pitcher, as it obliges him to pitch for the catcher, in measure, thereby, lessening his field for strategic play." But the game kept moving, and soon other clubs learned Decatur's lesson courtesy of an opponent. In 1865, the new Forest City Club of Rockford, eventually the state's best, foundered when its opponent, the Freeport Empire Club, "refused to remain quietly on the bases like gentlemen; and probably stole whenever they felt like it," gaining a 55–21 victory. And it was not until 1869, a year before Rockford's Forest City Club turned professional, that its catcher moved closer to the batter in order to better "pick 'em off the bat."[19]

Chadwick's opposition to bringing the catcher closer in his guidebooks explain why teams kept their catchers well behind home plate. Further, clubs played for fun, not perfection. Baseball was a social activity providing both exercise and local notoriety. Rising competitive teams like the Forest City Club learned from such experiences and adapted. Others, like Decatur's McPhersons, simply shrugged and played on.

Some players were better athletes and more determined competitors, though for most the game was simply an interlude between youth and adult responsibilities. What do we know of these young men of various skills and commitments who provided baseball's roots in Illinois?

Finding the Players

There were perhaps thousands of them, and most are lost to history. Peter Morris compiled mini biographies for players on the Forest City Club of Rockford, a club in Byron, Chicago's Excelsiors, and a team from Pecatonica.

But those clubs cover only a tiny percentage of all players between 1865 and 1870.[20] Several hundred teams were active in Illinois during this period, but detailed information beyond Morris's four exists for just forty-three clubs in nineteen communities.

Even when writers moved a paragraph or two beyond giving a game score to include box scores, players usually appear simply by last name. This practice complicates identification of baseball participants through city directories and US Census reports. Add to that challenge individuals' mobility during the era; people left little or no trace as they moved from a community after a short residence. Transients were the nineteenth century's equivalent of "dropping off the grid." Between incomplete names and mobility, most players remain unknown.

In twenty communities, as mentioned, sufficient detail exists in game reports and box scores that answers can be found in city directories, US Census reports, and news accounts. But without initials or first names, many remain lost. From those twenty communities, partial rosters for forty-three clubs were recovered in my research (including a few that were short-lived "muffin" clubs), yielding 223 players whose names and, in some cases, occupations could be determined. While obviously a small sample, the 223 players and club officials offer a picture of the game's demography.[21]

Players worked in a occupations as varied as business owners, livery stable workers, professionals, and printers. Among their ranks was one servant, a teamster, two barbers, fifteen appointed or elected government officials, seven who either owned taverns or worked in them, seven farmers, a butcher, two painters, and a cigar maker. In thirty-eight cases, sources are silent on a player's occupation.

Dominant occupational groups were clerks, business owners, and professionals, the latter encompassing lawyers, physicians, civil engineers, and educators. But there was significant representation among the skilled and unskilled, including bookbinders, pressmen, laborers, saloon and restaurant employees, and a livery stable worker. It is surprising, in light of the traditional image of baseball in this era as a game for white-collar workers, that these skilled and unskilled workers received time off when games and practices usually commenced around 2 or 3 p.m., seemingly precluding them from participation. Somehow, these men were able to get time away from their jobs, perhaps thanks to athletic prowess or simply connections with business owners.

Why so many in the unknown category? Minors, living at home and not working, provide one explanation. Also, with the rate of mobility, players might not remain in one place long enough to have occupations listed in city directories or census reports. On this detail, as with so many others, the contemporary documents offer little information. The number of elected or appointed officials (nine) was surprising but reflects yet another level of community involvement through baseball. Some were assistants or clerks in government offices. In those pre–civil service days, such jobs came through party or faction affiliation, in effect, patronage positions.

Club officials may have had links to players. Consider, for example, Stuart Dart, a member of Rock Island's Quicksteps Base Ball Club is listed as a clerk in a grocery store owned by his father, William H. Dart. The elder Dart was treasurer of the Illinois State Base Ball Association in 1867. Centralia had a father-son combination—James Cunningham and James T. Cunningham. James, the elder, was a Civil War veteran, serving as a captain the Eightieth Illinois before his capture and imprisonment in Richmond's Libby Prison until exchanged. By trade he was blacksmith, also operating a stable and serving not only as a town constable but, later, as mayor of Centralia. He played a few games at catcher for the town's top club, the Egyptians. His son, James T., distinguished himself in 1867's Great Tournament of the Western States in Decatur, Illinois. His image survives today, pictured in full uniform and holding the gilded ball his club won in Decatur.[22]

In Cairo, the Munns laid claim to the title of first family of baseball. The most prominent, Daniel W. Munn, played for the Independent Base Ball Club—as did the other Munns—Benjamin and James W. Munn. Daniel W. Munn—or, as his harshest critic, the editor of the *Cairo Democrat*, liked to refer to him, "Bill Dan Munn"—was a Republican, representing the city in the Illinois State Senate. Even worse, in the *Cairo Democrat*'s view, Munn was "an active radical Republican" who had opened his home to a Black doctor touring with a group of southerners who supported the Union during the Civil War. For this and his other perceived political and social sins, the newspaper termed Munn "a shallow-brained fool," someone whose military record "is as bare of honorable conduct as an undiapered babe, and his fast-wagging tongue is as innocent of truth as the Devil of righteousness." Public life in post–Civil War Illinois was not for the thin-skinned.[23]

Benjamin M. Munn, likely Daniel's brother, practiced law with him. James W. Munn was the assistant postmaster at Cairo, a political appointment. The ball field offered a relief from politics, a place where the hot shots came off bats rather than the pens of partisan editors.[24]

Three players for Alton's Shurtleff Collegiate Base Ball Club—F. T. Dubois, J. K. Dubois, and Charles A. (Alex) Starne—were the sons of two Springfield businesspeople, strong baseball supporters who created Springfield's largest venue for ball playing, Railway Park, at the end of the Capital Horse Railway Company's lines west of Springfield.[25]

Centralia Egyptian standout James T. Cunningham posed for a photograph, probably in 1867 or 1868, displaying his uniform, a large bat, and the gilded ball his team won for finishing second in the Grand Base Ball Tournament of the Western States in Decatur. Courtesy of the Centralia Historical Society and Museum.

Springfield's Capital Base Ball Club, taking its name from the horse railway company, had a roster heavily weighted with clerks and professionals. Of seven identifiable players, six were clerks and one, T. C. Mather, was an attorney.[26]

Other clubs, however, had more occupational diversity. Galesburg's College City Club included three laborers, two students, and a player with no

The Babe Ruth of his era, Pana attorney J. C. McQuigg was famous during the Excelsior Base Ball Club's brief existence for striking the ball so hard that it was termed a "humming bird," posing a danger to fielders who got in the way. Courtesy of the Abraham Lincoln Presidential Library and Museum.

listed occupation. Cairo's premier club, the Egyptians, put a barkeeper, a civil engineer, a barber, and an insurance agent on the field. Rock Island's Lively Turtle Base Ball Club included three laborers, three businesspeople, a public official, and three clerks in its lineup.[27]

Occasional examples of athletic skill echoed decades later. Attorney J. C. McQuigg earned renown during the brief life of the Pana Excelsior Base Ball Club and went on to have a long practice in that community. Memories of his home run prowess lingered two decades into the twentieth century. And in 1918, Isaac T. Archer regaled a reporter with details of what he claimed to be "the longest ball ever hit in Decatur" during his days with the equally short-lived McPherson Club.[28]

The Bloomington Base Ball Club was, for a time, one of the state's top three organizations in terms of talent. Its roster was a mixture of political and athletic skills. Lee Cheney, its best player, was already a source of controversy in the mid-1860s, but he brought an unusual background to the club. At the age of fourteen, he enlisted in the Union army as a drummer boy and suffered wounds in battle. When he joined the local club, Cheney was a clerk and later drove a beer delivery wagon.[29]

A gifted athlete, Cheney stood out as one of only two clerks on a roster dominated by business owners and professionals. Teammate Henry A. Ewing, the club president, became McLean County sheriff in 1868, a year after he was admitted to the bar and opened a law practice. Teammate Charters S. Roe was a deputy county circuit clerk, serving under his father, Edward R. Roe. And local coal dealer E. H. Rood was mayor of Bloomington.[30]

Cheney, Lackey, and Patrick J. Keenan, an Irish immigrant, constituted the club's talented core. Pitching prowess later led Keenan to the Chicago Excelsiors Club. The Excelsiors provided an off-field job with a private employer, allowing Keenan plenty of time for practice and play, making him one of the state's first professional players. Cheney, too, eventually turned professional.[31]

Two factors discourage drawing broad conclusions from these 223 players. First, newspapers of the time are missing for large areas of Illinois, especially its western and southeastern portions. Small towns without either a local newspaper or proximity to a larger town or neighboring city with one constitute an information black hole. The spread of the game throughout the state strongly suggests that there were probably more teams and players than have been recorded. Second, as mentioned before, the 223 players identified, even when combined with Morris's data on four other teams, surely represent but a small proportion of those who played the game.

Leavened a bit by those in the labor and tavern and saloon categories, clubs drew players largely among upwardly mobile groups. As well as being a healthy activity, the game represented opportunity for what is today termed networking and were like fraternal organizations in increasing contacts with like-minded and potentially helpful individuals.

Irretrievable from the yellowed, crumbling pages of old city directories and typed transcriptions of census reports is the joy that led and kept these men, ranging from fourteen years old to their early twenties, on those rough playing fields. And, as we peer into their world, straining to see their lives' shadows, we should remember above all, the fun they had and the joy they shared.

Baseball in Illinois between 1865 and 1868 existed, first, for fun. It was an activity that provided exercise *and* generated good times. The game was so enjoyable that at times everyone wanted in on it.

SHARING THE FUN

Then I went on a double quick to the field, and
tried to stop a hot ball. It came toward me from
the bat at the rate of nine miles a minute. I put
up my hands, the ball went sweetly singing on its
way with all the skin from my palms with it. . . .
It's a fine exercise—a little easier than being run
through a threshing machine and not much either.
—Brick Pomeroy[1]

Wisconsin wit Marcus "Brick" Pomeroy, like other newspaper editors, contributors, and letter writers brought a humorous perspective to baseball. They saw a phenomenon, one interesting to readers and providing ample opportunities for editorial comment. Baseball was godsend to editors looking to fill space by exercising their senses of humor. And so, from its beginnings, lampooning the game offered light counterpoint to gambling, competitiveness, and rule disputes stretching baseball's gentlemanly ideals. On-field lampoons augmented editorial winks and jests. These were, as Peter Morris notes, expressed through "muffin" games, contests celebrating mediocrity and incompetence.

Such humor reminded players, spectators, and readers alike of baseball's contagious fun. Envisioned as inclusive, it dealt like any other human endeavor with vanity and futility in the noble struggle for betterment.

Days after young men in Springfield and Princeton organized their cities' first baseball clubs, the *Illinois State Register* and Princeton-based *Bureau County* Patriot put editorial tongues firmly in cheek explaining the new game to readers. "The bat is a club built on the model of the club that Barnum [a reference to showman and serial exaggerator P. T. Barnum] killed Captain Cook with." The game featured much ball-chasing. "It is quite an intelligent game, depending upon the use of your legs. The first principle of the game is running. When you are 'in' you run away from the ball; when you are 'out' you run after it."[2]

Baseball's terminology provoked painful puns from editors and, at times, confused spectators. "Why are base ball clubs a benefit to the community in hot weather?" asked an East St. Louis editor. "Because they have fly catchers." The St. Louis Unions, a top club of the era, pounded Jacksonville's Hardin Base Ball Club and the *Illinois State Journal* shared a joke occurring during the game. "One of the spectators was a lady who had never seen a game of base ball played before. Noticing the strikers in their efforts to strike the ball and the catcher holding himself ready to catch it, she very innocently remarked that she did not understand 'why those fellows with the clubs were trying to keep that fellow from catching the ball.'" And the secular bible of Midwestern Republicanism, Chicago's *Tribune*, envisioned a game played by statuary around the US Capitol, featuring "Columbus, bareheaded, in tights and running shoes, and ancient base ball costume . . . 'chucking' the ball directly at the nude Washington, out in the park, who holds up his palms to receive it."[3]

The *Bureau County Patriot*'s editor, sitting in his Princeton office, surely marveled at his luck in having baseball to offer diversion from politics and local contretemps. Under the headline "Base Ball in the Family," he described a citizen who ran the family household like a baseball club. Dividing into "nines" for seating at the dinner table, each was assigned a position. The servant was ordered to "first base" and the wife, "whose word 'none dare dispute'" filled the role of umpire. As for the father, he was the "'batsman,' his duty being to flog the children." A cry at table from the youngest child became a "foul *bawl*." This worked until one evening when father returned home and found no dinner on the table—a distracted servant the cause. When he ordered the servant to work, the "'Umpire' put in and the result was fuss in the family," illustrating, the *Patriot* concluded, "that base ball is a game that don't work well in the family circle." The editor acknowledged baseball's resemblance to "that delightful game called 'driving an unruly pig out of the garden.' The dodging in both games is nearly the same."[4]

Editors lampooned the game's elaborate rules, rituals, and customs. Such was the case with the "Fat Contributor" to the *Woodstock Sentinel*, who foresaw "A Serious Rival of Base Ball" in another common youthful pastime—"mumble peg!" Americans must and would have a national game but soon, he predicted, popular favor for baseball would decline, replaced by the equipment of mumble peg,—a "jack-knife is a national emblem with us." This game even had its own history and rule book—"Stanberry on Mumble Peg . . . and if anybody knows anything about *mumbling* things, Attorney General Stanberry does [a reference to a US Cabinet member]." Throughout the United States, mumble peg contests flourished, the "Fat Contributor" assured readers. Just the other day, he received an invitation to a match between the "'Jack Knife Handle Mumble Peg Club' of Goshen, and the 'Bow Legged Mumble Peg Club' of Mud Lake, for the champion jack-knife of Ohio." Surely, a national convention of the game's adherents must follow, referencing baseball's national and state gatherings. Mumble peg was the coming game: "Any number of persons can play it. There is no running in the game, as in baseball, unless some outsider runs off with the jack-knife and the club has to run after him to recover it."[5]

Two western Illinois baseball clubs—Colchester and Tennessee—played each other and inspired fanciful reporting written in dialect. The author's seat was "in a retired corner ov the skoolhous frunten the feeld ov ackshun." The spectators—"Old foggies, including a doctor and a preacher, and a feamail with head lites onto her nose, 17 middle aged men, repersentin moder religion, go-a-heditiveness and other branches ov industry, 26 candidates for matrimony and femail suffrage, leanin agin the fense, 13 buners and grovery keepers, 18 young Amerikas without mustashes—total 94." Most players wore "red britches. This fact tu the untrained mind, or to the unthinen masses wuz, perhaps, looked onto as a matter ov no interest, but with one ov my ainshent frends and me, it wuz a perplexon question of whether a man kood run faster, hit harder or ketch a bawl better with red britches than he kood with kommon ones." Eventually, they concluded the pants were for "stile only."[6]

Soon, philosophical inquires by the writer and his "ainshent friends" turned to other matters—such as spectators' faces. "As the game progressed and waxed warm, one kood tell from the loutennances ov the by standers which side wuz ahead, that is if he new whitich town they liven in, or if he new how the tally stook, he kood tell whare each man lived jist from the expreshen ov his face. It is phunny how elashun or depreshun will show itself onto a man fase, unconshuly thus proven the selfhness ov man." Concluding, he apologized for his incomplete account of the game. "I don't know much about the game, and hav, therefour, give it *virbattum viterum* from the skoarers board, but I as satisfied that a boy settin near me kaut a good many flies that aint reported, and it seems tu me, that there was mor'n 8 run home when that shower cum up, but the skoarers ought tu no best."[7]

Two Peoria baseball clubs merged in 1867, forming a new club sponsored by a local flour mill and bakery. One newspaper saw an opportunity to poke fun. A letter to one of the editors, who often wrote under the name "Snooks," claimed there was still "enough dormant science and undeveloped muscle in Peoria to support more than one good base ball club." Offended by the commercialization of the game when the Excelsior and Enterprise clubs became the bakery-sponsored Fort Clark Base Ball Club, citizens met to protest and organize a new club. Their meeting convened on the local post office's cellar door. The first challenge, the writer recounted, was selecting a name with the same impact as the new Fort Clark Club. Finally, they hit upon the "Mrs. Raney Baking Powder Base Ball Club."[8]

The "Mrs. Raney Baking Powder Club" limited membership to "any person . . . who has no more respect for himself or friends than to join a club with such a name." Referencing the current battle in Illinois over the eight-hour day, the club's rules provided that any member "who goes out on three strikes" became an honorary member of the Eight Hour League. Broken-nosed pitchers must remain in games "but a pitcher without a handle [referring to the handle on a container used to hold liquids] shall not be permitted on the field." Other rules covered play. "Owing to the frequent practice of 'running the bases,' they will always be tied to the ground to prevent their being run." The club's shortstop must "exercise great caution in taking 'hot' balls . . . and should allow these to remain on the ground long enough to cool before handling them." "'Dead' balls" must be removed from the field "before they become offensive." And any catcher snaring a "'foul' ball" was allowed time to "'deodorize' and wash his hands."[9]

Criticism of the commercialization of baseball in Fort Clark's sponsorship, disguised in humor, underlies this fanciful account. In the twenty-first century, business enterprises affix their names to ballparks everywhere, and it is worth noting that the Fort Clark Base Ball Club, the Springfield's Capital Club, and Ottawa's Clifton Club (named for a hotel) were the only teams in Illinois during this period named for a commercial enterprise. "Great credit is due the Fort Clark Club for the original and novel system of base ball nomenclature adopted by them," the letter's writer concluded. "It is to be hoped that the National Association will second their efforts at reform in this particular."[10]

Honorary Members and Hapless Players

As honorary members of baseball clubs who sometimes even played baseball, editors wrote humorously of their forays into the game. An example comes from the editor of the *Ottawa Free Trader*. Taking the field one afternoon, he found "we could catch a 'fly' as well as molasses—caught ours in our neat, but not gaudy—mouth." Trying to umpire, he came close to a beating over a decision and, a result, he hadn't "dared to be seen on the ball 'pastures' since."[11]

His election as an honorary member of the Peoria Olympics Base Ball Club delighted another editor. "Visions of balls and bats, and bags and stakes floated over our imagination since we ascertained the fact that we were a base-baller," he confessed. Concluding that even honorary membership required some skill, he practiced in his parlor. Fifteen minutes later, he had "smashed the mirrors, knocked over the what-not, busted a hole in the picture of our revered dad, floored a picture of General Washington, sprained our finger, tore the carpet, busted our boot and several other minor achievements." Though he appreciated the honorary membership, he prayed never to step on the field.[12]

Another hapless baseballist, likely an editor, reported his adventures to the *Du Quoin Tribune*. "Jentleman Jenks" watched many games, studying rules and regulations, and became confident he could play easily and well. Reporting for practice, his assignment was right field. "But we didn't show off to much advantage and were ordered to close in. We closed in, and were afterwards called short-stop." New adventures commenced, constituting a series of miscues, miscalculations, and disasters all close enough in form to Brick Pomeroy's adventure to be a copy. But if Pomeroy's adventure, recounted later in this chapter, was its foundation, Jenks's story had its own additions.

Sent to play first base, Jenks delightfully found "a small pillow filled with sawdust, made on purpose for the convenience of players who are tired. We were tired. And took a sitting posture." Rebuked by the team's captain, he then spied a throw coming his way. Surprised, and "not wishing to get hit," Jenks allowed the ball to go to "where it had a mind to." After trying and failing at catcher, he was the object of derision from the captain, his teammates, and spectators. Finally, Jenks assumed umpiring duties. "This disgusted most every one, including us." Leaving the field, he decided "Not any more base ball for Jentleman Jenks."[13]

Jenks's contribution to baseball humor resembles a better-known piece from the pen of a prominent—and sometimes reviled—newspaper editor, Marcus M. "Brick" Pomeroy. A polarizing character in his times, Pomeroy is largely unknown today to all but Civil War scholars. During the Civil War, he published and edited an initially pro-Union Wisconsin newspaper, the *La Crosse Democrat*. But Lincoln's Emancipation Proclamation transformed Pomeroy from a supporter to a harsh critic, both of the president person-ally and of his administration. Before the Civil War, while editing another Wisconsin newspaper, Pomeroy's clever satire of a neighboring town drew the admiration of *Louisville* (KY) *Journal* editor George D. Prentice, who bestowed the "Brick" nickname. Through financial ups and downs, Pomeroy retained his fiery pen and appetite for political battle. Describing his style, one writer observed, "By its vividness, its personal combativeness, and politi-cal partisanship, it gained national notoriety." As the new game invaded the

Polemicist, partisan, and mauler of opponents in a manner befitting his nickname, "Brick," Marcus M. Pomeroy had a humorous streak that he used to great effect in lampooning his own experiences (real or imagined) with baseball. Courtesy of the Wisconsin Historical Society, WHI-85027.

Midwest, Pomeroy paused in lambasting Reconstruction policies to comment on the game then peppering the columns of exchange newspapers crossing his desk.[14]

Pomeroy's humorous reflections open with his own imagined or real experience on the ball field. As Pomeroy was thirty-four years old in 1867, it is plausible that he played the game on occasion. In light of his skill as a writer and his sense of humor, however, it is more likely that his testimony, reprinted in many newspapers, is fanciful self-depreciation.

Images of his battered body—hands, eyes, bruised cheeks—open the piece, the result of "Base ball. That is the row." His doctor recommended the game as a source of exercise. Trusting his physician, Pomeroy obtains an instruction book. After five days' study, believing he understands the game's principles, Pomeroy invests in a uniform—"a sugar-scoop cap, a red belt, a green shirt, yellow trousers, pumpkin colored shoes, a paper collar and purple neck tie." Thus gaudily attired, he took the field.[15]

Separating into "nines," he and his fellows were ready to play. "The ball," he explains, "is a pretty little drop of softness, the size of a goose egg, and five degrees harder than a brick." The game is "much like chess, only a little more *chase* than chess." Pomeroy examines another piece of equipment. "I took the bat. It is a murderous plaything descending from Pocahontas to the head of John Smith." The game commences when the umpire calls "play." "It is the most methodical play I know of, this base ball. Sawing hard wood is moonlight rambles beside base ball." Pomeroy allows the first pitch to pass— "it looked pretty coming, so I let it come." He struck the next ball "greatly upward," and the pitcher caught it. Not paying attention, Pomeroy was struck by the next batter's line drive hit. "A mule kicked me on the cheek. The man said it was the ball. It felt like a mule and I reposed on the grass. The ball went on." As the sides changed, the editor took a position in left field, "standing on my dignity" when a "hot ball . . . came skyrocketing toward me. My Captain yelled, 'take it!'" Pomeroy noticed "how sweetly the ball descended. . . . I felt something warm in my eye! 'Muffin!' yelled ninety fellows. 'Muffin be d . . . d! It's a cannon ball!' For 3 days I've had two pounds of raw beef on that eye, and yet it paineth!"[16]

He wanted to leave, "but my gentle Captain said, 'nay.' So I nayed and stayed." At the striker's line once more, he swung at and missed the first pitch. The second came in "neck high. It struck me in the gullet," though the umpire called the ball a foul. He drove the third pitch into right field, "through a parlor window—a kerosene lamp, and rip up against the head of an infant who was quietly taking its ---- nap in his or its mother's arms." Pomeroy "slung the bat" aside and "meandered forth to the first base," only to hear "high words." In flinging the bat, he struck the umpire, breaking his jaw. For this the fine was ten cents. Still, "the game went on and I liked it. . . . Base ball is a sweet little game." At his next at-bat, "I noticed everybody moved back about ten rods! The new umpire retreated twelve rods. He was timid!" After taking a few pitches, Pomeroy drove another ball to right field, where "a fat man and his dog sat in the shade of an oak tree enjoying the game. The ball broke one leg of the dog and landed like a runaway engine in the corporosity [*sic*] of the fat man. He was taken home to die."[17]

Once more in the field, Pomeroy tries to "stop a hot ball. It came toward me from the bat at the rate of nine miles a minute. I put up my hands, the ball went sweetly singing on its way with all the skin from my palms with it." Reflecting on the game, he realized "I've played five times and this is the result: Twenty-seven dollars paid out for things; one bunged eye, badly bunged; one broken little finger; one bump on the head; nineteen lame backs; a sore jaw; one thumb dislocated; three sprained ankles; one dislocated shoulder, from trying to throw a ball a thousand yards; two hands raw from trying to stop hot balls; a lump the size of a hornet's nest on the left hip, well back; a nose sweetly jammed and five uniforms spoiled from rolling in the dirt at the bases." After two weeks' exposure, he did not like the game. "There is not a square inch on in or under me but aches. . . . I never worked so hard since Ruth stole wheat, and never was so lame since the burning of Luther."[18]

Yet he was proud of his proficiency. "It's a fine exercise—a little easier than being run through a threshing machine and not much either." Examining the scorer's book, Pomeroy found he'd broken "seven bats, made one tally, broke one umpire's jaw, broke ten windows in adjoining houses, killed a baby, broke the leg of a dog, and mortally injured the bread-basket of a spectator, knocking five other players out of time by slinging my bat, and knocked the waterfall from a school-marm who was standing twenty yards from the field, a quiet looker-on." He also accounted for "fifteen bottles of arnica liniment, five bottles of lotions, half a raw beef, and am so full of pain that it seems as if my bones were but bats, and my legs the limbs of a dead horse-chestnut, instead of the once elegant trotters of Brick Pomeroy."[19]

Fanciful baseball contests and self-depreciating field performances, real or imagined, amused and whetted the public's appetite for information and fun from the new game. They lightened other news of wins, losses, and, sometimes, disputes. Articles like Pomeroy's demonstrate the serious mistake in underestimating the sheer attraction of the game's "fun" element. And as teams organized, set match games, reviewed rules, and purchased uniforms, these chores were made endurable by a desire to share in the game's joys.

Muffin Games

In his work on baseball's early decades, Peter Morris identifies the muffin game as a way to satirize and critique the official game while having a good time. The term *muffin* identified an inexpert player. Obviously, muffin games focused more on enjoyment for participants and spectators than on who won. Morris persuasively argues that muffin games nationally were a reaction to a growing professionalism and competitiveness. Making a direct connection in Illinois is complicated by the limited sample of the 1865–70 period. Some games do fall into this category, but others simply manifest a desire to join in the fun.[20]

Morris asserts that the game's post–Civil War growth increased the emphasis on winning by the end of the 1860s, creating "first nine" teams on clubs. This phenomenon diminished playing roles for less-gifted ballists. Those less-talented members footed the bill for the top nine and received less playing time. In response, club members got up muffin games not only in order to lampoon the game's direction but to "play baseball for the simple pleasures it afforded." Likewise, a public, tiring of conflict and winning-above-all attitudes, enthusiastically watched these inferior players "bumble their way through a burlesque of the national pastime."[21]

A classic muffin contest, as described by Morris, pits fat versus lean players or two teams of heavyweight players, often with humorous rules emphasizing the inability of the players to perform at the game's highest level. For example, an 1868 game in Clinton pitted the local Eureka Club's second nine against "a heavy nine of 'muffins,' whose uniform included a "tight fitting" shirt inscribed with red lettering, "let 'er be" on the shirt's back. Illinoisans enjoyed these matchups as well as occupational pairings such as physicians versus lawyers, editors versus printers, bachelors versus married men, and other contests based on age or other factors.[22]

Because progress of the game through Illinois was uneven, greater emphasis on competitive goals arrived sooner in some areas than in others, and many of the state's muffin games simply were an enthusiastic response to a new activity, a desire to join in the fun even at the expense of looking foolish.

Boasting ten clubs, Cairo was especially smitten with baseball. Its citizens also enjoyed satire and fun. Two 1867 muffin teams drew local newspaper attention by highlighting their athletic inferiority while celebrating the joy of play. "Challenges, gracefully written on perfumed note to the number of a dozen have passed between the 'Grasshopper' and 'Caterpillar' clubs," the *Cairo Democrat* told its readers. Exaggerating both the formality of rituals and the fire of competition, the captain of the Caterpillars challenged his counterpart, "The quivering anxiety of my noble nine to 'wax' the 'Hoppers' is irrepressible!" Grasshopper captain Sherry Gillett, fired back, "My elastic nine are in the waxing business themselves, some, and propose to apply the glutinous substance to your'n." The newspaper shared an important fact—none of these players had ever played baseball. Aside from avoiding a wax coating, the game's winner was assured "sixty-eight dollars in city scrip, a patent cork-screw and a sack of oats." If the contest continued past the sun's setting, "moonshine" would illuminate the last innings.[23]

Selection of an umpire highlighted the anticipated incompetence. The choice had "never saw a game played in his life and has been peremptorily denied the privilege of informing himself." Spectators should "please restrain all undue levity should there be an occasional mistake or blunder." As it was more than likely that "every man who takes the bat will . . . knock himself on the head, it is hoped the bystanders will be considerate enough to give him falling room."[24]

After pregame rituals, play commenced, ending in a 14–8 victory for the Grasshoppers. Spectators savored the supposed "feats of fleet-footedness" or the moment a player held up a "hissing" fly ball he caught, which were "to excite the applause such an accomplishment deserved." The *Cairo Democrat*'s owner, J. H. Oberly, congratulated himself for joining the winners as scorer. As the losing club, the Caterpillars, faded, its first baseman "became fatigued" and the right fielder sought relief under a shade tree. Soon after, the game was called.[25]

A rematch spurred more fun. Once again, captains penned elaborate challenges and responses. The newspaper was overjoyed. "The 'worms' and 'insects' return to the ball and bat, each desperately bent on victory or exhaustion." Caterpillar captain A. Sweeney ended his challenge "With the highest appreciation of the nerve and muscle which delude you into the notion of base-ballistic equality with the Caterpillars." Sherry Gillett responded for the Grasshoppers: "We can give you 'cats' 'rats,' and . . . we can hop more muchly than you can crawls." The September 21, 1867, game promised to be a "sweating ordeal," made interesting by a "wager of $25 and a supper for the party."[26]

Another poke at the national pastime's emerging language came under the headline "Forbidden Slang." Perceiving an "evident inclination on the part of some to degrade the beautiful game of base ball to the level of the prize ring," the two muffin clubs agreed to ban "slang appellations" such as "daisy cutters" [a term for a hard-hit ground ball], "muffins," "skyscrapers" [high fly balls to the outfield], "taking it on the fly," and "gobbling the huckleberry [possibly meaning to catch the ball; "huckleberry" was sometimes used to describe a small object]." Anyone using such terms "will be peremptorily expelled from his club."[27]

Muffin matches bestowed another blessing on the *Cairo Democrat*—a chance to editorially bash its Paducah, Kentucky, rival. When Len Faxson, local editor of *Paducah Herald*, wrote a detailed account of the rematch, the Cairo journal refused to use it. "It is peculiarly Faxonish, and *therefore* of too immoral nature for reproduction in these columns," the *Democrat* explained, banning all save a few sentences describing the play of Fagin, the local editor of the *Democrat*. "The temporary local of the Democrat made a home run on all fours, in regular Kangeroo style, which 'feet' was greeted with tremendous applause," Faxson wrote. "Thereupon Mose Harrell held up his paddle and stopped a ball and then called for a dray, upon which he reclined his graceful form, and gave directions to the driver to drive all over the bases until he got back to the place where the feller was standing with the paddle. He did so, and Mose scored one." In mock outrage, Fagin declared the *Herald* was "stricken from our exchange list."[28]

One slow news day, an editor of the *Ottawa Free Trader* announced an addition to the river city's ball clubs, the 'Hefty' Base Ball Club, containing "the most solid and substantial in the material of its make up as will be seen by the list and averdupois [*sic*] of its members." Collectively, the first nine weighed 2,100 pounds—in the writer's exaggeration. Adding in the second and third nines, the club tipped the scale at "5,424 pounds." Not surprising considering the club's solitary rule: "no member weighing less than 200 admitted. . . . The club challenges any other of equal weight to a match game to be played with the thermometer not below 85 Fahrenheit."[29]

Taking the field within weeks, the new club played at least two games, its only casualty a ballist who dislocated a little finger "trying to catch a pretty swift ball." The "Hefty" Club or an offshoot of it, the Avoirdupois, played in August with the Infants, whose members were around fifteen years old. On a 100-degree day, the Infants arrived early, but their opponents dallied, the game commencing when two spectators filled gaps on the Avoirdupois roster. "Five innings were agreed upon as the game, the 'hefts' well knowing that ambulances would have to be called into requisition should they attempt a much longer game." As expected, the Avoirdupois players were poor on defense and unfamiliar with the "laws of the game." Spectators enjoyed the game, "which to be appreciated must have been seen."[30]

Three years later, other ample-bodied Ottawa baseball enthusiasts stepped onto the field and, as a "rotund nine," challenged the city's finest club, the Shabbonas. An Ottawa editor umpired the game and confessed an attempt to even the odds by ruling against the Shabbonas. The game ended with a 28–24 win for the Shabbona but "had we been umpire two minutes longer, the avoirdupois men would have been the victors in that fight."[31]

"Fat" clubs like the Avoirdupois adopted special rules newspapers took delight in printing. The rules banned anyone over 300 pounds from playing, allowed the use of "express wagons" to "carry the players from base to base. . . . No player will be allowed more than three men to help him to his home base." A player taking more than fifteen minutes in going from one base to another was out. No spectators were allowed within twenty feet of the bat. "Players can stop for refreshments at each base, where a small bottle will be found." In various versions of the "rules," the bottle was either a "*base vial*" or a "*beerconical*." A meeting in a Champaign butcher shop planned such a team. "No one admitted who weighs less than two hundred and ten pounds." The goal of the fictitious team was to defeat the "Nationals of Washington, who are now in this state playing for the championship."[32]

Two northern Illinois cities paired up in a "fat" match featuring Dixon's "Quiet Club" and the "Lummux Club" of Sterling, both teams "composed of parties opposed to violent exercise in whatever shape it may come," hence, special rules. Any player making first base would be "carried the balance of the distance around." Play would commence when the weather cooled enough so players could walk ten yards without perspiring. In Pana, a Catholic priest announced another "large" club. "Father Vaughn informs us that there is to be a Base Ball club started in this place, which no person weighing less than 200 pounds will be allowed to join." Later that summer, Pana looked forward to a new team, the Wallapus club, "a heavy institution. It is thought they will be able to 'Wollop' something if they practice long enough."[33]

"Fat versus lean" matches offered a variation on the "fat" club tradition. Mound City's Monitor Base Ball Club hosted a match between its light and heavyweight members. A similar match between fat and slim nines in Jacksonville promised to be "comic, elegant, unique, eccentric and *recherché*, as well as grand, gloomy and peculiar." Later, the newspaper reported that the fat nine's captain had procured someone to field for him. Sadly, or fortunately for baseball's standards, no account of the game survives.[34]

Age versus Youth

Another muffin matchup, youth versus age, was equally popular.

Two teams contested in a July 1867 match on the DeKalb County fairgrounds in Sycamore. Both teams—the Juvenile Athletics of Sycamore and the Innocent Infants of DeKalb—were adults rather than teens and toddlers. "Phineas Joslyn Sr." and "Major Whorry" were among the Athletics, and the Infant roster included "Rev. Hoisington." One play supports this conclusion: "Hoisington went to bat and sent a splendid ball over towards the brewery in left field. Paine went for the ball in splendid style, and returned . . . with the ball in one hand and a glass of Corkings' ale in the other."[35]

A player was put out between second and third base two hours after he started from second. Continuing, the newspaper described "most wonderful feats . . . performed ever recorded on athletic sports, ancient or modern. Some of the players could jump fifteen feet high and catch a ball," while others turned "somersaults backwards" and caught balls "in their teeth." Of course, these displays were fanciful, as, "the weather being warm, they [the players] concluded not to perform these feats until some other day." When the game ended in a tie, several local men, "who had bet heavily on the result of the game, demanded the return of the stakes."[36]

The entire game possibly sprang from an editor's imagination, a chance to poke fun at local citizens while satirizing the baseball's increasing seriousness. Telling is his acknowledgment of gambling's growing role by creating a postgame uproar among bettors dissatisfied with the tie.

Contests based on age divisions were common in other Illinois communities. Jacksonville's baseball organizations included, for a time, the Relic Base Ball Club. The aged Relics met a local junior club, the Alert Base Ball Club, and an editor laced his reportage with humor. When the Relics took the first bat, the "Umpire was the busiest man in the ring. He calls nine strikes in rapid succession, after which violent exercise, he refreshes himself with an umbrella." The Relics moved onto the field as "Scorers disconsolately whittle their pencils." The Alerts then sent the Relics to "chasing the ball about like mad with ineffectual efforts to catch flies." As this dance became "wearisome to spectators," the Alerts allowed "their opponents to come in and rest awhile," while scorers filled the pages with Alert home runs.[37]

The Relics enjoyed some success batting. After one player hit safely, rather than running to first base, he headed to second base "straight over the pitcher and short stop." After the game, no member of the Relic Club could purchase life insurance "on account of damage received in the great match of to-day."[38]

In Stark County, two clubs likely composed of out-of-shape adults, the Old Fogies and the Greenhorns, played in October 1869, resulting in the "most amusing and laughable game of the season." The Old Fogies managed to squeeze out a one-run victory. The writer noted, however, that Dr. Chamberlain of the Greenhorns, who "showed his rejuvenated activity to the delighted multitude by rolling to the first base and past but did not get back in time to prevent being put out."[39]

Baseball mania's first blush sometimes emboldened older men to test their skills. During the summer of 1866, new baseball clubs popped up every week in Springfield, even the likely imaginary Veteran Club. Its listed members included Alexander Starne, Jesse K. Dubois, O. M. Hatch, and Newton Bateman—all current or former state officeholders. Starne and Dubois, of course, were owners of the Capital Horse Railway Company and the land used as the main baseball grounds but also the fathers of prominent players. The new club's members met for practice one day and, days later, received a nudge from the local Democratic newspaper to "enter the lists and show these youngsters that muscle is not yet extinct among us." The same newspaper welcomed the Veteran club, observing, "In England, the best cricketers are men of middle age, whose muscles are firm, and whose nerves are well strung. Base ball, being our national pastime, should be enjoyed by young and old."[40]

Quincy considered forming a club composed of "ancient settlers." "Quite a number of venerable athlests [*sic*] have enrolled themselves. . . . The aged citizens talk seriously of teaching the youth of the city how to play base ball." Perhaps with more humor than sincerity, the newspaper account ended with the hope that "our young men will go to work in earnest and not be outdone in the matter of playing base ball by the patriarchs of the city."[41]

Another "old" club emerged on the state's eastern border, according to the *Danville Commercial*. Its members had never played the game in its modern form. As a result, "the regular clubs anticipate a good time and some rare fun at the expense of the Muffins in their ludicrous attempts to play their old fashioned game." The "old" club was sensitive and "somewhat bashful. . . . Don't everybody go to laugh at their blunders the first game, or they will get discouraged and play no more." Perhaps there was too much laughter that day, for there is no further mention of the muffin players or the club.[42]

Bachelors versus Married Men

Aligning teams by matrimonial status proved popular—bachelors versus married men, heads of families against singles, and so on. In 1866, two Cairo clubs—the Independents and the Egyptians—reassembled to create married and unmarried teams. Their match attracted a good crowd. The Bloomington Base Ball Club offered intraclub matches along the same lines in the spring of 1867. The bachelors lost. Marengo's married men also prevailed, though not without cost. "Elder David Teed was making his last run" when he sprained his ankle. "He will be without the use of his foot for a long time."[43]

In Lincoln, "Heads of Families" challenged local bachelors to a game in late August 1867. After the challengers won the first contest, a rematch was set. A prize was offered to the winning team's fastest runner. Avenging their previous loss, the bachelors won the game, "Dr. Hunting" taking home the prize cradle. "What use the Doctor will ever have for it if he continues his present style of living we know not." The newspaper encouraged him to "get married and find use for it."[44]

Lawyers against All Comers

Illinois lawyers were known for their verbosity, and muffin games involving them inspired florid descriptions in local newspapers. Lawyers in the twin cities of Champaign and Urbana contended in 1867, delighting a local newspaper. The *Champaign Gazette and Union* began its extended account with an observation. Where quinine once was the best-selling drug in local markets to relieve malaria "chills and shakes and coughs and sniffling sneezes," the fever was now supplanted by the "great national game." As a result, tincture arnica, a treatment for sore muscles, was in great demand, "generally ascribed to the muffin game of base ball played in our city between the lawyers of Urbana and those of this place." Two lawyers, "Frank Jaques and J. C. Sheldon," the "*heaviest* lawyers in the county, their aggregate weight fetching down 400" received special attention. During the game, they "floated over the field like zephyrs and as gracefully as gazelles." As to the other players, "Indeed, it presented one of those fearful sights which beggars description." Fielders slid through the wet field's muck on all fours trying to stop the ball. One fielder's ball-stung fingers led to a muff. The "sleek, bald" head of "Judge Ayers . . . bobbing along between the bases" proved particularly memorable. True to their profession, "We heard all those eighteen lawyers bossing the game and at the same time. We heard eloquent disciples of Blackstone and Chitty demur to the decision of the umpire and argue side of the question a la court house." Darkness ended the game, giving the Urbana lawyers a 68–61 victory. "If this muffin game was played as a muffin game, then the Champaign bar is ahead on the principles which govern the mule races where the slowest mule takes the purse."[45]

Equally enjoyed by whimsical editors and readers were contests pitting physicians against lawyers. The *Monmouth Review*, stirring the pot for such a game, announced that local physicians were challenging "lazy lawyers." Game attendance was "15,000; there may not have been so many—I know there were no more. In fact, the census would probably reduce the number," admitted the newspaper's correspondent, "Timothens Moonshine."[46]

"Moonshine" asserted confidence in his report but admitted it was not from the score sheets. Inaccuracies, he promised, stemming from a defective memory were well-intentioned. His lampoon follows the lines described by Peter Morris, touching all the points—umpiring, betting, and unscientific, laughable play by the participants. The umpire, selected from among seven men, was too poor to gamble on the game and therefore trustworthy. After reaching first base, players sometimes refused to proceed. One player approaching first base stopped to adjust his collar. A physician ambled on the basepaths with the gait of a buffalo. A lawyer hit the ball "toward the railroad" and it was termed "dead." But the physician's team's pitcher "administers something and it recovers. Great joy." Another player's "*epidermis* peeled off the *pyramidalis nasi*, immediately below the *osbicularis palpetrarum*."[47]

The crisis arrived in the ninth. "The 'limbs' [physicians] came up full of *elan* and attacked the enemy's works but were repulsed at all points." The lawyers made a few more tallies and won the game. "I think the game was a success," "Moonshine" observed. "A good deal of 'bawling' was done by various parties."[48]

Other occupations jumped into the fun. The *Chicago Tribune* reported Springfield's druggists challenging local physicians to a game. In Amboy, a club of young retail clerks organized as the Counter Jumpers and went on to win the Lee County championship. Monmouth's painters challenged "any street, trade or profession" to a match game. Rock Island's "grocery men" beat the "dry goods men" 45 to 28. And Champaign's insurance agents offered a game to their counterparts in Urbana.[49]

Bloomington's drugstore clerks played their dry-goods counterparts at the fairgrounds. The game may have served as a distraction from the troubles of the city's crack club, the Bloomington Base Ball Club. "We advise everybody to go out and enjoy a good old muffin game," the local newspaper advised. "Scientific base ball will be nowhere by the side of this one in the fun to be extracted from it. Go and see the exhibition of broken noses, barked shins and bunged eyes that deadly fray will make among the contestants. . . . We predict this will be the high game of the season."[50]

Game day found the *Pantagraph* still beating the drum. "Splinters, bandages," and tonic for sore muscles were ready. In practice, the competing nines suffered skinned fingers. "The game will afford an unlimited amount of fun." Rain showers held down attendance, but the competing nines persevered, playing in the mud. "The players immortalized themselves by the zeal they displayed and utter disregard of all the 'fine points.'" Science was at a discount and victory went to the drugstore clerks, 44 to 37.[51]

Muffin clubs organized in Monmouth were based on streets and occupations. Two picked nines—one from Broadway, the other from Main Street, contended for ice cream. The clerks, mechanics, and businesspeople from the two streets had never played the game. Even with three-digit temperatures that July 1870 day, a large crowd turned out. Main Street won, but the aftermath found members of both nines "oiling up stiff joints, patching sore thumbs, poulticing stone bruises, and washing off tan and freckles."[52]

Rock Island grocers and dry-goods clerks jumped into the fun. The first rule for the contest—"No man shall be allowed to play who now is, or ever has been, a member of any base ball club." Determined to keep out "ringers," the rules allowed a club to select an experienced "base ballist" as captain, but he was barred from playing. And, if a player was hurt, no substitutes were allowed.[53]

Catching the spirit as well that year was a collection of Bloomington professionals. Local lawyers issued a challenge to "any nine Ministers, Doctors, Professors, and Bankers." A hastily assembled team of physicians, professors, and ministers accepted. Apparently forgetting its earlier description of the drugstore clerks versus dry-goods store clerks contest, the *Pantagraph* encouraged readers not to miss "an opportunity of witnessing the great contest of the season." After five of the lawyers' nine failed to show up, experienced players took their places. Surprising no one, the "lawyer" team won 55–26. Classic muffin terms peppered the game story, humor taking precedence over actual detail. "A muffin game played by lawyers, who made a brief game, or a game of briefs of it, against kid-gloved professors who demurred to holding red hot balls, and yet stole marches undismayed by the presence of the limbs of the law in the presence of sixty-three spectators and two small boys watching intently the men who physic and tormented the community, strive to make each others [*sic*] own dead beat."[54]

Greatest press attention to muffin games appeared when printers and, especially, editors were involved. The *Chicago Tribune* carried a lengthy account of an editors versus printer's muffin match in August 1867 and the same month took note of another in Springfield. It gleefully anticipated the downstate editors-printers match. It "bids fair to be one of the funniest affairs of the season," if only because both clubs were made up of men unfamiliar with the game. It also urged players from regular clubs to attend and "see the way in which the game *can* be played by parties who (don't) know how to do it."[55]

Ottawa's competing Democratic and Republican newspapers carried their rivalry to the ball grounds. Printers from the Democratic *Free Trader* and the *Republican* arranged a match of seven innings with eight players to a side because the *Republican* could muster only that number. On game day, triple-digit temperatures threatened, nearly postponing the affair, especially as the *Free Trader* club also was short players and forced to bring in two inexperienced replacements—the senior editor and the printing foreman. When clouds arrived and obscured the sun, the game commenced.[56]

After the *Republican* took the lead, the Democrats came on, led by the "senior editor, making his maiden bat." He hit safely and scored. The teams stayed close, "the Republicans, not yet disheartened, went in *wicked*, sending several flies of amazing altitude and swiftness across the field." Buoyed by his success at the plate, the Free Press "senior editor . . . recklessly confronted one of the most savage of these flies and essayed to stop it. He might as well tried to stop a cannon ball. It simply touched the third finger of his left hand

and stopped in the grass about five or six rods behind him." Looking down at his finger, the editor found "the first joint turned back at right angles, and the inside of the joint badly lacerated. He then and there came to the conclusion that base ball, and, particularly, catching flies, was not 'his strong hold.'" The Republicans suffered similar mishaps. Their pitcher "undertook to gobble a fly by receiving it between his eyes, a feat in which he signally failed; and one of their fielders undertook to gobble a similar bird by receiving it on his forehead—another failure."[57]

At Decatur's Grand Base Ball Tournament of the Great Western States in September 1867, the weak performance of the host club, the McPhersons, plus controversy on the field, and a poor financial return placed a cloud over the multiday event. But its last day provided a commodity all too rare during the hot, dusty, and disappointing week—fun, delivered via a muffin game between local editors and printers. The game lampooned athletic skill and deportment. At one point, the editors "left the field for refreshments and returned refreshed, most of them whipping their mouths as if they had been drinking water," a probable reference to beer. One of the printers knocked a ball into left field, where the editors' fielder, dozing, failed to get it. Another outfielder, chasing a fly ball, tumbled into a creek that ran through the playing field. "Demoralized," he gave up the effort. Winning the game 24–22, the editors retired from the playing ground "in a two-horse wagon, the band playing, 'See the Conquering Hero Comes.'" Yet victor and vanquished shared a common fate. "No bones were broken, but a worse crippled set of men never walked the streets of Decatur than the green players of this game. Stiff joints and sore muscles were the prevailing complaint and arnica was in great demand."[58]

Satires of the game written and played out by muffin games offer insight into baseball's formative years in Illinois. Increasing emphasis on athletic skill, as Morris notes, saw a counterreaction in games where fielders fell or stumbled, injured fingers and heads, yet were in on the fun. Base runners refusing to advance because of fatigue or disinterest were laughed with and at rather than booed. An increasingly disputatious environment on the field became humorous when satirized in muffin games or editorial comment. And the "gorilla in the room"—gambling—earned chuckles at a light-hearted distance.

Although editors, players, and spectators alike would eventually lose the battle to restore the shared fun and enthusiasm of the 1865–69 game, it can be said they went down not with a whimper but amid smiles and laughter.

Humor was a distraction from the game's problems, not only the disputes and gambling but the absence of those not deemed fit to compete with white males. Seeking to play and enjoy the game, Black men, and some white women, instead encountered condescension and denigration.

BARRIERS OF RACE AND GENDER

Our colored brethren can play base
ball, and do it well into the bargain.
—*Chicago Tribune*, August 24, 1870[1]

B aseball knew no color line as it spread over Illinois in the post–Civil War years. A LaSalle reporter visiting Bloomington observed that "Base ball is all the rage—clubs of boys from five years up to men of forty" playing the game. The game's contagion filled vacant lots, alleys, and even the public streets with ballplayers, transcending class, trade, and professional barriers. "All nationalities, both white and black, meet on an equality of the grounds of the base ball clubs."[2] But the LaSalle reporter exaggerated. "Equality of the grounds" did not exist in Bloomington or other Illinois cities, towns, and villages.

Racial questions triggered raging controversies that coincided with the game's growth. Would both former southern slaves and free Blacks in the North play against whites when significant opinion both in the former Confederate states and in the North demanded a white-only standard? On a larger scale, fostering reconciliation with the Confederate states by allowing racists in both sections to ensure inequality for Blacks culminated in 1877 with the abandonment of Reconstruction by the dominant Republican Party, leaving the southern freedmen at the tender mercies of their former masters.

Baseball was ahead of this curve. A decade earlier, the National Association of Base Ball Players met and unanimously approved a recommendation "against the admission of any club which may be composed of one or more colored persons."[3]

The 1867 convention's action is sometimes viewed as the beginning of discrimination in baseball, but Ryan A. Swanson's *When Baseball Went White: Reconstruction, Reconciliation, and Dreams of a National Pastime* reveals a complex process. First, there was tenuous acceptance of "colored" clubs by white clubs in some cities, but it was succeeded by increasing racial discrimination to attract southern participation in the game and its national organization.[4]

Swanson's study, focusing on Philadelphia, Washington, DC, and Richmond, Virginia, recounts the policy of exclusion. Black men too caught the baseball mania sweeping the nation in the post–Civil War years. But another obsession—-"sectional reconciliation"—simultaneously advanced through the North and South. A handful of white northerners did see the game as a means of promoting equality, but their voices were drowned out by others' determination to make baseball a truly national game. Achieving the latter goal required banning Blacks from organized baseball. That was the price demanded by baseball's southern proponents. This also required driving integration's proponents from leadership in the game's national organization and forcing Blacks off ball fields used by whites, in some cases violently.[5]

Arthur Poe Gorman was a key player in drawing baseball's color line. A Maryland native and future US senator, Gorman became president of the National Association of Base Ball Players (NABBP) in 1866, "representing Southern sentiment." Later, he applied his talents to promoting segregation through the US Congress. As the NABBP's president, he played a leading role when baseball chose between integrating the game or building another bastion of segregation.[6]

Baseball's integration reached the NABBP's 1867 convention's floor in a roundabout way. The Philadelphia Pythians, a Black club, achieved success and respect while playing other Black clubs in the East. It also formed a friendly relationship with Philly's leading white club, the Athletics. This was particularly important in gaining access to a playing field—challenging in a growing urban area. Hoping that membership in the Pennsylvania Base Ball Association would ease its difficulties in finding a field suitable for hosting visiting teams and charging admission, the Pythian Club sought entry to the NABBP. The Pythians' proficiency on the field and gentlemanly behavior off it appeared to strengthen the club's chances.

Convention leaders at first delayed action and then pressured the team's representative to withdraw the request. Gorman's allies would not allow the Black team to make its case before the full convention or even to its credentials committee. While that committee deferred action on the Pythians, white clubs' applications sailed through. Soon it was clear that even the expected arrival of pro-Pythian delegates would not overcome their opponents' numerical advantage, and the Black club's representative withdrew its request.[7]

Why? Segregation's proponents, called "reconciliationists," feared the Black club's admission would lead to integrated baseball, something they were determined to prevent. Gorman led the reconciliationist faction at the 1867 national convention held, ironically, in Philadelphia, home of the Pythians. Dashing hopes for an integrated game came peacefully—a simple committee report setting a precedent retained in professional baseball until 1946. With strong Black clubs like the Pythians and Chicago's Uniques in mind, the nominating committee unanimously reported "against the admission of any club which may be composed of one or more colored persons." The decision's announcement drew "hisses" from the audience as Gorman threatened to clear the galleries.[8]

Regardless of the NABBP's new guideline, one thing is clear in Illinois during this era: Blacks joined the game and played it skillfully. Scattered coverage documents their involvement, often phrased in racially derogatory terms and marked by condescension. There are only a few accounts of matches between white and Black clubs, though a vague report hints at the possibility of one in Bloomington. As with whites, it is reasonable to assume Blacks played in more impromptu, unorganized contests. It is likely that occasionally Blacks and whites played together but, if so, outside the strictures of the official, organized game.

Acknowledging local baseball fever, one of Jacksonville's newspapers described a game involving "young American citizens of African discent [*sic*] from three to five feet in length," referring to their height. On the field, they moved in "large style," superintended by an "'umpire' of the midnight persuasion of color and of advanced year." The reporter was the only white present. In Ottawa, an editor used a term signifying holding an opponent scoreless. "Does it change the complexion of a colored base ball club to be 'white washed'?" On the western edge of Illinois, a Quincy newspaper announced a new club organized by "negro boys." The Grant and Coalblacks Club had a small roster, reducing to four the number of players on each side. The players deployed "just as much profane and vulgar language as ingenuity and natural talent of the person will admit." Condemning the "obscenity and profanity" during the contest, the reporter observed, "We didn't know how many 'fly catches,' tallies, etc., were made, but are inclined to believe that a number of the lady residents in that portion of the city would have been greatly pleased and relieved if the Coalblacks had all made a 'home run'"[9]

Once, a newspaper reported that Blacks contended successfully for the right to play baseball.

Home to one of the state's best clubs, Bloomington was a baseball hotbed by 1866. After notching a stunning second-place finish at a tournament in

Rockford, the Bloomington Base Ball Club prepared to host its own event in September. The city's *Pantagraph* noted the new Gray Eagles Club, their only uniform "a belt with the words 'Gray Eagle,' formed by "the Africans of this city," hard at practice and hoping to compete in the tourney. "They probably will be allowed to play . . . now that the Civil Rights Bill is being so generally put in execution." Regardless, the Gray Eagles faced challenges. On Sundays, the club practiced in a wooded area south of town. There a group of white men clashed with the Black ballplayers. Accounts of the dispute disagree. One version has the whites abusing a Black child until the "ball players pitched in" and drove the whites from the grounds. In another version, the Black ballplayers were abusing the boy and the whites intervened, "driving off the darkies" at first. But both versions agree the whites eventually fled from the field. "One darkey who has been in the army is said to have knocked down four town boys." Any whites planning future disruptions of Gray Eagles practices needed "to take along enough clubs to be fully on par" with the Black players.[10]

And with that, the Gray Eagle Club disappears from public notice. But another Black club emerged, perhaps either descended from the Gray Eagles or simply the same players with a new name. Those players, the Independent Base Ball Club, gave a ball in 1867. The following year, it challenged any team in McLean County, except the Bloomington Base Ball Club's starters, to a match game. Independents named in the challenge notice were James Sacley, Clinton Dudley, Marion Holley, George Brown, David Downs, James Holley, George Harris, Frank Thomas, William Franklin, and Witteor James. Two years later, the Independents faced a black Springfield club, the Dexters, for "the colored championship of the state." After the Dexter Club won the three-game series, a Springfield newspaper celebrated in the typical racist language of the times. "The Springfield n——rs against the whole country, Chicago Whites Stockings included. . . . Springfield now has the champion n—r base ball club of the United States which didn't cost $20,000, or us 20 cents, who now proudly wear the champion belt and would like to see that darkey club that can take it."[11]

A rare integrated contest came in 1870, a victory by the professional Forest City Club over a Black club, the Blue Stockings Club of Chicago, termed by one writer as "scarcely worth mentioning." The *Chicago Tribune*, however, devoted unusual space to a game that summer between the Blue Stockings and the Rockford Base Ball Club, a Black team from that city, known as "*proteges* of the Forest City boys, who have made it a special point to put them through the details, and have looked upon them as appendages, in some sort."[12]

The *Tribune*'s writer, acknowledging the rarity of the game, asserted that some believed it was an anatomical impossibility for Blacks to play the game with skill. "This fallacy, like many another with reference to the same subject, was thoroughly exploded at Ogden Park yesterday afternoon. Our colored brethren *can* play base ball and do it well into the bargain." The Blue Stockings, composed of waiters from various hotels and restaurants, first had to overcome a "rowdy element," whites who insisted the grounds used for play and practice by the Blue Stockings was "a 'white man's park'" and off limits to Black players. The Blue Stockings eventually secured practice space and "mastered the preliminaries" through a match challenge with the Rockford Club, winning the first game. About four hundred spectators, largely Blacks, gathered at Ogden Park for the second game along with a small number of whites drawn by curiosity. In contrast to the noted tardiness of the city's professional and leading amateur clubs, both black clubs were on the grounds early, allowing the game to commence at the announced starting time. "Such conduct could only be properly punished by expulsion by the State and National Associations," the reporter sarcastically observed, before noting that white state and national associations ostracized these players on racial grounds. "They should be admitted at once in order that such reflections upon the practices of their betters [sic] might be rigorously dealt with."[13]

Chicago's Blue Stockings, taking its name from the stockings it wore, was not the only Black club in the city. Others included the Uniques, the Oaklands, and the Gordons.[14]

The *Tribune*'s game report included descriptions of team uniforms. The Blue Stockings' "tasty uniform" consisted of a cap with broad white and blue stripes, blue shirts with the team monogram on the breast, and pants of white flannel with blue stockings. Rockford sported blue caps, white shirts, and full-length blue pants. The umpire, R. C. Rickhoff of the white Potter Palmer Club, presided at the game, termed an "unusually interesting one throughout, besides being extremely creditable to the Chicago lads." Without doubt the play of the Blue Stockings was equal to that of any amateur club in its 48–14 victory. "Outplayed in every respect," the Rockford club lost its chance for the $100 promised by the Forest Citys for defeating the Chicago nine. "To sum up the game in general it need only be said that, saving the single item of color, it was like other well-played games." One "peculiarity," however, was noticeable. The Blue Stockings somersaulted while making outfield catches or running the bases, any of which "would have permanently doubled up and disabled a White Stocking" (Chicago's professional club).[15]

"A Colored Club of Inferior Capacity"

Field success did not ensure the winning club's acceptance by the city's white amateur teams. When the Blue Stockings were barred from a Senior Amateur Championship Tournament, the *Chicago Tribune*, the Republican organ of the Midwest, struggled to explain the action. Though the club, in beating Rockford, played "a much better game than anyone would have supposed a party of hotel and restaurant waiters capable of doing," nonetheless, it was deemed inferior to white clubs. The Blue Stockings bid was rejected, "mainly because the Blue Stockings were not deemed of sufficient strength to be entitled to consideration." Yet the newspaper suspected something else behind the rejection, a combination of race and class discrimination. Though excluding the entertaining Blue Stocking Club meant lower attendance, the young white men of "respectable and good standing" in charge had the "unquestioned right and power" to ban the Black club. Accepting the Blue Stockings, the *Tribune* claimed, would "burlesque the tournament by the admission of a colored club of inferior capacity." And, it added, the whole affair would have passed quietly save for the "ill-natured and purely gratuitous comments of the evening contemporary," which attempted to damage the tournament. But by deeming the Blue Stockings "inferior," the *Tribune* ignored its own report of the August 24 Rockford game that categorized the club as "fully equal to that of any amateur club in the city."[16]

That "evening contemporary," the *Chicago Times*, a Democratic newspaper, though far from friendly to Blacks, disagreed. Denigrating the upcoming event as the "So-Called Amateur Tournament," the *Times* reprinted the club's protest to the *New York Clipper*, a popular sporting newspaper. W. F. Johnson, Blue Stockings Club secretary, complained of his team's exclusion from the tournament "for what reason I cannot tell, unless it is because they are afraid to play us." If that was true, how, he wondered, could the participants term themselves champion amateur clubs? Although excluded from a "one-horse tournament," the newspaper pronounced the club equal to any club in Chicago save the professionals.[17]

One Chicago white club, the Independents, defied the race barrier, agreed to play the Blue Stockings and came away with a 17–15 victory. Historian Leslie A. Heaphy indicates that, in a rematch, the Blue Stockings prevailed 17–9 but lost two subsequent games to the Independents.[18]

Although the Blue Stockings won city honors against the Rockford Black team and had one victory in a series with a white club daring to cross the color line, it opened no further breach in the ramparts of white supremacy.

Decatur, where newspaper attention to the game faltered when the McPherson Club disappeared after the 1867 season, had a Black club in 1869 whose name is unknown according to the *Bureau County Republican*. Condescension greeted its emergence. "We had fondly hoped that the enfranchisement of the colored people would tend to elevate their ideas and aspirations," the *Weekly Republican* observed, "but our anticipations have come to grief. The young colored men of Decatur have, we are sorry to say, taken a step backward—they have organized a base ball club!"[19]

Decatur's Black ballplayers were twice rebuffed: first by receiving less attention than local white clubs, none of whom had any remarkable success on the field and, second, by seeing their embrace of the game presented as categorically negative—"a step backward" for their race.

The Diana and Soror-Sisters Clubs

Equally dismissive treatment, though without racial insults, greeted women's baseball clubs.

Debra Shattuck's *Bloomer Girls: Women Baseball Pioneers* describes how baseball became a "men-only" sport. "In a culture that routinely attributed childlike emotions and physical weakness to women, advocates of the fly rule, longer base-paths and (eventually) overhand pitching, must have realized that if their evolving game was not suited for children, then it was not suited for women, either." Many prebaseball bat-and-ball games, she argues, included women, albeit children, but as US baseball evolved in the 1830s and 1840s, it was gendered to exclude females.[20]

Swanson, in his examination of baseball's color line, noted a similar boundary based on gender. "Women in the 1860s and '70s had few roles in 'official baseball.'" Although banned from the field, women were valued as spectators. Their presence in the stands restrained rowdiness among male spectators and brought respectability.[21]

Only small glimpses of women's baseball appear in Illinois newspapers from the 1865–70 era. "The ladies of Woodstock are organizing a base ball club," the *Ottawa Free Trader* announced. "To what base uses will they come at last!" The *Cairo Democrat* also proved unable to avoid a pun in noting the existence of a "young ladies" club in Niles, Michigan. "We suppose they are now open to engagements for a home match. We know of some girls in Cairo that are might [*sic*] good on the catch."[22]

Tantalizingly short accounts exist showing young women responding to the game with enthusiasm. "Next year we may expect that the ladies will figure extensively as base-ball players," commented the *Pana Gazette* in reviewing the just-completed successful season of the town's prime club, the Excel-siors. "Our reason for believing this to be the case is the fact that we often see them practicing now." Their skill in ball handling, the editor continued, demonstrated proficiency in the game. One twelve-year-old member of the unnamed group hit a ball "corner ways across a 180-foot lot last Thursday." And women proved unafraid of catching fly balls in a manner "that would have been an honor to some of the [Pana] Excelsior's first nine." But the temptation to condescension proved irresistible—"as catchers (if they have their aprons on) they can't be beat." He warned the local Excelsiors to practice lest the "darling little creatures" outshine them next season.[23]

In October 1869, the *Chicago Times* reported women at Evanston's North-western Female College organizing the "Diana Base Ball Club." A boys team challenged the women to a game. Shattuck describes the match invitation as "patronizing and dripping with gendered allegory," referring to the goddess Diana as "the goddess of the chase, so may you, the modern goddesses, con-sent to become the protecting deities of our national game." When the Diana Club rejected the challenge but offered to play any senior club, the *Times* quipped, "it is older game they are seeking." There is no evidence, however, that the Diana Club played any men's club. The same year, a "picked nine of maidens" bested a team of married women in a game at Rockford.[24]

Only one match between male and female clubs left an account. The occa-sion was the Marion County Fair in southern Illinois and the game between the Centralia Egyptian and "Soror-Sisters" clubs became part of a larger controversy over a fair prize.

During the 1869 fair, the Egyptians played—and lost—a game to the Soror-Sisters. The *Centralia Sentinel* attributed the loss, tongue-in-cheek, to the women's "strong minded proclivities." After a loss to the Egyptians, a Mount Vernon team was denied the fair's top prize in the baseball tournament. It complained that since the Egyptians were not "entered on the Secretary's books" and therefore not officially a competitor, the loss to them should not count. At that point, the "lachrymose Sorosisters" entered the fray. Having "played and defeated the Egyptians with honorable intentions," the women "insist that they won the prize and are loudly demanding their rights." In what was likely a made-up newspaper fuss, at least in the case of the Egyp-tian–Soror-Sisters argument, the newspaper brushed off the men's loss to the women. "All we can say in their [Egyptians] defense [is] no doubt their respect for the sex forbade their winning."[25]

It would be another decade or two before women's teams organized at the college level, though the game's popularity transcended gender boundaries. On empty lots in town or fields at the edge of villages, it is likely that girls and young women took up bats, hitting, and fielding bare-handed just like boys and young men. But unlike the organized game as played on the other side of racial and gender lines, their games were paid little attention. It would take another century and a half before athletics for Illinois women would gain regular and widespread attention.

As the national pastime, Illinois's 1860-era baseball reflected America's faults as it trumpeted its association with the country's perceived virtues.

Segregated on the margins of white society, Black baseball players persevered, though any hopes for a racially level playing field were crushed by prejudice and fear. Clearly, Black teams like Chicago's Blue Stockings and Bloomington's Gray Eagles and Independents had the talent to compete. Displaying their skills in games with white clubs could raise questions about assumptions of racial superiority, making Black clubs a threat to racism's underpinnings.

Questions of race and gender receded as the emerging game found other sources of contention, dulling the early enthusiasm.

TROUBLE IN BASEBALL'S EDEN

At the third innings, in consequence of the ruling of
the umpire . . . the spirit of discord arose, and the
Bloomington Juniors refused to bat another ball.
—*Illinois State Journal*, September 20, 1867[1]

C hallenging baseball's spirit of fraternity and sportsmanship, incidents
like one at a Decatur tournament on September 19, 1867, referred to in
the epigraph to this chapter, reveal another side to the new game—angry
outbursts spurred by disputes, rule violations, and intense rivalries. Such
incidents tarnished baseball's allure.

Promoted as the "Grand Base Ball Tournament of the Western States," the
event illustrates the increasing tensions accompanying the thirst for victory.
Ballyhooed in newspapers throughout the state, and organized by Decatur's
McPherson Base Ball Club, the tourney at the state fairgrounds (now Fair-
view Park) not only proved disappointing for its financial backers and the
McPherson Club but also spawned angry recriminations.[2]

During that hot, dusty September week, only a few of the fifty invited
clubs appeared, though the potential for excitement remained. Two long-
time rivals—the Bloomington Base Ball Club's senior team and the Chicago
Excelsiors, still seen as the team to beat despite its earlier embarrassment
at the hands of the Washington Nationals—were in the field. Bloomington's
club had good reason to anticipate meeting with the Excelsiors at Decatur.
After its success in the Rockford tournament the previous year, the Bloomington Base Ball Club aggressively and unsuccessfully pursued the Excelsiors.
Bloomington especially took offense at the *Chicago Tribune*'s assertion that
the Excelsiors team could "whip the hind sights" off it and other downstate
clubs. Decatur's tournament offered what "they have tried twice to secure
and failed—that is a game with the Excelsiors," Bloomington's *Pantagraph*

INSIDE VIEW OF THE STATE FAIR GROUNDS

Showing the West side of Ring and immediate surroundings from its center

This lithograph illustrates the rough, tree-filled location of the playing field used for Decatur's Grand Base Ball Tournament of the Western States in September 1867. Not visible in the dark shading of the racetrack infield is the creek into which a player tumbled while chasing a fly ball. Then known as the state fairgrounds, it is now Fairview Park. Portions of the racetrack infield are part of a baseball field, one of the few places in Illinois a field from that time remains. Courtesy of the Illinois State Library. The image was created by Homes and Hodgen of Philadelphia, Pennsylvania, in 1865.

wrote, a chance to defeat the Chicagoans. Foreseeing victory, Bloomington's citizens sent their team off after a night of dancing.[3]

The showdown's widespread anticipation makes it curious that, after reaching Decatur, Bloomington's senior nine did everything possible to avoid the game. Rather than readying themselves for the match, the Bloomington senior players lobbied other clubs to keep the Chicago Excelsiors out of championship competition because they would arrive after the first-day 4 p.m. deadline for the championship bracket. When the other clubs rejected the scheme, the Bloomington senior club pulled out of the tourney. Its junior team, however, remained only to stir new controversy. Perhaps angry over the Excelsiors' recruitment of their former pitcher, Patrick J. Keenan, the Bloomington team thought that blocking the team might clear the path to victory for them and punish Keenan. But the weakened field eased Keenan's and the Excelsiors' march to the tournament's championship.[4]

Under Section 31 of the 1867 Rules of the National Association of Base Ball Players, all ballists in a match had to be a member of their respective club for thirty days prior to the game. Designed to deter all-star teams playing under the name of an existing club, the rule also outlawed switching players between their club's senior and junior rosters. Players taking the field for a senior club and later appearing on the junior roster gave the latter an unfair advantage, having skills above the average junior club member. Lee Cheney was with the Bloomington the Star Base Ball Club, a junior club when it took the field against Springfield's Athletic Club. But Cheney, who would later play professionally, also was a mainstay on the senior club. His presence violated the rules, the Springfield juniors insisted, in their refusal to play. The umpire declared a forfeit win for Bloomington's juniors, irritating spectators who wanted a game. Pana's Excelsiors, having just defeated the host McPhersons in a lop-sided, five-inning contest, pleased the crowd by stepping up to play Bloomington.[5]

Soon new troubles arose. Bloomington took an early lead, but Pana rallied, gaining the advantage. At that moment, "the spirit of discord arose" when Bloomington's captain persistently questioned the umpire's decisions, though, according to the Decatur reporter on the scene, spectators felt his calls were correct. Bloomington's captain finally refused to obey the umpire, who, fed up, called the game after three innings in Pana's favor. Summarizing the Bloomington senior and junior clubs' actions during the tourney, the *Decatur Republican* urged spectators to attend the remaining games and ensure the event's success "in spite of the unmanly efforts of the Bloomington clubs to prevent it."[6]

Word spread quickly through the Illinois baseball community about the two Bloomington clubs' behavior. Even Bloomington's daily newspaper questioned their actions. And, after the Bloomington newspaper denounced Chicago's Excelsiors for stealing the local club's star pitcher, the *Illinois State Journal* fired back, labeling Bloomington's attempt to play Lee Cheney on the junior club's roster a "sharp practice" and advised the Bloomington clubs to examine their own shortcomings before condemning Chicago's.[7]

Roster jumping and loading one club with the best players from other local clubs created problems too. In the fall of 1866, Cairo's Egyptian Base Ball Club challenged Centralia's club of the same name to a match. When Cairo's players arrived in Centralia, the match nearly expired at the train depot. Centralia's captain presented his counterpart with a certified list of his players who "were and had been members for thirty days in accordance with a regulation of the National Association." But when asked for his list, Cairo's captain admitted he had none, confirming what Centralia's players suspected, "the Cairoites had selected the best players from three or four clubs and intended to pass them off as the First Nine of the Egyptian Base Ball Club of Cairo!" There was grounds for canceling the game, but to avoid that, the clubs agreed to refer the matter to *Wilke's Spirit of the Times*, a leading sporting publication in New York City.[8]

The game itself sparked more disagreements. During play, the Cairo captain "took the liberty to instruct the Umpire," resulting in the official's alleged favoritism toward the visitors. "Out of fifteen points of issue referred to the Umpire, only two were decided in favor of the Centralia Club." After two back-to-back decisions against the Centralia Club, including one acknowledged as an error by a Cairo player, the hosts found themselves on the wrong end of a fifteen-run inning and lost 41–26. Responding to a boastful account of the game in the *Cairo Democrat*, the *Centralia Sentinel* suggested the victors "look at the facts a little and see how much you have to brag of." Rituals restored good feelings among Centralia's players, who took the loss in stride and hosted their visitors that evening at a supper. Seven months later, the Cairo newspaper again gloated. After Centralia's victory over Decatur's McPherson Club in July 1867, Cairo's *Democrat* criticized Centralia for "putting on sundry airs" and reminded them that Cairo's Egyptians "flazed out [*sic*]" their rivals "without half as hard as they can try." The two clubs never met again.[9]

Centralia–Mount Vernon Conflict

Largely generated by newspaper comment, the Cairo-Centralia fuss placed another strain on the game's ideals, but one later overshadowed by Centralia's on-the-field conflicts with Mount Vernon, a town located roughly thirty miles southeast. The trouble's roots reach back to 1867 in a game between the Egyptians and Mount Vernon's Star Base Ball Club during the Jefferson County Fair. Coming off a strong finish at the Grand Base Ball Tournament of the Western States in Decatur, where it lost the championship match to the state's reputed best club, the Chicago Excelsiors, the Egyptians entered the fair's competition for a cash premium.[10]

Darkness forced calling of the Egyptian-Star game at seven innings with Centralia ahead, but the Mount Vernon Club disagreed. The *Mount Vernon Free Press* then assumed the Star Club's cause and the cash prize's donor gave it to the Stars because, in his view, the Centralia club did not deserve it. The called game's final two innings must be played, the newspaper asserted. Striking back, the *Centralia Sentinel* invited the Star Club to enter the next week's Marion County Fair at Centralia and face the Egyptians. Or the Centralia club "will play them on any occasion they may select only excepting that they conduct themselves a little more like gentlemen than they did on Friday."[11]

Clarification of its club's side came through a letter appearing in the same issue by Egyptian team captain Horace Van Cleve. According to Van Cleve, the trouble started when the Star captain believed the Egyptians were determined to take advantage of his club. In Van Cleve's view, the Star captain and his teammates were completely ignorant of the game's basic rules, "twice he [the Star captain] acknowledged that he had 'never seen that book before'" (likely referring to *Haney's Base Ball Book* by Henry Chadwick). The Egyptians shot to a 27–4 lead after two innings but then let up and the Stars scored 17 runs before darkness arrived, ending the game. The Star captain refused to accept the umpire's ruling, insisting on completion of the full nine innings. "It was all in vain that I read him the regulations to prove that we had fairly won the game." Next the prize's donor told Van Cleve he would not award it unless all nine innings were played. Replying, Van Cleve said winning the prize was not Centralia's goal "but to beat the Star club of Jefferson county was and. . . . we had DONE IT." Overhearing threatening talk among the Stars players, Van Cleve and his players quietly left the field and returned to Centralia. The next day, a Star Club representative came to Centralia, indicating his club's willingness to award the prize to the Egyptians. But a night's reflection soured Van Cleve, and he considered acceptance of the premium "a disgrace," writing that if the money did show up the Egyptians would return it to the donor or give it to the Jefferson County Agricultural Society, the fair's sponsor.[12]

The next year, the two clubs resumed their competition. The format in 1868 was a best-of-three series, the first game played at Centralia. One Centralia newspaper favorably described the Star Club as a "fine lot of boys" and another, the *Sentinel*, promised that, regardless of the outcome, the Egyptians "will learn their visitors a lesson in hospitality which they will not soon forget." The opening game's final score, 34 to 28 in the Egyptians' favor, indicated an evenly matched but uncontroversial contest.[13]

The following Saturday, the series resumed in Mount Vernon, the Egyptian Club met there by the Stars and the local cornet band. After enjoying a meal courtesy of their hosts, the clubs and spectators moved to the playing grounds. The weather was cold, the field muddy and uneven. Gamblers gathered around as the hometown crowd lustily cheered the Star Club's successes, falling silent when the Egyptians did well. At the end of the eighth inning, the score was 24–24. Tallying seven runs, the Star Club had one out remaining when its batter, Pace, asked the Egyptian pitcher, Munn, for a "shoulder ball." The rules and customs of the time allowed batters to indicate the general area in which they wanted the ball. Pitcher Munn complied and Pace struck the ball with "tremendous force," hitting Munn near his right shoulder. Munn staggered and then, clasping his shoulder with his left hand, but never taking his eyes off Pace who was running to first base, retrieved the ball and threw him out. A spectator cried out, in jest, "Fifty dollars on the Egyptians!" Players and spectators ran on to the field to assist the obviously distressed Munn. A doctor bandaged the injured player's shoulder, and a carriage took Munn to a hotel. In the top of the ninth, the Egyptians managed a single run, losing 31 to 25.[14]

Although acknowledging minor grousing about an umpire's call in the ninth inning and unspecified incidents on the part of the Stars, Centralia newspaper accounts primarily expressed gratitude for the kindnesses of the Mount Vernon physician and the hotel keeper who cared for the injured player. "The Egyptians said they were fairly beaten and have no excuse to offer for their defeat," the *Sentinel* conceded. Attention now focused on the next Saturday and the deciding match set at Ashley, a village between the competing towns.[15]

To ensure a friendly crowd at the neutral site, the Egyptian Club chartered a special car on the Illinois Central Railroad's branch line to Ashley, with round trip tickets at one dollar ($20.58 in 2022). "Ho! For Ashley," headlined the *Centralia Democrat*. Mounting interest in the game by both clubs and their supporters promised an exciting day. Large numbers of ladies and friends of the Egyptians made the trip to Ashley, where they found ideal weather conditions—"bright, calm and pleasant." But the atmosphere troubled gamblers. Egyptian backers took offense when Star supporters demanded favorable odds all the while boasting loudly about their club. The game proved thrilling, the lead changing hands several times until, in what was becoming a pattern, a dispute arose late in the game. In the eighth, the Egyptian pitcher fielded a ground ball by a Star batter and, rather than throwing to first base, tagged him on the basepath between home and first. The umpire declared the batter out and the Stars loudly protested his call. To prevent the game's end at that moment, the Egyptians agreed to their opponents' position, though insisting on appealing the play to the *New York Clipper*, a leading sporting publication. When play resumed, the Star Club scored five tallies and then held the Centralia club scoreless in the bottom of the inning, leaving the game tied, 27–27.[16]

The Egyptians held the Stars scoreless in the top of the ninth, creating a do-or-die situation. Scoring two runs, the Egyptians emerged with the victory becoming, in the judgment of the *Sentinel*, the "CHAMPION CLUB OF SOUTHERN ILLINOIS." The immediate off-field action did not appear in the newspaper account, unspoken of for fifty-seven years. In a 1925 interview, Henry Condit of the Egyptian Club remembered that emotions before the game were at "a high point, so when we went to Ashley, we got every roughneck in town to go with us." It turned out to be a wise move, he added, because "Mount Vernon brought along just as many." With the on-field contest over, "a harder fight started" among spectators and players. One participant pulled a revolver, a free-for-all ensued, and "some heads were cracked but no fatalities resulted." Simmering resentments building over two years found release that day, shattering baseball's image as a game that calmed competitive passion.[17]

Why was the Egyptian-Star rivalry so fierce? Perhaps jealousies of pride and commerce between the two towns fired it. But any number of other cities in similar situations avoided the free-for-all seen at Ashley. Certainly, disputes over the rules played a significant role.

Gambling proved the elephant in the room that day and other places in mid-nineteenth-century Illinois baseball. Sometimes mentioned to slur the opposing team's followers, gambling lurked on the sidelines at nearly every game. With stakes high and money changing hands, anger and frustration led to confrontation and, at Ashley, a free-for-all.

Pointedly, in reporting the final score of the deciding game, the *Sentinel* refused to credit the Star Club with the disputed five runs from the eighth inning. While the Egyptian Club would continue into the 1869 season, the Star Club played its last game that day in Ashley.[18]

Although Centralia's Egyptians emerged as winners of the 1868 series and Mount Vernon's Stars the vanquished, the real loser was the rituals created to ensure good feelings rather than fisticuffs. Beginning with the darkness-shortened first game and continuing through the eighth inning of the Ashley game, the Star Club consistently sought to undermine the authority of the umpire, ignoring Henry Chadwick's ideal of gracious acceptance.

Competition, Rivalries, and Erosion of Rituals

Period newspapers reveal lack of restraint becoming common as tempers increasingly flared and baseball teams and their communities viewed games as a new opportunity for economic and political contests with their neighbors. Onarga's Senior Base Ball Club failed to receive the advertised $30 premium for winning a county fair tournament and the village's *Iroquois Republican* newspaper demanded satisfaction. A fair official promptly responded, explaining the money would be paid in full. Discussing a game's outcome, newspapers in Warsaw, Illinois, and Keokuk, Iowa, vied over whose team had the least amount of time to practice due to, said the *Warsaw Bulletin*, "constant and arduous business labors." Choosing an umpire for a game between Rock Island's Wapello Base Ball Club and the Scott Base Ball Club of Davenport, Iowa, churned up another newspaper fuss succeeding an earlier one. The *Rock Island Argus* asserted its rival across the Mississippi River, the *Davenport Democrat*, and the city's Scott Club along with it, fell into the category of "people who get beaten sometimes [and] assign reasons for their defeat which are rather ridiculous, when a frank admission of defeat would appear much better."[19]

A club in tiny Butler groused that a Pana nine evaded its challenges, raising the "dander" of Pana's team. After a loss to the Achilles Club of Morrison, the Geneseo Farmers Base Ball Club challenged the victors to a rematch. Dismissing the invitation, Charles H. Down, the Achilles Club's spokesman, wrote, "You are, I see, quite ignorant of the rules." The loser of the match, he explained, had no right to challenge the victor to another game. He closed with condescension: "Hoping by practice you may so improve that the coming season you will be worthy of our best efforts to defeat you." Earlville's baseball club clobbered its La Salle County rival, Leland's Dirigo Base Ball Club, 51–33 in 1868. But when the clubs met again in Leland, Earlville baseballists found a surprise. According to the *Sterling Gazette*, the visitors "expected the same persons who played in the first game would play in the rest, and it was not expected to have to play two or three different clubs at the same time or, members of two or three different clubs." Violating the game's rules, the Dirigos loaded up with the best players on other teams. Even the Dirigo captain admitted a request from the new team that he not play. The Earlville Club caught on to the ruse and some Dirigos confessed the scheme. Outraged, the Earlville players returned home.[20]

Support for the game's rituals remained high in 1867, indicated by the Hickory Base Ball Club of New Rutland's reaction to the Wenona Base Ball Club's third straight win over it. A Wenona writer, though not providing specifics, complained "bitterly of the treatment" by the Hickory Club, including "not even showing us the respect due from one gentleman to another."[21]

Slights like these, real or imagined, promoted hard feelings sometimes aired in newspapers. In August 1867, just such a contretemps spilled over into the columns of Springfield's *Illinois State Journal*. In a "card," a device more associated with dueling, the Sheridan Base Ball Club of Chatham, a small village to the south of the capital city, announced it would no longer play teams from its larger neighbor. "We have lost all desire for the honor of winning a game from any club in that place." The Chatham team traced the history of its meetings with Springfield clubs. Earlier that season, the Sheridans played the Active Base Ball Club of Springfield. But rather than the expected club, players from several teams filled the Actives' roster on the field that day—good athletes but not enough to defeat the Chatham club "had it not been for their pitcher." The ringer appeared on the roster as "A. B. C. Dick," but he was actually "a son of [US] Senator [Lyman] Trumbull, a very swift pitcher, and as fine a player of any of the [Washington] National nine." Even the talented "Dick" failed, and the Sheridans left the field with a ten-run victory, but their mouths carried a sour taste from the attempt to pack a junior club with a superior player.[22]

Things got worse when the Sheridans played the second nine of the Athletic Club. "This game was a disgrace to the city of Springfield," the Sheridans charged, blaming an unnamed hostile umpire from Springfield who seemed partial to the Athletics. During play, the Chatham club's frustrations fulminated, and its captain finally calmed his team to keep them "from knocking this umpire over with a bat." His success allowed his nine to remain gentlemen even to the point of cheering the Athletics. But more trouble brewed on the sidelines, where "lots of Springfield 'roughs'" tried to entice "honest old farmers" from Chatham "to put their money up" on losing bets. Next came an invitation from Springfield's Empire Club to play "a friendly game" with the Sheridans at Chatham. But, the writer claimed, the Empires showed up without notice late on a Friday afternoon. Scrambling for players, the Sheridans managed to put a team on the field, though this meant taking any available player and certain defeat. As to the Sheridans' future with Springfield clubs, we "desire that they will honor us no more hereafter with challenges or notices of friendly games of base ball."[23]

Though publishing the card, the *Illinois State Journal's* editor expressed misgivings and claimed to know nothing of the controversy. He was "only sorry that any ill feeling should exist among the Chatham boys" and assured "none but the most kindly sentiments are entertained by our clubs toward their Chatham brothers." His hopes proved ill-founded.[24]

A response from the "Empire Nine" appeared in the next day's edition of the newspaper. Rather than surprising the Chatham club, the visitors dispatched representatives to alert the Sheridans the Springfield team was on the way. Furthermore, the Sheridans were the ones violating the game's rituals when they didn't escort the visitors to the playing field. Chatham's club, he charged, also exaggerated its lack of players because six of its starting nine players were on the field. Worse, after five innings, the Sheridans abruptly quit the game.[25]

Ending the exchange, another Chatham resident weighed in, signing as "Base Ball." He termed the Sheridan Club's card "vain glorious . . . singularly wanting in good taste and sense, and overburden [sic] by conceit." Instead of complaining about Springfield clubs, the writer recommended the Sheridan Club work on its own shortcomings. During the game at Springfield against the Athletic Club's second nine, he countered, the Chatham team violated the game's etiquette by threatening the umpire. Seeing "bad grace" behind the card, the writer concluded it was Springfield clubs who should avoid Chatham.[26]

Such contretemps spread over newspaper columns cast a spirit of discord, transforming a game into yet another source of contention like the era's hard-edged partisan politics. Underneath the ideals, these disputes revealed the sour side of competitiveness and arguments over what appeared to readers to be minor details.

Illinois baseball clubs embroiled in disputes like those of the Sheridans followed a path blazed earlier in the decade by eastern teams. George B. Kirsch recounts an 1860 dispute between Brooklyn's Resolute Base Ball Club and the Jersey City Mechanics, the latter allowing "foul language and open gambling" on their playing grounds during the clubs' supposedly friendly contest. Soured by the experience, a Resolute Club official reluctantly presented the game ball to the victors and a few days later denounced the Mechanics in a local newspaper. This, in turn, launched a battle in newspaper columns between the opposing sides until the editor, tiring of it, cut off access. Now Chatham's Sheridan Club, the Springfield clubs it denigrated, and other teams and editors in Illinois discovered for themselves the gap separating the envisioned game and the one played with "the all-too-frequent reality of contention and bad feeling."[27]

Umpires under Fire

Piggybacked on the growing spirit of competition came a new attitude toward the umpire from players and spectators alike. Henry Chadwick's idealized view of the game prohibited questioning an umpire's decision. The model player is careful to "never wound his [the umpire] feelings by implying that his judgment is weak, his partiality apparent, or his integrity of character doubtful." Chadwick's perfect ballist would never question through expression or posture an umpire's call because such displays were "as expressive . . . as words." The player is to greet all decisions—good or bad—with quiet acceptance.[28]

Intercity competition and gambling passions undermined the umpire's pedestal, as decisions once unquestioned received criticism from all sides. Five hundred people turned out in 1870 for a game at Livingston County's Five Mile Grove settlement between the Morning Star Base Ball Club of Forrest and the Pontiac Mechanics Club. Taking an eight-run lead in its first at-bat, the Mechanics, a juvenile club, according to a correspondent for the *Ottawa Free Trader,* "began to hector the umpire and bandy words with the multitude" until the umpire "became disgusted and declined serving further." Amid the confusion, the Forrest Club revived, eventually winning 78 to 37. By the rituals of the game, the losing club at this point was supposed to yield its ball to the victors. The Mechanics, however, refused, pleading that, as a junior club, they were exempt. "They possess an abundance of impudence all will admit," concluded a reporter.[29]

A year earlier, a game to decide the so-called junior championship of the state illustrated the collapse of old strictures protecting the umpire from verbal abuse. The Occidental Junior Club of Quincy split a home-and-home series with Springfield's Liberty Club, and the deciding game was set for August 17, 1869, in Quincy. This junior championship was a self-determined title, not the result of any playoff system with junior clubs statewide but simply a speculation accepted as fact by the teams and their supporters. Still, illusion overcame reality, and public interest ran high. Admission to the contest at the Quincy fairgrounds cost 25 cents ($5.37 in 2022) with "no extra charges for carriages." Also, buses ran from Quincy to the game site throughout the afternoon.[30]

By game time, August's sun and humidity combined, creating a classic prairie scorcher. Mental temperatures too rose. As the visiting Liberty Club members inspected the fairgrounds field, they discovered second base was only 120 feet from home base, not the required 127 feet, four inches. The shorter distance favored the home team's pitcher. After measuring the base lines, proper distances were set.[31]

Controversy next sprang up among spectators, who composed, a reporter claimed, one of the largest crowds to ever watch a baseball game in Quincy. More than simple anticipation of a tightly contested game fired the crowd. "Bets were freely offered two to one," one account noted, with an estimated $2,500 ($53,725 in 2022) changing hands. With the lead switching several times throughout the game, "the excitement became intense, and numerous persons, great and small, volunteered advice to the umpire and sometimes questioned his decisions." Worsening this discourtesy was the umpire's status.

George W. Lackey, a founder of the Bloomington Base Ball Club, former president of the state association, and "a distinguished player himself," received constant criticism. By the top of the sixth inning, the Liberty Club held an 18–15 lead, and "the excitement . . . reached a 'fever heat.'" At this point, according to the *Whig and Republican* reporter, "some roughs from Springfield. . . . tried to raise a disturbance but order was soon restored." Later, rebutting the charge against its hometown compatriots, Springfield's *Illinois State Journal* countered that "the disturbances were caused by the profane, hooting ruffians of Quincy." Regardless of the source, the result was an angry and unruly crowd.[32]

Under the rules, an umpire only called foul balls. Fair balls drew silence, creating a potential for confusion, especially if noisy spectators gathered close along the foul lines. In the eighth inning, an Occidental Junior player struck "a splendid grounder close down to left field," seemingly a hit. Someone in the crowd, however, shouted "foul!" Mistaking the voice for that of the umpire Lackey, the player left first base, preparing to return to strike again. An alert Springfield player fired the ball to the first baseman, who then tagged the Quincy player. Immediately, the Occidental Junior was "declared out by the Umpire, who said it was a fair ball and *he* had not called the foul." The Liberty Club batted in the top of the ninth, emerging with a one-run lead. The narrow score, a last chance for the Quincy club to snatch victory, betting in the stands, and the heat of the day all combined, raising pressure to the climactic point. The first Occidental Junior batter hit safely and came home on another hit, tying the game. Amid the crowd's shouts, the next batter struck a towering fly ball misplayed by the Liberty fielder. Another hit sent the winning run across home. "No words can express the scene of excitement which ensued," the *Quincy Whig and Republican* wrote. "Hats were thrown in the air; men and boys rushed hither and thither, screaming at the top of their voices; while the ladies waved their handkerchiefs and even joined in the cheers." His counterpart on the *Herald*, sitting at field level amid the spectators, lost his chance for description when "the crowd rushed before the reporter's stand, making a detailed report impossible." Though the victory was assured, the game was not over. Under the protocol of the time, the inning continuing until the third out, accounting for the final 34–29 score.[33]

But spectators crossed a line during the game, a fact noted by Lackey in his remarks while announcing the score. Admonishing the crowd, Lackey sharply noted this was "the first time that a decision of his was ever questioned" in any game he umpired. Even the *Quincy Herald* expressed shame at the crowd's action. "We trust no enthusiasm for a Quincy club may hereafter lead any to so far forget the proprieties of the occasion as to act the part of self-appointed umpires." While putting no blame for the violations of the "proprieties" on the Quincy players, the *Illinois State Journal* condemned the "profane, hooting ruffians of Quincy" for creating an atmosphere denying the Liberty Club "fair play. . . . A portion of the people present at the game were determined that the Occidentals should win either by fair or foul means." In addition, the "threats and unbecoming language towards him [Lackey] goes far to strengthen the opinion that the Libertys did not have fair play in the game."[34]

It is worth noting that no problems arose between the Occidental Junior and Liberty Clubs during the game after resolving the second base distance problem. The two clubs celebrated together after the match, according to one report. This game's problems came from a new source—the spectators. To be sure, the see-saw pattern of the game was a factor, especially in combination with significant gambling. No doubt, a rivalry between the two cities played a role. Local boosters perhaps weaving their own hopes into their team's fortunes quickly hitched onto the rising trajectory of the Occidental Junior Club, even if its junior championship was solely a matter of regional competition.[35]

Lackey was not the only Illinois umpire under fire in the game's early days, despite Chadwick's injunctions. Such incidents could lead to lengthy disputes between rival newspapers, as was the case with a July 1867 game involving the Pioneer Club of Geneseo and the Wapellos of Rock Island. Baseballist E. M. Hughes was at the center. Hughes, a member of a Davenport, Iowa, ball club, volunteered to umpire the game played in Atkinson, Illinois. In the bottom of the seventh, with Wapellos batting and the Geneseo club holding a two-run lead, the whistle of the last train back to Rock Island sounded. Both clubs' captains called for the game to end, and spectators and players alike dashed to the railroad depot. Umpire Hughes called the game, awarding victory based on the score at the end of the last completed inning—the sixth—when the Wapellos held a one-run lead. But the Pioneer Club thought the score at the end of their half of the seventh left them victorious. This misperception led some to "stir up ill feelings between the clubs." Hughes jumped into the fray via a letter to the editor of the *Rock Island Argus*, citing three sections of the rule book that justified his actions. As the grumbling continued into late July, the *Rock Island Argus* quoted the *Geneseo Republic*, which entered the fray on behalf of its defeated team. On July 13, the publication to which disputes were often submitted—the *New York Clipper*—declared that "No game can be called at the request of one club, and no club has a right to stop playing till the game is finished. If the matter is brought before the National Convention, the P. [Geneseo Pioneers] will receive the ball, no doubt." The

Geneseo Republic welcomed the news but cautioned, "Will the Wapellos give it [the ball] up now? Of course not." But, after E. M. Hughes sent his statement to the *Clipper* and the New York newspaper reversed its ruling, the Geneseo paper ceased fire and conceded (the *Rock Island Argus* quoting): "the umpire was justified in calling the game."[36]

This weeks-long editorial fight over the Pioneer-Wapello dispute did not quench fires along the Mississippi River. In late August, another controversy flared—this one involving a game between the Wapellos and the Scott Base Ball Club of Davenport, Iowa. The *Davenport Democrat* alleged that a Wapello victory came after the umpire, a man named Hakes, favored the Rock Island club to the extent that a fence post bearing a sign "Decision for the Wapellos" could have replaced him. Apparently umpire Hakes was a Rock Island resident, leading the Iowa newspaper to question the honesty of the recent game and another, earlier loss. The newspaper wondered whether a Rock Island umpire had presided over that contest. The *Rock Island Argus* dismissed the complaint as an effort to avoid admitting that the Scott Club was fairly beaten. It attacked the motives of the *Democrat*'s editor, who had served as an umpire himself on occasion and "has been suspected of an undue prejudice against" the Wapellos.[37]

Although not rare, selecting a member of one of the contending clubs as umpire did not always end well. When the Greenville Independent Club and Athletics of Trenton met and the former emerged a 30–25 victor, a spectator spoke out. "Had the umpire acted half way fair," the Trenton club would have won easily. But during the fifth inning, the umpire, a Greenville player, saw that his club could not win fairly. At one point the Trenton team had to "put seven out to get three judged out." The lesson? "Never . . . accept as umpire one of their opponents, however gentlemanly may be his appearance."[38]

Like George W. Lackey at Quincy, F. D. Beach found his decisions in a game questioned, in this case one between the Young America Club of Aurora and the Dundee Base Ball club. "Mr. Beach certainly meant to give all his decisions fairly, and at any rate he was entitled to be treated as a gentleman . . . and . . . the Dundee boys certainly failed to do so." The umpire of a game between Monmouth's Clipper club and the Amateurs of Princeton also was accused of favoritism. When Edgar Gleim of Rock Island officiated at a game between the Active Club of Moline, Illinois, and the Mississippi Club of Davenport, Iowa, someone charged "the inattention of the Umpire" led to a Moline victory. A "Mr. Gould" of Somonauk allegedly gave the Amateur Club of Sandwich a 53–11 victory over the Plano Union Club. After a 44–36 loss received by his village's Active Club at the hands of Minonk's Enterprise

Club, the losers left the field in protest. A Hudson spectator termed the decisions of the umpire—a member of the Minonk club—"palpably dishonest."[39]

On rare occasions, an umpire received praise, usually in game descriptions commending his decisions as "fair and impartial." An Ottawa umpire received "a splendid Gold pen and Holder" for his work. Another umpire—E. F. Bradford of Mascoutah—gained praise both for his firmness and his willingness to change a call when convinced he had erred on the rules. "Mr. Bradford filled the position with dignity and impartiality," leaving the defeated club "no reasonable objection to his decision."[40]

Exceeding such praise was criticism and character aspersions as competitive fires consumed the game's ideals.

Baseball and Intercity Competition

Baseball, then, provided another bone of contention for rival communities and their respective newspapers. Rather than hurling charges and countercharges over quality of life, healthy conditions, commercial advantages, and politics, editors had a new topic with which to bash their neighbors.

In October 1867, Carrollton and Jerseyville, two small communities in southwestern Illinois, used baseball as tinder for local jealousies. Jerseyville's *Democrat* fired the first salvo, predicting its club heading to Carrollton would "take the socks off" their rivals. "Well, they came and were beaten nearly three to one," gloated the *Carrollton Gazette*. Jerseyville next dispatched its "brag club" to restore civic honor, and the *Gazette* twisted the knife, only to have that contest end the same way. "Socks should always come off the way they are put on and not pushed over the head," advised the *Gazette*'s editor. Rubbing it in, he added the Jerseyville team was on a fool's errand. "It is hardly probable that a club from a village like Jerseyville would be able to play with that of a city like Carrollton without getting badly used up."[41]

For Illinois towns and villages, a baseball team offered opportunity to prove superiority, indicating it was up to date with the times. When Pike County's seat, Pittsfield, finally organized a club, a local editor rejoiced the town was "emerging from the only cloud that rested upon her fame as a 'national' town." Until then, Pittsfield had no citizens to assign to the game's positions. "Now she is possessed of all of these and more, and the great game, the great national game of base ball is played scientifically . . . within her limits." To the north and east in Bureau County, baseball intertwined with Princeton's image. After its Amateur Base Ball Club lost to an Arlington rival, an editor warned, "it won't do to have Princeton behind any other town in any respect." A winning club was as important to a striving town as a powerful politician or good railroad connections. Such resources needed encouragement. Acknowledging his election as an honorary member of the Oquawka Base Ball Club, a local editor anticipated "frequent opportunities to do big blowing" after victories. "Don't be beaten, Gentlemen."[42]

Editors viewed members of successful baseball clubs as ambassadors and heroes. Centralia's Egyptian Base Ball Club, an editor claimed, was "composed of the best young men of the city." Contending Republican and Democratic newspapers in Champaign County took a brief respite to agree on local clubs. The Republican *Champaign Gazette and Union* boasted the local Empire Base Ball Club was demonstrably better than any "in the Congressional District." And Urbana's *Illinois Democrat* bragged that, in baseball, "Champaign need be behind no place." Baseball could level the playing field on which mismatched communities competed. Or at least it did one day for the southwestern Illinois village of Greenville. The St. Louis Imperial Base Ball Club anticipated an easy victory when it crossed the Mississippi River and traveled miles inland to play the Greenville Independent Base Ball Club. Instead, the St. Louis visitors "found to their hearts content that 'Country Muscle' was too much for them by a score of 70 to 20." No doubt, loungers around Greenville's courthouse savored bragging rights for days, if not weeks.[43]

With baseball mania sweeping the state in 1866 and 1867, frustration rankled in towns and cities where the game had yet to arrive or who lacked a consistently winning team. Viewing the nation as well as Illinois, the *Quincy Herald* wondered why its club lagged. "Why is it? Why has not Quincy rivalled her western competitors and stood ready to give battle with any Eastern club?" Pride prevented blaming lack of talent. Instead, it criticized local citizens for not providing encouragement and financial support. One hope shimmered—the Dexter Base Ball Club. The time was coming, the editor predicted, when it "will do credit to Quincy." It did not. Up the Mississippi River, Rock Island kept a sharp eye on the baseball pretensions of its Iowa neighbor, Davenport. The *Rock Island* Argus reprinted the *Davenport Democrat*'s brag that its city's Scott Base Ball Club had "gained some little notoriety for playing," and the *Rock Island Argus* fired back. "If we recollect right, they got their reputation up and something else down in Rock Island last season." And to the southeast, Springfield's *Illinois State Register* bellowed that the city's Athletic Base Ball Club "is rapidly preparing to take rank among the first-class clubs of the state."[44]

Dixon alleged that its rival's (Sterling's) baseball club ducked a challenge to play the Dixon Riverside Base Ball Club. A Sterling editor treated the remark as a personal affront. "You fellows are getting mighty anxious to get cleaned out," he wrote. "Come and see us when you boil over and we'll try and exercise you a little on a ten acre lot." After the Darlington, Wisconsin, club stopped in Warren to play a game on its way to meet a Rockford team, the outcome delighted the smaller town's editor. Having no organized club, Warren managed to get enough boys together. The pick-up club "gave them a turn, making 11 tallies to Darlington's 6." Apparently, the visitors swaggered a bit before the game. "Come down here putting on base ball style and then get badly beaten by a club that has never been organized," the *Warren Sentinel* crowed. Assuming a club's inferiority—by implication, its community's— could rebound on the offending club. A baseball tournament in conjunction with the Iroquois County Fair sparked resentments. First, Onarga's newspaper charged, the host Watseka Club purposefully pitted the Muffers of Onarga against the perceived "crack club" of Chenoa, apparently hoping to tire out the Muffers before the game with the Watseka Base Ball Club. Instead, the Muffers defeated Chenoa and went on to "beat the Watseka club, the umpire and the citizens beside taking a little sass. . . . Here is a subject for you, Mr. Republican [referring to the editor of Watseka's newspaper] as soon as you have exhausted your gas on the band question." Losing to a rival, of course, embarrassed newspaper editors and their community. Recognizing that, the *Warsaw Bulletin* cautioned its local Mutual Club before a game with a Keokuk, Iowa, team. "Look out boys, for you will have hard work to hold the good name you have already won." And when victory came, the editor stuck the symbolic knife in his Iowa rival. "Let the base ball boys of Warsaw alone."[45]

Even when defeat was likely, in fact almost certain, a local club must uphold the town's reputation as well as its own. Touring downstate in 1869, the powerful Forest City Base Ball Club of Rockford scheduled a game in Jacksonville. Although Jacksonville had baseball history dating back to 1866, producing competitive senior and junior clubs in that time, the looming Forest City Club was professional and proved it was the best in Illinois by defeating all rivals. Encouraging citizens to attend the game, a Jacksonville editor promised, "the playing, on one side at least, will be by far the best ever seen in this city." He admonished the local club, "Relics, don't go back on your town or the game. . . . A terrible defeat must be expected but play, practice and let the score be the best our town can make." As the Forest City Club had upcoming games with teams in Quincy and Springfield as well, "our score must compare favorably with theirs or our town will be disgraced."[46]

Like the river town it served, the *Cairo Democrat* was rough, brawling, outspoken, and quick to take offense. To its editor, baseball was yet another weapon for pummeling southern Illinois rivals and, most especially, its Kentucky competitor, Paducah. Reading surviving issues of the *Cairo Democrat* and the *Paducah Herald*, one gains the impression that, if not for the intervening Ohio River, one or both editors might have faced homicide charges. A series of games between the Quickstep Club of Paducah and Cairo's Eclipse Base Ball Club in 1867 spurred an editorial skirmish lasting three months, complete with charges, countercharges, promises, accusations of drunkenness, and a large serving of humble pie that the Cairo editor managed to throw back at his Kentucky antagonist.

Although the newspapers dueled over other matters, baseball spawned their best efforts. Innocently enough, the fight began when the *Paducah Herald*, as quoted in the *Cairo Democrat*, boasted of the Quicksteps Club's victory over an Evansville, Indiana, rival. "There are no base ballers like ours. Evansville, if you have any more ballists bring 'em along," the *Herald*'s editor, Len Faxson, taunted (again as quoted in the *Cairo Democrat*). If they did, it would be easy for the Quicksteps to give "them a squamperization [*sic*]." Faxson's counterpart at the *Cairo Democrat* jumped in, inviting Paducah to challenge a local club if the Kentucky club wanted its smooth feathers ruffled by the Illinoisans. Without waiting for Paducah's challenge, a Cairo club, the Eclipse, challenged Paducah. Faxson, with an editorial smirk, said he doubted the Cairo players "will sleep much until the Quicksteps flax the conceit out of them." The *Democrat* countered that it was the Quicksteps who "will have to be carried from the field" suggesting that if Faxson wasn't "too drunk" before the game started, afterward he would surely retreat to a "convenient whiskey shop."[47]

Paducah, in the Cairo newspaper's view, dragged its feet in accepting the challenge, and the *Democrat* explained the delay, noting "Talk is cheap, and Len Faxson indulges in it to about the same extent that he does cheap whiskey." On September 11, the Quicksteps arrived in Cairo to settle the matter. After all the editorial explosions, the actual game was a disappointment—to Cairo's Eclipse Club and its backers—as Paducah won 43–16. Deploying humor, the *Cairo Democrat* responded. Under the headline "Why They Beat Us," the *Democrat* explained that "much to the surprise of everybody there were only two members of the Eclipse first nine on the ground." Seven players came from bystanders, including "a man with one eye; a club-footed Missourian; a man with a cork hand; two men on crutches; a McCracken county merchant with the itch, and the 'local' of the Paducah Herald [Faxson] drunk." The fanciful account continues, reporting various failings, passing outs, and general incompetence of the thrown-together team. In a straight version, however, appearing on the same page, the newspaper recounted the Quickstep's arrival on a steamboat, their welcome by the Eclipse Club, and a dinner for the visitors. Witnessed by "at least four hundred spectators," the real game proceeded without incident, the Eclipse players giving "three rousing cheers" for their opponents. "It is but justice to the Eclipse Club," the article noted, "to say that their pitcher, and best player, was out of the city." The *Democrat* urged the boys to practice.[48]

The lopsided victory took the edge off the rivalry and, in its account of the game, the *Paducah Herald* demonstrated restraint, according to the *Democrat*, whose editor allowed that the Quicksteps not only played well but "are fine looking men." For the return match at Paducah, it was the Cairo team's turn to board a steamboat, which at least provided a nice ride on the Ohio River and back. On the field, the Eclipse were pummeled once more, losing 65 to 30. "The explanation for this defeat has not reached us," the *Cairo Democrat* reported. "We are quite certain, however, it *can* be explained and *will* be." A day later, with no explanation, the newspaper concluded merely that the Eclipse ballists "didn't play their *best*." Out of courtesy to Cairo's defeated finest, the newspaper ended speculation.[49]

In this, just another of its many battles, the *Cairo Democrat's* aggressive posture toward the relative merits of its baseball players in comparison with those of Paducah demonstrates how perception of the game evolved. The coin of civic pride had two sides—support and criticism. Seeking explanations for failed expectations, local newspapers often found answers within the local teams.

Practice, Practice, Practice

The most common admonishment to faltering local teams, as seen by Quincy's editors' repeated comments in the prologue to this book, is one word—*practice*. Only a few weeks after baseball arrived, a Jacksonville newspaper urged its local teams to practice—"that practice which will be of so much use to you in time of need!" Failure to do so signaled "a lack of discipline." When one local club lost badly to a Quincy rival, the newspaper recommended steady practice until the players recovered their old skills. In northern Illinois, practice acquired an adjective. "*Systematic* practice," that being what the Woodstock Base Ball Club required after a series of losses. The intriguingly named Lively Turtles of Rock Island also needed practice. And three years after its first bit of advice to local teams, a Jacksonville newspaper bemoaned one of its club's "listless, lazy and careless playing. No improvement can be expected save as the result of sharp, active, earnest work." Even victory failed to disguise sloppy play. After Quincy's Occidentals defeated a St. Louis team, a local editor observed it was still unfit to face the state's leading clubs. Why?—"want of practice." Similarly, Harvard's club would keep losing to local rivals until it learned to "practice a little more." And after Decatur's junior club, the Centrals, fell to Clinton, a disgusted Decatur editor observed, "We would advise our boys to either practice enough to make themselves proficient, or spend their time at something which pays better."[50]

Such disgust was common. As we saw earlier when Quincy's Occidentals continued their losing ways, a local newspaper dubbed them the "Accidentals." After Ottawa's best club, the Shabbonas, lost a key game to the Illinois Club of Morris, one writer explained, "The fact is that the Shabbona boys have become very negligent of late have had little or no practice, hence they evince a very little skill in playing." A particular embarrassment to one Peoria editor was the Olympic Base Ball Club. Noting that a Davenport, Iowa, club recently lost a game 118 to 7, the editor urged that the Olympics challenge the losers "in order to get a club that they could beat." Noticing a South Bend, Indiana, tournament featuring a $25 prize for the "worst beaten club," the editor urged the Olympics to enter. "They are the worst beaten club we know of in these parts." Incompetence appeared contagious in Peoria, as its Fort Clark Club also proved a stranger to victory. Promoting an upcoming game between the Fort Clarks and a Rock Island team, the newspaper said victory by the former would create a new sensation, which is "to have our club beat another city's club. We shall have to break the news gently to our readers. We live in hope."[51]

It was no surprise that disdain found most forceful expression in Chicago, where the Excelsiors continued to disappoint. In its July 6, 1868, issue, the *Chicago Republican* loosed a drop of editorial vitriol. "Excelsior Park, located at the corner of State and 22nd sts is an enclosure rented by a base ball club of this city, formerly known as the Excelsior club." The team excelled in "nothing except the uniformity with which they are beaten by other clubs." A name change was in order, but the team has "not yet exhibited sufficient sense or modesty to do it."[52]

Some thought the Woodstock Base Ball Club also needed a new name, and a local editor gave it one. After repeated stories recounting the team's defeats, he suggested "as usual," meaning defeated as expected. One of Rock Island's teams, the Lively Turtle Club, rarely tasted victory. When a Davenport newspaper reported it was "a fair and square club to deal with," the *Rock Island Argus* embraced the praise: "This is very kind and will be capital enough to set up business with. Without this the Turtles would have no standing at all."[53]

As seen in these examples, the success or failure of a local club could reflect on a community's self-image, especially in a time of local boosterism. With that identification came challenges. A leisure activity took on more importance than usual. Winning gained a higher priority, raising the costs of failure. Losing could mean public humiliation. As competition increased, aligning with civic pride and criticism, the old game lost part of its allure. And as winning became paramount, the game's joy and fun receded.

REPRESENTATIVE TEAMS

Wanted immediately at the offices of the Tribune and Republican newspapers, a base ball
club that the Excelsiors can beat, and that will
agree not to win or carry off any Chicago money.
—*Freeport Bulletin*, August 1, 1867[1]

S tinging criticism, like the above, became more common in 1868 and
1869 as baseball players and fans alike focused on winning rather than
celebrating the game's higher purposes.

Not only Chicago's Excelsiors, ironically the state's winningest club, but
others scattered around all sections of Illinois faced new expectations and
problems. By 1870, nearly all the pioneering clubs had disappeared or transi-
tioned to junior clubs. More often, teams appeared for a season, until eventually disbanding or losing the local newspaper's attention.

Some clubs persisted, like the Egyptian Club of Centralia, and others
organized, raised funds, traveled, and competed for a short time before,
without explanation, they disappeared from the record. Examining a small
number of them opens a window to their world.

The Egyptian Base Ball Club
of Centralia, 1866–70

Centralia's Egyptian Club was one of the state's most successful, not only on
the field but in longevity. Organized in 1866 from remnants of an 1865 club,
it played every year through 1870, a rarity in Illinois.

Constructing the Illinois Central Railroad in the 1850s created the town
of Centralia. Besides platting the town, the railroad placed its shops and a
roundhouse there, ensuring transportation's key role in its development. An
early historian described it as "pre-eminently a railroad town." Rails gave
Centralia connections to both the Ohio and the Mississippi Rivers to the
south and west, north to Chicago, and places between. Blacks fleeing the

South arrived by rail around 1864 to a community already divided ethnically. Earlier arrivals with New England and Mid-Atlantic antecedents gathered on the east side, Germans on the west. "Southtown" attracted upland southerners to the city's edge. Like other Illinois communities, Centralia had problems, some irritating, a few deadly. A local newspaper complained that "Centralia is a free pasture field for hogs." A cholera outbreak in August-September 1866 put twenty-one people in the local cemetery during nine days in August alone. Quiet days allowed editors to wax poetic about a local fair's side show, particularly the "Circassian Girl." "Her complexion is wonderfully fair, causing her face, neck and bust to appear almost like wax work or ivory." And her charms weren't limited to looks. "She is 21 years of age and speaks six different languages."[2]

New Englanders, mid-Atlantic states natives and upland southerners probably composed the original roster of the 1865 Liberty Base Ball Club. Most of its players were either in their teens or early twenties and wore long trousers, white shirts, and caps. After a successful opening season, the club fell apart when some players couldn't pay road-trip expenses. A few formed the Egyptian Base Ball Club.[3]

First notice of the new club appeared in June 1866, and the next month brought news of a nine-inning intrasquad game. The same article named the club's starting nine. Front-row seats were reserved for ladies at the grounds, the city's park at the time (now the site of the local library). The club name is a common nickname for the southern third of the state, "Little Egypt," the source of which is disputed. As a matter of course, the new club competed with others of the same name in southern Illinois communities. "It is rather unfortunate that the word should have been selected by three clubs of Southern Illinois—in Centralia, Carbondale and Cairo," a local newspaper noted in claiming rights of discovery. "Our boys were the first to organize and assume the name, and if there is any virtue priority [sic], the Centralia Club has the strongest claim."[4]

That November, the Centralia Egyptians contended with another claimant to the name—Cairo. But the controversial loss (see chapter 7) to the Cairo club did not end the season. In 1867, after opening with intrateam games, the club traveled north on the Illinois Central Railroad to play Decatur's McPherson Club. A tight game's momentum shifted after seven innings when an Egyptian player shouted to his teammates that a loss was unacceptable, prompting the next batter, Henry Condit, to promise a home run, who then fulfilled it, igniting a rally and leaving the Decatur team's "goose cooked." On the way home, the team stopped at Pana, where they eked out a one-run victory over its Excelsior Club.[5]

Enthusiastic community support buoyed the Egyptians. In September, young ladies presented the team with "a beautiful flag, with the emblems of the fraternity ingraved [*sic*] in the field," encouraging players to carry the banner to victory. As had the victory at Pana, the flag story appeared in newspapers outside Centralia and Marion County, indicating the growing appetite for baseball news and boosting the Egyptian Club's reputation. More positive press appeared later that month when the Egyptians returned to Decatur for the much-ballyhooed Grand Base Ball Tournament of the Western States. Although the event disappointed promoters, the Egyptians' fame rose despite losing in the senior club division to the Chicago Excelsiors. The Chicago team described the Egyptians as "skillful players who with a good pitcher could give them a close game." Second place was worth a $250 cash prize (the equivalent of $4,937.50 in 2022) plus a gold gilded baseball said to be worth $50 ($987.50 in 2022). Another intraclub game in late October concluded the Egyptian's season, followed by a postgame supper and singing.[6]

Egyptian mainstay Henry Condit recalled in a 1925 newspaper interview that the match with a club in Salem, which "had got up a team for the express purpose of licking us," was the highlight of that 1867 season. Before the game, one spectator requested an exciting game, promising "Every man that reached third base will get a glass of beer." To show he wasn't jesting; the man carried a "ten gallon can filled with beer" over to third base. The inducement brought out the best in the Egyptians, who scored 112 runs to 9 for the Salem team. Condit alone tallied 13 runs that day, managing to "get to third base a few more times than that," claiming his share of the beer prize. "It was an awfully hot day," he explained.[7]

But the 1868 season started without scheduled matches, prompting the *Centralia Democrat* to wonder "what has become of *us* Egyptians? Isn't it about time *they* were stealing a march on some club? . . . How is it, boys?" Finally, in late August, the Egyptian Club played its first match against another local club, the Unions, who fell 51–28. Next, the club traveled to Carlyle for a tournament. But the 1868 season's real excitement came in a three-game series with the Stars, a strong Mount Vernon club.[8]

The series between the rivals featured tight scores, injuries, and a free-for-all (see chapter 7). This best-of-three event colorfully illustrates the positives and negatives of the early game. The Egyptians emerged victorious, taking two out of three games, becoming, according to a Centralia newspaper, "THE CHAMPION CLUB OF SOUTHERN ILLINOIS." Just before the Mount Vernon series, the Egyptian Club crushed the Okaw Club of Carlyle, winning a $50 prize (worth $987.50 in 2022). A "feast" and dance on December 11 closed out the club's 1868 activities, the *Sentinel* observing that the club excelled "not only in playing balls, but also in dancing halls."[9]

After three successful seasons, the Egyptians assembled in April 1869 to set a schedule minus their old rival, Mount Vernon's Stars. A new team, the Resolute Base Ball Club, now carried Mount Vernon's honor on the field and challenged the Egyptians.[10] But no surviving records indicate that the game—or any others—occurred in 1869. The club continued into 1870, playing at least two games—one against the Mount Vernon Resolutes, the other with the Trenton Athletic Club.[11]

Sixty years later, Condit fondly recalled the Egyptian Club's spirit. "There were no such things as masks or chest protectors or mitts for the catchers. The infielders and outfielders played barehanded." And while the pitcher tossed the ball underhand, "that didn't ease it [the ball] up when a heavy batter leaned on one and sent a sizzler to the infield or outfield." Occasionally, the club lacked substitutes. "Maybe a fellow would get hurt, but he was game, and unless he got killed he got back in the game." Still, "we had fun, lots of it. . . . We had a good time." This spirit explains why Centralia was among the handful of senior clubs surviving until 1870.[12]

Excelsior Base Ball Club
of Chicago, 1858–68

On Lake Michigan's western shore, another baseball club gained regular, often critical, attention from Chicago newspapers. Though the best in its community, its roster filled with local players, and accumulating more wins than losses between 1865 and 1868, a nagging air of disappointment surrounded the Excelsior Base Ball Club. A scroll through Illinois newspapers reveals no club more disdained and disparaged by other communities and players than Chicago's Excelsiors. A historian of the club described it as "the recipient of far more abuse than any other baseball club of the era," despite winning more games than it lost. But in its detractors' eyes, one loss revealed the club's fundamental weakness, rendering it unworthy of an emerging metropolis. Moreover, the Excelsior Club's penchant for dispute and disparaging language toward opponents secured its bad reputation. For example, while understandably trying to avoid a flurry of games against weaker clubs, the Excelsiors indiscriminately insulted other teams. Accepting such challenges, the Chicago club sneered, would lead to an endless series of games "with clubs of questionable ability." Historian Peter Morris terms the language "deliberately provocative," and it created controversy—as if the Excelsiors needed more.[13]

Chicago pioneered organized baseball before the Civil War, its participation stretching back to 1858, when the Excelsiors defeated the Chicago Unions in two matches. After sitting idle in 1859, the 1860 club lost two of three games to a local rival, the Atlantic Base Ball Club. It also staged an intrateam game, dividing its players by political affiliation—one team favoring US Senator Stephen A. Douglas, the other, the Republican presidential candidate, Abraham Lincoln. In contrast with the political contest in November, the Douglas team won the match. The next year, most Excelsiors joined the Union Army.[14]

After the war, the Excelsiors reorganized and, in September 1865, entered a Rockford tournament. The Excelsiors stalked off the field during the championship game after a disputed call at third base. With the Excelsiors clinging to a one-run lead in the third inning, a player on Freeport's Empire Club was called out and then, after an appeal, was declared safe. Refusing to accept the umpire's reconsideration, the Chicago team "gathered up its bats and coats and left the field," which began its controversial reputation. Regardless, the Excelsiors enjoyed support from leading citizens and met in the offices of prominent banker George C. Smith.[15]

Their uniform of white trousers and white shirts ensured regular laundry charges and consumed $1,399 out of a $1,453 budget in 1866 (in 2022 dollars, $25,718.62 out of $26,706.14). Charging admission to games might have raised funds, but that required a permanent home field. The club lacked one. Open ground in the city was, Morris observes, "prohibitively expensive." Two 1866 events—tourneys in Rockford and Bloomington—sowed the next controversies. After Chicago defeated Detroit at Rockford, the losers offered the Excelsiors a best-of-three series. Even after Detroit promised to pay its hotel and travel expenses, the Excelsior Club spurned the challenge. It also rejected a challenge from the tourney's hosts, the rising Forest City Club. The Excelsiors insisted that the Rockford team was just one of many "clubs of questionable ability" and that playing such teams might overextend both Chicago's players and the club's treasury.[16]

In Bloomington, ill will boiled up later between Chicago and the downstate city with its own rising club. The resentments first arose at the 1866 Rockford tourney, where the Bloomington Base Ball Club defeated Chicago's second team, the Atlantics, and was set for the championship match against the Excelsiors. The match never took place, one explanation being a requirement that the injury-hobbled Bloomington team needed to play—and defeat—the Atlantic Club again before the championship contest. Never satisfactorily detailed in any account was how the Bloomington club still managed to leave with the second-place trophy. The confusing outcome sparked Bloomington's simmering resentment against both Chicago clubs. In its rain-marred tournament that September, the Bloomington Club again came within a step of the long-awaited match with the Excelsiors. First, it had to defeat the Atlantic Club. Going into the final inning, the score was tied. In its at-bat, the Atlantic Club scored three runs. Despite its confidence, the Bloomington Club fell short in its at-bat when team captain George Lackey, reportedly "under too much excitement" was tagged out in a rundown between third and home, ending the game.[17]

For the 1867 season, the Excelsiors debuted a new uniform, "blue shirt, cricket flannel pants, a web belt, and a white hat with a blue star." Growing pressures came too, related to an increasing identification of baseball teams with a city's pride and an "awkward transition to professionalism"—significant problems in ambitious cities like Chicago, Morris notes. Hoping to attract more local fans, the Excelsiors scheduled a rematch with the Atlantic Club, which it had narrowly defeated for the 1866 Bloomington tourney championship. The Excelsiors added one professional player, pitcher C. J. McNally, imported from the East. Excelsior victories over the Atlantics and the Forest City Club of Rockford raised local spirits for the biggest baseball event played in the city—a two-day visit by the Washington Nationals, an essentially professional team touring the Midwest.[18]

The National Base Ball Club's players were employees of the US Department of the Treasury, their jobs allowing generous time for practice and play. Tearing through the best the region had to offer, the Nationals shattered hopes and egos from Cincinnati to St. Louis and places in between. Excelsior supporters confidently expected the showdown in Chicago would end the Nationals' streak. Anticipating huge crowds, the games were moved to a racetrack, Dexter Park, near the stockyards. But before being conquered (or so local fans assumed) by the Excelsiors, the Nationals must play Rockford's Forest City Club.[19]

What happened in those two games—-Nationals versus the Forest City Club and Nationals against the Excelsiors—proved catastrophic for Chicago's top team. "It is difficult to overstate the extent to which this single game served to transform Chicago's top club from a source of pride into the object of scorn and ridicule," writes Morris. Newspapers in Illinois built up the Excelsiors-National's game, reporting the Washington club's progress through the Midwest, noting each overwhelming victory, each assuming its eventual defeat by the Excelsiors.[20]

Most thought the preliminary game with Rockford simply offered the Nationals a chance to loosen up after their long train ride from St. Louis. Another reason that the game's outcome shocked the baseball world was one important witness. Henry Chadwick, sometimes referred to as the "father" of baseball coverage, who traveled with the Nationals, reported the game for the *Baseball Player's Chronicle*. He watched and wrote as the Forest City's teenaged pitcher, Albert Goodwill Spalding, and the rest of his "country club" upended the Nationals 29 to 23—the touring club's first loss.[21]

Even the *Warsaw Bulletin* on the banks of the Mississippi River noticed the stunning outcome. The Nationals, it wrote, contrary to expectations, "have been badly beaten." A larger surprise was coming. The next day, the Nationals, considered underdogs by some bettors after the loss to the Forest City Club, rebounded to humiliate the Excelsiors, 49–4. Cynics on the *Chicago Tribune* suspected the Nationals purposely lost to Rockford in a scheme to rig the odds for the next day's game, thereby creating a windfall for bettors and themselves. After an angry response from the president of the Nationals, the *Tribune* withdrew the charge. Painfully, it became clear the Excelsior Club simply was outplayed by a superior club. And if Chicagoans thought the humiliation would die away, newspapers around the Midwest disabused them of the notion. "The newspapers published in the villages of Springfield and Milwaukee seemed to think" the city was "dreadfully cast down" over the loss. The *Tribune* sniffed that a "fourth-rate trotting horse will excite ten time the amount of local feeling any day than was bestowed on the base ball match," distancing itself and the city from the vanquished club. While the *Waukegan Gazette* used its columns to praise Forest City for its victory, many more newspapers gloried in the defeat of Chicago's top team. Danville's *Commercial* crowed that the Chicago team was "whipped to death." Bloomington reiterated its long-standing challenge to the Excelsior Club. Despite not having a dog in the fight, downstate's leading Republican newspaper, Springfield's *Illinois State Journal*, unleashed its delight. "Chicago has had its comb cut," an editor chuckled. "Poor Chicago; foolish Chicago. . . . Let Chicago hold its tongue and be still, and not make a fool of itself."[22]

A satirist in Peoria saw opportunity in the loss, using it in a series on life in the fictional village of Dudalville. "Snooks," the community's leading character, challenged the Excelsiors to a game. "The Snooks club consisted of our fellow townsman, Mr. Snooks, his lovely wife, and their seven sagacious children, forming a nine that would be hard to beat anywhere." Stretched over two columns, the game played out. Attendees included the fictional "Lieut. Governor Bross," who, at game's end, hinted that the Snooks Club members were professionals and in league with gamblers "for which Mrs. Snooks threshed him." After the game concluded in a scoreless tie, all parties were treated "to a cold collation of cod fish balls at the Snookian mansion and the Excelsior Club left for Chicago very much pleased with their reception."[23]

At Freeport, whose Empire Base Ball Club had won the Rockford tournament in 1865 when the Excelsiors stormed off the field, an editor termed Chicago's loss to the Nationals "unparalleled." Preferring to use ammunition from Chicago editors rather than its own, the newspaper endorsed a mock advertisement in the *Chicago Times*: "Wanted immediately at the offices of the Tribune and Republican newspapers, a base ball club that the Excelsiors can beat, and that will agree not to win or carry off any Chicago money." More was to come.[24]

A team in the northern Illinois village of Pecatonica entered the 1866 Rockford tourney and was smashed 49–1 by Detroit. Its fellow competitors awarded the unfortunate Pecatonicans a tin horn, a gift usually reserved for young children, inscribed with the word "Practice." Now Pecatonica's baseballists "decided that they had held the 'horn' as long as they were entitled to it," the idea being that the Excelsior Club, with its lopsided defeat by the Nationals, had usurped the village's reputation. Courtesy of Pecatonica's club, the Excelsiors received the tin horn. Piling on, a group of Chicago newspapermen, calling themselves the "Editorial Nine," challenged the Excelsiors "with the view of showing to the world that the Excelsiors are not the worst players in the State."[25]

Embarrassed, assailed by local critics, and the laughingstock of newspaper editors around the state, the Excelsior Club sought professional help. With cooperation from local merchants, the Excelsiors imported players by guaranteeing phantom jobs—their pay would come from an employer, but their work was to play baseball and play it well. A saloon business lured John Zeller, a mainstay of the New York Mutuals. A trip downstate seeking the Bloomington Base Ball Club's catcher and star pitcher failed with the first target but succeeded with the second, Patrick J. Keenan. "This scurvy trick of the Excelsiors we publish, that the base ball clubs of the West may know what kind of an honorable crowd they have to deal with in the Excelsiors," fumed the *Bloomington Pantagraph*. But the real story was the acquisition of the Forest City's young pitcher, vanquisher of the Nationals, Albert Goodwill Spalding, who now clerked in a Chicago grocery store for $40 per week at a time when the store's senior clerks made but $10.[26]

During Decatur's "Grand Base Ball Tournament of the Western States" that fall, Zeller and Keenan helped the Excelsiors sweep the field. The long-awaited match with the Bloomington Base Ball Club occurred later that month, and the Chicago team came from behind to win. In October, the Excelsior Club took two from Detroit to settle the question of which city had the best ball club. At the second game in Detroit, jubilant Chicago supporters embraced the embarrassment of the Nationals loss by "enthusiastically blowing on the famed Pecatonica horn."[27]

As Morris explains, the Excelsior Club suffered only one defeat in its first three postwar campaigns and then suddenly tumbled to five more. Insecurity became its constant companion. Its future appeared clouded even with four professional players at the end of the 1867 season. Baseball was plunging ahead, professionalism was growing, and, if the Excelsiors were to represent the burgeoning metropolis in the manner its civic boosters and fans expected, it must keep pace. Before the 1868 season, Spalding and Keenan departed, returning to their original clubs. Two new Philadelphia players were added—Harry Lex and James Hoyt—keeping the number of professionals at four. Would that be enough? The negative reply came amid dissension among the team's players and unremitting public hostility.[28]

A new field, located at State and Twenty-Second streets, was surrounded by an eight-foot fence and served as the club's 1868 home. Spectators now had to pay. Hoping 1867's post-National's momentum would carry over into the new season, the Excelsiors planned a busy schedule. But losses to the Forest City Club (again led by Spalding), as well as to the Philadelphia Athletics and Brooklyn's Atlantics, inspired a local wit to dub the team the "Inferiors." The club's fortunes quickly went downhill. On the Fourth of July, Spalding and the Forest Citys defeated the Excelsiors in Chicago before 2,500 spectators. Two weeks later, the Cincinnati Buckeyes drubbed the Chicagoans 43–22. By the end of July, Chicago's leading newspaper warned the Excelsiors that it was time either to quit or "practice." Too many once-great players were lackadaisical and should not be on the roster. Better to lose with hardworking amateurs than suffer continual humiliation with poorly motivated professionals. Even worse, the *Chicago Times* termed the Excelsiors "the celebrated muffin nine."[29]

Losses and criticism took a toll. Two veteran players resigned from the club. Finances and fund-raising floundered. Although dues assessments on both honorary and active members raised enough to keep the club on the field, a loss to the Unions of Morrisania of New York was devastating. John Zeller, one of the Excelsior's professionals, suffered a knee fracture during the game. After recruiting more New York professionals, the club launched a tour of Michigan, Ohio, and New York. Losses to Detroit and the Cincinnati Red Stockings compounded damage already done. Returning to Chicago, the team "received the chilliest of welcomes." Another trip to St. Louis produced three victories, but a game in Bloomington reinforced the Excelsior Club's bad reputation. After a dispute with the host club, the Excelsior captain pulled his team off the field in the fourth inning. Worse yet, upon returning to Chicago, the bedraggled and dispirited Excelsiors found the fence surrounding their ballpark dismantled and carried off by thieves.[30]

The purloined fence proved the team's coup de grace. It disbanded. The *Chicago Tribune* hoped some of the players would remain next year to form "the nucleus for a stronger organization." Linking success on the ball field to the city's reputation, it added, "It is imperative that Chicago should boast of a base ball club which can not only beat anything in the West, but which shall be able to vindicate Chicago's importance as the first city on the continent, by bidding defiance to any and all clubs in America." But no such team emerged in 1869, leaving the local game to amateurs. Even the second-class Atlantics were booted out the door by the *Chicago Times*, describing its players as "a gentlemanly but awkward and somewhat indolent group of ball tossers." Much of the city's baseball energy and enthusiasm went to company clubs, more than fifty by 1870.[31]

Demoralized and bitter, the Excelsior Base Ball Club's prime backers left the game entirely. In 1870, a new set of promoters formed the Chicago White Stockings, forerunner of today's Chicago Cubs, and put a fully professional team on the field that tried to live up to the *Chicago Tribune's* demand for team "to vindicate Chicago's importance."

Baseball did not disappear from Chicago with the demise of the Excelsior and Atlantic Clubs. The game continued on open prairies at the city's edge or undeveloped lots within its boundaries. Balls flew off bats, runners dashed around the bases, spectators cheered and moaned. The lessons learned brought a new game, one in which good spirits, good intentions, and practice did not ensure success. Talent, the best money could buy, was necessary. On a smaller scale, the experience of Chicago's Excelsiors repeated in other Illinois cities, towns, and villages.

Vermilion Base Ball Club
of Danville, 1866–67

About 150 miles south of Chicago, Danville organized its baseball club in 1866. Near the state's eastern border, Danville later enjoyed political power and federal largesse during the long congressional run of Joseph Cannon, who became speaker of the US House of Representatives in the early 1900s. Those glory days were decades in its future. Postwar Danville's afflictions included hogs stampeding through its streets and recurrent fires. Fighting the latter, one fire company had baseball players in its ranks. First notice of the city's Vermilion Base Ball Club, named after the county of which Danville was the seat, came in October. A month later, the club played its first game—an intraclub contest. Optimism reigned, the *Danville Commercial* predicting the new nine "will soon be able to compete successfully with the crack Clubs of the State."[32]

Vermilion Club member C. G. Harris wrote an account of the match for the local newspaper, noting a larger-than-anticipated crowd, including a "goodly company of smiling ladies." Harris's game story rambles, typical in 1860s-era coverage, and defeats a modern reader's hopes for searching out exactly what happened. For example, "Buhl sent a splendid ball to Lowell, who relieved him of his willow" (possibly meaning that the batter hit a fly to the outfielder who caught it for an out); "Devore received a like hint through a ball cleverly caught by Mann"; and "Hessey received a quietus from a tip bound to Gregory"; and so on. J. G. Kingsbury, editor of the *Commercial*, played for the club, scoring five runs and making two fly catches at shortstop. After the game, the losers hosted an "oyster supper at Buhl's Hall." Honored guests included representatives of the city's press and the Danville Band. "Altogether the affair was a pleasant innovation upon the humdrum-do-nothings of our little city."[33]

The "pleasant innovation" continued the following spring as the Vermilion Base Ball Club announced its challenge to the Hoosier Club of Lafayette, Indiana. The same article mentioned the next day's match game between the club's best nine players and a "*chosen* nine" from the remainder at their grounds west of the fair grounds. If the challenge to Lafayette was accepted and a game played, no record of it survives. In July, the newspaper urged readers to attend practice sessions. "Other clubs may have acquired more skill and precision in their movements than ours, but we venture to say but few can excel the Vermilion Base Ball Club in celerity and promptness of action required in this charming sport." The newspaper also noted the Vermilions entering a tourney at the upcoming Champaign County Fair.[34]

Joining the Vermilion Base Ball Club and their Champaign hosts, the Empire Club, at the tournament were the Blue Jackets and Red Jackets from Paxton, the Continental Club of Urbana, and Arcola's Pioneer Base Ball Club. The Danville, Urbana, and Champaign clubs emerged as first-round winners and played among themselves for the championship. The first match put the Vermilions against the Empires. "Excitement ran high," spectators anticipating a close match. Instead, they watched the Champaign club build and maintain a strong lead. One writer attributed the Danville team's slow start to lack of experience, relating that the tournament offered its first match games. Darkness fell in the seventh inning, and the game was called with the Empires holding an 84–54 lead. Indicating the lack of hard feelings—at that time—Danville ceded second place to Urbana's Continentals because they "had played a much better game than the Vermilion" and deserved it.[35]

Despite the lopsided loss, the Vermilions believed they could do better, and even defeat the Empires, in a rematch. A Champaign newspaper saw little hope for the challengers, commenting that "nothing remains for them but defeat." Champaign's Empire Club traveled by train to Danville for the rematch, where "the great contest . . . on which the ultimate fate of this mundane sphere is supposed to hang." The venue was set for the Vermilion Club's grounds on the first Friday in October. Again, poking fun at the pregame ballyhoo, the *Commercial* pleaded with local shopkeepers "to conceal everything in the shape of rope about their premises because if our boys should get beaten (which will not happen) they may be prevented from going off and hanging themselves at once." There was no need to worry. The Danville team did not lose the game; yet neither did it win. The Empires arrived on Thursday night and awoke Friday to rain. The visitors agreed to stay over another night and play the game early Saturday. For unknown reasons, the Empire Club changed its mind and departed. "When morning broke clear and fair and the Vermilion Base Ball Club sought their friends of the Empires, behold! They had 'folded their tents in the night like the Arabs/ And as silently stolen away.'" Disappointment shifted toward anger when a Champaign newspaper referred to the Danville group as a "country club." Champaign's abrupt departure combined with the condescending reference hardened resentment. "We cannot but consider their haste to leave in an unfavorable light." For its part, the Champaign newspaper vigorously defended the Empires, casting their own aspersions on the Vermilions. "Week after week, since this last affair, they [the Vermilion Club] have slurred the Empires, most shamefully and have even taken the pains to send papers containing such items to the different clubs in this part of the state." Quickly, good memories of fellowship and sportsmanship from the two teams' meeting at the county fair dissipated.[36]

At least one game remained for the Vermilions. In November, the club played a team in Homer, a small village between Champaign and Danville, mauling its Eureka Base Ball Club 92–37. After its lopsided victory, the Vermilion Base Ball Club expired. No mentions of the club or baseball can be found in Danville newspapers in 1868 or 1869. Time obscures the reasons for its abrupt end. Perhaps sour feelings over the Champaign controversy, the difficulty in finding opponents from towns of equal size, the simple departure of key players, competing interests of potential members, or some combination thereof killed the club. Certainly, the combination of ruffled feelings and injured civic pride left a sour taste, overwhelming the joy of organized competition. Yet it is perplexing that the team and the game welcomed as "a pleasant innovation upon the humdrum-do-nothings of our little city " passed so quickly and quietly.[37]

Excelsior Club of Pana, 1867

Equally mystifying is the rise and disappearance of Pana's Excelsior Base Ball Club, which lost only two games during its brief existence and included on its roster a player later termed "the Babe Ruth of Central Illinois."[38]

The Excelsior Club gained first notice in 1867 when the Centralia Egyptian Base Ball Club stopped off at Pana on its return from a match in Decatur. The game with the Egyptians was indicative of the Pana players' skills. Centralia, the dominant team in southern Illinois, squeaked out a one-run victory. A Pana newspaper attributed the victory to the Egyptian players' superior fielding, though "the Pana boys . . . were decidedly the best batsmen." Days after winning a match against its junior affiliate, the Athletic Base Ball Club, and playing an intraclub game, the Excelsiors attracted a crowd to its practice, including "quite a swarm of fair ladies," perhaps lured by the club's new uniforms which "blossomed out" and "look well."[39]

A local druggist took advantage of the team's growing popularity. "Ed Weinstein wishes us to inform base ball players, generally, that it takes three barrels of arnica, mixed with a quart of—of—well some other drug, we disremember what kind it is, to enable a man to make a 'home run' these hot days." The same day of Weinstein's plug, the newspaper announced an upcoming match with Decatur's McPherson Club. "Wake up, 'Red Caps'!" the *Pana Gazette* urged. "Arouse! Shake off your lethargy! Gird on your armor and be ready for the conflict." Keeping with the military theme, Pana's players must brave the "whizzing balls from the McPherson battery. . . . Don't dodge the 'flies'[,] muff 'hot balls' nor try to catch them in your mouth." Decatur druggists needed "a large supply of arnica," and hopefully physicians were on call in case some player was struck by a "humming bird" off the bat of J. C. McQuigg, a powerful Pana home-run hitter. The game was envisioned as more than a mere athletic contest; it was a celebration, filled with fun and the promise of civic honor.[40]

Pana's team and several enthusiasts left from the town's Illinois Central Railroad depot in a special car reserved for their use. At Decatur, they were met by a delegation from the McPhersons and taken to a local hotel, where they paid 25 cents each (almost $5 in 2022 dollars) for a meal "that was supposed to be free." With plenty of time before the game, the Excelsiors wandered about the town, picking up street talk indicating "that the Pana boys would stand a poor chance in the hands of so formidable an antagonist."

Once play started, however, on the field tucked between the north-south and east-west railroad lines, the visitors blossomed. "The McPherson boys began to complain that they could not bat a ball but in the field any place, no matter how far, without one of the Excelsior fielders would start it back just before it reached the ground. This proved to be a serious annoyance to them." The *Decatur Weekly Republican* put responsibility for the 57–19 loss literally in the hands of the McPhersons—"it is but justice to the Decatur boys to say their fielding was much worse than usual." But an estimated one thousand spectators, predominantly Decatur residents, found plenty to admire: "the audience never failed to cheer the Excelsiors when a good play was made."[41]

A few days later, a rematch in Pana was arranged. The McPherson Club arrived by train at 7:30 a.m., "accompanied by the Silver Band." Though the game's first inning was played poorly, the Excelsiors soon pulled away to win 41–26. After a dinner hosted by the Excelsiors, Decatur's junior club, the Centrals, played Pana's juniors, the Athletics. Once again, Pana won. Unlike some town rivalries, the short-lived Decatur-Pana competition produced no ill feelings, their respective newspapers and club members proclaiming mutual respect.[42]

September showcased the Pana Excelsiors. First, the club traveled south, along the Illinois Central Railroad line, to Vandalia, gaining a lopsided 93 to 50 victory over the Active Base Ball Club. Marking the game was another impressive hit by McQuigg, Pana's catcher, that "lit up on the top of a high hill about two hundred yards distance." The ball's resting place was so far from the infield that McQuigg rested at third base for "half a minute" before easily proceeding home. McQuigg had plenty of help, with Pana knocking twelve home runs against four for the Actives during the four-and-a-half-hour game. In mid-September, the Excelsior Club was back in Decatur for the Grand Base Ball Tournament of the Western States. Not only did the club win the junior championship, it kept the tournament alive when disputes threatened its continuance. The strange series of events left the Pana nine as champion of its division after winning only one contest, a 56–20 drubbing of the host McPhersons, which was covered in chapter 7. Amid all the discord arising from use of ineligible players and the attempt to bar the Chicago Excelsiors from competing, the Pana club earned much goodwill in addition to a "gold pitcher." One tourney account especially noticed the Pana team, "who have nobly come up to the work every time, always ready to do anything to render the tournament a success."[43]

Pana's youth club, the Athletics, traveled to Taylorville a few days later, taking only five innings to convince their hosts, the National Club, that "Pana was too much for them." With baseball fever bearing such fruits, the *Pana*

Gazette bragged, "Ball clubs around in various sections of the country that contemplate beating our Pana clubs will please bear in mind that it takes a 'full team' to beat any of them." Next, Vandalia's Actives traveled to Pana, this time losing by a slightly smaller margin, 48–18. Seeking to regain local pride, the Taylorville Nationals also came to Pana, only to lose by eighty-seven tallies. For Pana's Excelsiors, the season ended in late October with another train ride, this one to Mattoon and a 67–14 victory. Further proof, the *Pana Gazette* editor proclaimed, contradictorily, of the Excelsior's "world-wide reputation throughout this section of the State."[44]

By all indications, the Excelsior Base Ball Club was on its way to becoming competitive with clubs in larger cities like Springfield and Bloomington. It might take another crack at the Centralia Egyptians, the only club to defeat them in 1867. But, when the Pana club met in mid-November at Pana city hall, there were indications of trouble, a newspaper article noting the "decimated ranks of the Excelsior Base Ball Club." Further clues came the following May. "They have had several meetings," the *Pana Gazette* explained, "and liquidated all the indebtedness of the Club." Though its trips to other cities involved relatively short distances, rail tickets still had to be purchased, meals arranged, time taken off work, equipment bought or replaced—all potentially creating a burden.[45]

After that point, the Excelsior Base Ball Club drops from the record. The *Pana Gazette* made no mention of either the Excelsiors or baseball after the May 22 article. Like their friendly rival, the Decatur McPherson Club, Pana's Excelsiors disbanded after the 1867 season. Perhaps the Excelsiors (and other disbanded clubs) continued to play among themselves in informal contests. What is curious about Pana's demise, however, is not only its success on the field—only one loss—but its strong community support. J. C. McQuigg, the "Babe Ruth" of his time, remained in Pana, engaging in a successful law practice. His days of awe-inspiring blows with his bat were, like the Excelsiors, a momentary interruption in the life of a small rural Illinois community. His legacy, however, lingered in the mind of a local historian, who fondly recalled and shared his story a half-century later.[46]

The Shabbona Base Ball Club
of Ottawa, 1867–70

Even clubs surviving for several seasons faced challenges and eventually collided with the harsh competitive realities created by baseball's evolution.

Ottawa, the seat of LaSalle County, at the confluence of the Fox and Illinois Rivers, is a classic river town. At its northern edge, the Illinois-Michigan

Canal carried cargo to and from Chicago. Unlike other trade centers, the city failed to organize baseball clubs early, though, once the game arrived, it persisted until the club confronted the emerging professional era on a disastrous road trip.

The game is first noticed in the May 9, 1867, edition of the *Ottawa Republican* announcing the O.K. Base Ball Club's challenge to another local team—the one that would dominate the sport in Ottawa—the Shabbona Base Ball Club. The game on grounds east of the Fox River attracted "hundreds of spectators," ending with the Shabbonas on top, 37–24. The *Republican* speculated that the O.K. Club would seek a rematch and wondered why more merchants and clerks did not attend. If they did so in the future, "They would not so look as though a *puff of wind would blow them away*."[47]

A few weeks later, the second nines of the two clubs played on the Fox River grounds. Ignoring hot weather, another crowd turned out to see the O.K. Club reverse roles, beating the Shabbonas 30 to 14. A third game between the rivals occurred later, and this time the Shabbona Club won again, 37–20. Between those matches, the Shabbonas traveled to Peoria to meet that city's Enterprise Base Ball Club. The outcome of that match is lost.[48]

In July, the Shabbonas played games against actors and others employed by the Black Crook, a theatrical production touring Illinois that summer. Down 44 to 4 after five innings, the Black Crook players "threw up the sponge." The *Republican* was jubilant, predicting that, with practice, the Shabbona Club could be among the best in Illinois. Neighboring LaSalle sent over its club, the Little Vermilion, at the end of the month. Perhaps reading its press notices in the *Republican*, the Shabbona Base Ball Club came on strong and won 89 to 17. "Evidently, one great cause of their [Little Vermilion's] being so badly beaten in this contest was that want of practice in batting swift as well as slow balls," indicating that, even in Illinois, pitchers were varying speeds. Their role under the rules was to simply put the ball where the batter could hit it, and perhaps they changed speeds and used other tricks to confuse batters. Some spectators traveled with the team from LaSalle. Although the defeat was lopsided, one reporter presumed that the ladies, at least, were consoled that "the Shabbonas are a rough looking set of fellows, anyway."[49]

It was a good week for the surging Shabbona Base Ball Club. Its second nine clobbered the Eagle Base Ball Club of Dayton, a LaSalle County town, 55 to 22. In August, another victory by the Shabbona reserves came against the first nine of the Illinois Base Ball Club of Morris, 75–63 after four and one-half hours.[50]

A second game between the Little Vermilion and Shabbona Clubs proved the first victory margin to be no fluke, the Shabbona Club winning, 98 to 48.

But, in another rematch, the Illinois Club of Morris beat the Shabbona reserves by 17 runs. "Our boys have supposed that they were invincible," moaned the *Republican*. In truth, the loss did not come as a surprise, as "the Shabbona boys have become very negligent of late and have had little or no practice."[51]

The Shabbona first nine also suffered a setback, losing 48 to 34 to the O.K. Club. "Shab-*Bi-nice*, where art you now?" the *Free Trader* mourned ungrammatically, playing on the name of the legendary Native American from LaSalle County who aided early settlers. "*Abbor-gine* from whence cometh the breeze that hath thusly ruffled your plumage?" The writer pointed to the trouble. "'Pride cometh before a fall'; he that exalteth himself shall be abased." The game account following emphasized humor more than criticism. For example, one player was knocked to the ground a couple of times by hard-hit balls, the last one's impact causing him to faint, and a physician was summoned. "Bob [the player], resting his head upon the protruding abdomen of the surgeon, and straining the nerves of his battered peepers in the directions of his friends, exclaims with anxiety, 'Don't give up the game.'"[52]

During the 1867 LaSalle County Fair, the Shabbona Club again defeated the O.K. Club, this time 56 to 45, and also won at the Grundy County Fair to end the first nine's season. Remaining was the Shabbona second nine's rematch with the first nine of Morris's Illinois Club to decide the split in their first two games. In late October, the clubs played the deciding game in Morris. Reporting in florid fashion, the *Free Trader*'s writer scattered classical references, humor, and feigned seriousness. His account began with "twelve alarm clocks striking simultaneously at 5 o'clock on Tuesday morning last" to roust the players from bed and follows the sleepy-eyed team and its supporters to the depot and onto the train to Morris. The rising sun drinking "up the dew of Tuesday morning" portended good things. On the other hand, "The Illinois nine . . . doubtless slept on the stern resolves of their guests, as did Webster on the speech of Hayne—soundly." Illinois Club players met the Shabbonas at the depot and "gave us a cordial greeting and . . . a good warm breakfast." But the game's course quickly indicated the laurels would remain in Morris, and the Illinois Club won by seventeen runs. Signing himself "Third Baseman," the correspondent explained the loss. "The greeting they [the Illinois players] gave us *in uniform* was, if anything, a *little warmer* than that of the early morning." But the writer, acknowledging the hosts' hospitality, promised "to give Morris another specimen of his batting, when they will agree to treat our second nine just as they did throughout Tuesday last."[53]

With winter, a skating park, enclosed by an eight-foot-high, tightly boarded fence, opened on the Fox River ball grounds. As ice covered the field, the Shabbonas recalled their first season ending with victory for its first nine and a defeat, accepted good-naturedly, by its reserves. Good press accompanied the inaugural season; Ottawa newspapers limited their criticism and often framed losses as an opportunity for humor rather than censure. Important to note is that the rituals and feelings of friendship superseded the desire to win. In its friendly journey through 1867, the Shabbona Club avoided the pitfalls, controversies, and hard feelings afflicting its baseball comrades in other parts of the state.[54]

Spring's approach in 1868 brought the Shabbona Base Ball Club back to the courthouse to ratify a new constitution and elect officers. Twelve days later, it reassembled for unspecified business above the Bradford and Bryant store. An uncooperative Mother Nature prevented practice and games, as noted by the headline "Dull Times," over the *Free Trader's* complaints that "abominable weather" gave Ottawa its "dullest spell" in ten years. "There would be some relief could one even play base ball but there is no code of the game we ever heard of that permits it to be played with umbrellas." But it voiced confidence that drier days—and a new look—were ahead. "The Shabbonas will appear at the coming match in handsome new uniforms." And an advertisement announced, "Boys Base Ball Shoes just received" at a local dry-goods store.[55]

Victory over the Illinois Club of Morris launched the season, though a few days later, the Shabbonas fell to Morris by five runs. Rebounding the next month, the Shabbonas easily handled Geneseo's Pioneer Club, 33–22, before several hundred spectators. In its game account, the *Republican* regretted that the loss to Morris cost the Shabbonas championship for the Sixth Congressional District. The next game with Geneseo was tight in the early innings before Ottawa's ten-run ninth inning secured victory.[56]

Buoyed by their triumph over Geneseo, the Shabbonas challenged any club in its congressional district or in the cities of Bloomington, Peoria, Galesburg, Aurora, Princeton, and Monmouth to play a match in Ottawa on fifteen days' notice. The only team taking advantage of the offer was the Farmers Base Ball Club of Farm Ridge [today Grand Ridge], a tiny village between Ottawa and Streator. As a surprise to no one, the Shabbonas were victorious, 31 to 11. The next game, against the Live Oak Club of Peru, brought the team near disintegration. Having defeated the Live Oaks 39–11 earlier in the season, the Shabbonas traveled to Peru and lost, 38 to 16. E. A Nattinger, the Shabbona Club's secretary, called a team meeting to determine "whether the Club shall *go under*, or maintain its old reputation."[57]

The Shabbonas survived and beat another village team, the Oak Base Ball Club of Deer Park, 60–36, though there is reason to believe that the Shabbona Base Ball Club brought in outside players to augment its ranks. An early-season story reported the team "strengthened" by the addition of William L. Bryant, formerly of the Enterprise Club of Pittsburgh; William Jenkins, described as being from a "New York club"; and a player named Murphy from the O.K. Base Ball Club, which hadn't returned in 1868. The Shabbonas were following in the footsteps of other top clubs—notably the Chicago Excelsiors and Rockford's Forest City Club. The evolving game threatened clubs stocked solely with local talent.[58]

General interest in baseball on the part of the *Ottawa Free Trader* newspaper as well as the Shabbona Club faded in 1869. Only one game was reported and that not until September, when the local favorites nipped Chillicothe, 25–24. Some five hundred spectators watched the contest, including three justices of the Illinois Supreme Court then holding session in Ottawa. The river city's infatuation with baseball, though diminished, continued, as evidenced by five separate advertisements over the summer from H. Walther, who sold baseballs and bats at his ice-cream parlor. The newspaper also noticed clubs in Earlville and Leland, both small LaSalle County communities. In the latter article, the newspaper worried the game was "nearly played out." The only other mention of baseball in the *Free Trader* columns came in October in a promotion for an upcoming game in Morris between the Illinois Club of that city and the famed Forest City Club of Rockford. A railroad offered return tickets at one-fifth the normal cost for all traveling to the game.[59]

A rejuvenated Shabbona Club emerged in 1870 to inflate—and then puncture—its boosters' hopes for competing with the state's finest. These dreams commenced in late June when some "lively young gentlemen" met in the county courthouse and reorganized the Shabbonas. A reporter noted the club applied for membership in the Illinois State Base Ball Association.[60]

The "new" Shabbona Club's first test came when Chicago's Garden City Base Ball Club arrived. Maintaining the rituals in a time of increasing competition, the Shabbonas met the Chicagoans at the train depot and escorted them to the Clifton Hotel on the western banks of the Fox River. Later, across the river, the Shabbonas "astonished their city neighbors by very good play," making the 31–17 loss seem a moral victory to Ottawa's supporters and players. Any potential hard feelings melted away in the continuation of the observed rituals. Overnighting in Ottawa, the Garden City team "enjoyed the hospitalities of Ottawa, without cost, of course." The afterglow perhaps prevented Garden City players from warning the next visitors, the Chicago Eckfords, about the Shabbona Club's surprising skill. Referring to their hosts as a "country greenhorn team" before the game, the Eckfords were in for a surprise. Initially, the Shabbonas looked at their foes "with fear and trembling," hoping to simply give the Chicagoans a decent game before, a reporter estimated "a couple of thousand people." But, by the end of the sixth inning, the Eckfords were ready to 'go home and see ma' and were let off" on the short end of a 47–11 score. Entertained that evening at the Clifton, the Eckfords returned home the next morning "in a dilapidated condition."[61]

Shabbona supporters, not the least among them the *Free Trader*, were ecstatic. "Ottawa has a club she may well be proud of," crowed the newspaper. Ottawa's favorites traveled to Henry, easily topping its Star Club before moving on to Peoria to play the Fort Clark Base Ball Club. In six innings, the Shabbonas ran up a 59–6 score, demoralizing their Peoria hosts, who "quit the game in disgust and left the field . . . so intensely mad that they did not even treat the Shabbonas with common respect." The next opponent, Springfield's Liberty Club, already had topped a St. Louis club and the Lone Stars of New Orleans, "the champions of the South," raising betting odds two-to-one in its favor. Another large crowd turned out, first enduring a storm that delayed play for thirty minutes. When the game resumed, the Shabbonas outplayed the Springfield club. Final score: Shabbona, 15; Liberty Club, 8.[62]

Riding on the high hopes and spirits of players and supporters, the Shabbona Club joined in a "muffin game" against the "rotund nine." Members of the latter club were limited to those "over two hundred pounds" or "less than one hundred pounds." Drafting a newspaper reporter to serve as umpire increased the game's frivolity (see chapter 5).[63]

The *Free Trader* shared more serious club news. Emboldened by its success, the Shabbona Base Ball Club planned an August tour of ten games in seven cities. Starting on August 17 against Springfield's Liberty Club, the projected tour would travel south to play two St. Louis clubs, then turn north to Quincy and Rockford, on into Janesville, Wisconsin, then over to Milwaukee, and concluding in Chicago with three games in as many days, the finale with the professional Chicago White Stockings. "The boys have a large contract but are not afraid of being able to fill it."[64]

Apart from Rockford's Forest City Club, no Illinois team attempted such a lengthy tour or one involving outstanding teams. Though the Shabbonas had defeated the Eckfords of Chicago and the Liberty Club, many of their projected opponents had better records. Its surprising earlier success led the Shabbona Club to underestimate the opposition.

Things began smoothly. A tongue-in-cheek-account written as if it were an Indian legend told in clichés and faux romanticism reported that "at the settlement known as Springfield the Shabbonas bravely scalped another tribe of savages known as the 'Libertas.'" The storyteller continued, "Elated with success and fearless of danger, they boldly and fiercely assaulted the 'breastworks' of a village known as St. Louis." But there the ballyhooed tour halted in its tracks.[65]

"Here they came to grief; here they were tommy-hawked; here they were martyred; here they died." Some observers attributed the losses in St. Louis to players drinking or eating too much. One player, the reporter implied, was drunk. When admonished for not catching balls hit his way, he replied, "I generally catch two or three of 'em each time, but how's a feller going to catch a (hic) 'leven to wunst?" The tour abruptly ended. Returning Shabbona players were depicted as "straggling along." In the fanciful account, the "only surviving member of the club" was to be honored by a parade, "deemed a matter of justice, owing to the brilliant career of the Shabbonas." But this parade consisted of a "blind mule, a band of music, a dozen base ball bats and such remnants of the Shabbona uniforms as could be procured," all waiting to greet the survivor at the train depot. From there, he was marched through the streets as the maids of a local hotel "threw down bouquets of the choicest quality"—perhaps dirty water from wash basins and commodes. While no results of any games played after the Springfield victory exist, the fanciful tale contained elements of truth. The tour did collapse in St. Louis after a thrashing or two at the hands of the experienced St. Louis clubs, compounded by money trouble.[66]

Chicagoans offered another explanation for the tour's sudden end, one shedding light on the "blind mule" parade. The *Chicago Times* account judged the Shabbonas the champion "Club That Can Walk . . . east or west." Ottawa's players having raised $200 to fund the tour by "chipping in," discovered in St. Louis that their "treasury became exhausted, and the result was that they disbanded and 'flat-footed-it' home." Anger inflamed the humiliation when the club's captain found funds for his travel home by rail while his teammates walked. Although footsore and fatigued, the walkers reportedly retained some energy, for they seized "their late superior office[r], placed him on a mule, and rode him around town."[67]

On the same day as the fanciful account of the Shabbona Club's downfall, another humorous reference to it appeared. Reprinting a brief about a DeKalb player suffering a broken leg, an editor quipped, "We know of a worse case at Ottawa: a whole club, while playing base ball, got *dead broke*." Proof that the Shabbonas were not literally killed or scalped in St. Louis came in late September when the Forest City Club of Rockford arrived in Ottawa. The professional club played a "picked nine" team, winning 12–2. "It is due to the Ottawas to say that they were able to gather up but four or five of the old Shabbona Club and had to fill out with scrubs."[68]

Dashing the Shabbona Club's ambitions to compete with the top teams of Illinois were the harsh, unforgiving realities of top-level competition. By then, most Illinois clubs already had discovered such truths, which, combined with the game's declining faddishness, ended many early baseball clubs. Ottawa's Shabbona Club simply persisted longer. Baseball remained but left scores of crushed dreams like those of the Shabbona's three-state tour, stinging disappointments eased only through humor and the passage of time.

Each of the clubs of this chapter is representative in the sense that its rise and problems repeat in other sections of the state. Most had some success on the field, but their stories also reveal the challenges and frustrations faced as the game became more competitive.

Contrasting the consistent support for the Centralia Egyptians Club are the editorial poundings endured by the Chicago Excelsiors. The successful rise and sudden disappearance of Pana's team likely was linked to costs associated with travel and hosting games, as well as the players' shifting attention to work, families, and careers. And Danville's end models the disappearance of other clubs after unpleasant experiences in competitive play.

By 1870, baseball's future, at least at the highest level, was clear. Possessing the best players, not necessarily the most practiced, predicted success. Towns were lucky to have one or two gifted athletes. Communities with the necessary funds—Chicago and Rockford—could fill talent deficiencies with good players by giving them salaries. Unless a club had deep pockets, hopes for local glory were unrealistic. Better to move on to other venues, such as commerce or luring railroad connections, and leave baseball to junior players. The adults moved on.

THE THRILL DEPARTS

> There is nothing to censure in ball playing, as
> an exercise, or a recreation, on occasion, for
> students or persons of sedentary habits for the
> glow of pleasure which it inspires when once in
> a while a spirit of emulation is excited. But pro-
> fessional base ball playing—bah—what is it?
> —*Bloomington Pantagraph*, October 28, 1870[1]

While competitiveness and professionalism provoked this 1870 editorial rebuke, baseball fever receded in many Illinois communities as early as 1868. Freeport's *Bulletin* newspaper ran no articles about the game in 1868. Waukegan and Galena newspapers also are silent on the game that year and 1869. During 1868, Rock Island's *Argus* observed a lack of enthusiasm, and its surviving 1869 issues are bare of baseball. "Base ball fanaticism is perceptibly on the decline," an editor noted in June 1868. "The men who but one short year ago were proud to carry a broken finger or a frowning eye from the hotly-contested field now don't seem to care whether they get into a field at all."[2]

At Cairo, the cooling also continued. "Last summer base ball flourished in Cairo and men and boys played base ball, talked base ball, and pitched their balls around the streets so persistently that the City Dads were obliged to adopt an ordinance forbidding ball playing on the streets," an editor of the *Cairo Democrat* recalled in 1868. "But the mania has passed away, vanished like a summer cloud."[3]

The game was not quite dead, nor would it ever be. Baseball continued in many Illinois communities and emerged in others during 1868 and after. Nevertheless, these commentators did reflect reality. The game was transition-ing. The fad phase cooled beside temporary enthusiasms like croquet and velocipedes. Novelty attached itself to other activities, drawing newspaper attention. Baseball lived, though with less editorial notice, moving unevenly from an object of public curiosity to a simple recreational activity interesting only to players and their supporters. Entering the decade's final years, a few places discovered the game or revived dormant interest. But overall, baseball interest faded in most communities as familiar problems again filled news columns.

A Few Outposts Persisted

Dogs bedeviled the southern Illinois community of Carlyle in 1869. Its streets plagued with "more thieving, barking, worthless dogs than any place of its size this side of the moon. . . . 'Let us have peace,' and fewer dogs," one of the town's newspapers declared, echoing U. S. Grant's presidential campaign slogan. The same issue offered hope—if not for the elimination of the canine menace at least a distraction from it. A baseball club had organized. A report of its fourteen members came in the next issue. Rising enthusiasm for the game encouraged a local merchant to advertise his stock of baseballs.[4]

In north central Illinois, an editor noted in 1869, "Base ball fever is becoming very prevalent again. But it is like working in harvest and getting no pay." That summer, his local competitor announced the reorganization of the defunct Princeton Amateur Base Ball Club, and both newspapers covered the team's fortunes. The same year, Freeport saw a revival of the game there.[5]

But Jacksonville, an early adopter of the game, experienced diminishing enthusiasm. After betraying mixed emotions about the game's rumored revival, the *Jacksonville Journal* reluctantly welcomed the effort. "If they will do so 'without running the thing into the ground,' as of yore, it is a happy idea. Otherwise, we say let it alone." Resuscitating the city's old Union Club produced little on-field success but spotlighted another club, the Alerts, a junior organization, who defeated "the weather-beaten relics of the old Union club" twice that summer. Another sign of junior clubs surpassing their seniors, these victories set the stage for the Alert club's rivalry with their Springfield counterparts, the Liberty Club.[6]

Even in Aurora, a newspaper once expecting the imminent demise of the old Black Hawk Base Ball Club, now reported its revival and a new junior team that summer.[7] To the west, a Quincy newspaper looked to the future. "Here we have little of the intentions of our senior clubs, but they seem to have given up the field entirely to the juniors who are practicing regularly and have already won at least two victories."[8]

As Illinois teams rose, revived, or faded, the nation's best teams toured the prairies from Brooklyn, Philadelphia, New York City, and an Illinois city just up the road, Rockford. Between the baselines, their level of play proved impossible for most Illinois teams to match. And the ways such teams added talent, by either providing off-field jobs with little work for good players or paying them outright, were unavailable to amateurs. The contests of the era with touring teams exposed the game's emerging harsh reality—practice could go only so far. Superior athletic skill was no longer rare and was now a commodity bought and sold in the market.

Located on a railroad line between Chicago and St. Louis, Bloomington hosted touring national teams in the late 1860s. Besides providing a convenient stop, the city's team, the Bloomington Base Ball Club, enjoyed a good reputation, potentially offering moneymaking opportunities for visiting clubs. Within two years of its 1865 founding, the club had become the second- or third-strongest in the state. A second-place finish in the 1866 Rockford tournament, its 1867 defeat of Rockford's Forest City Club, and strong showings against leading Chicago clubs made it attractive to touring teams.

For reasons unknown, the Bloomington Base Ball Club stopped playing local and area competition after the 1867 season, reserving its match play for the few teams it deemed suitable. Lack of regular competition, however, weakened the club, the resulting rustiness doing it no good against top teams, beginning with the Philadelphia Athletics on June 15, 1868.

During what historian Peter Morris termed a "troubled transition to professionalism," the Athletic Club earned praise by promoting the game through tours like its 1868 swing. Considered a powerhouse on the East Coast, regularly competing with clubs like the Washington Nationals and Brooklyn Atlantics, the Athletics inaugurated the game's future in 1865 by playing the Resolute Club of Brooklyn in that city's first enclosed ballpark, the Union Grounds.

Admission charges followed, with spectator access limited by board walls. But the club's strength came at a price—literally. In 1866, it was accused of paying three players twenty dollars apiece contrary to the game's rules. And, in 1869, it hired an infielder from another Philadelphia club to join it against the Brooklyn Atlantics.[9]

Professionalism roiled Philly's Athletic Club and angered its former president, who resigned from the club in a fiery letter. "Gentlemen, we have broken every law of the game, and we have defied public opinion. Six of our nine are regularly paid—are 'Hired Men,' in fact." The Athletics taking the field in Bloomington were professionals. Several would go onto major-league careers, the most famous of whom would be Al Reach. Second baseman Reach became a successful sporting-goods dealer, accumulating enough wealth to launch the National League franchise in Philadelphia, the modern Phillies.[10]

Nothing suggests the Bloomington Base Ball Club contained anything other than businessmen, lawyers, and clerks playing for fun and exercise. In a refrain repeated throughout the summer, Bloomington's leading newspaper proclaimed the upcoming Athletics contest "the greatest game of base ball that ever came off in this city." At the fairgrounds west of the city limits, the newspaper predicted, the Philadelphians would encounter a club "never in better trim for efficient playing." With Bloomington's best catcher, pitcher, third baseman, and right fielder in the lineup, such optimism, though naïve, is understandable.[11]

Spectators numbering between a thousand and twelve hundred gathered to watch the game under warm temperatures cooled by cloudy skies. Bloomington's supporters took hope at the end of the first inning with their club's 5–3 lead. But, by the end of the third, after some "fine play on their part and poor play on the part of the Bloomingtons," the Athletics pulled away, creeping "along from base to base, sure, swift and noiseless" to a 31–6 victory. As for the Bloomington Club, "it was easy to see that they were in the hands of those who were the superior in all points of the game." Or, as the *Quincy Whig and Republican* put it, "The Athletic boys . . . played smash with the Bloomington nine."[12]

Another lesson followed later that month when the Brooklyn Atlantics arrived. The state's best team, the Forest City Club of Rockford, had lost by only two runs to the Atlantics, piquing local interest in the game with the "champion club of the East." "The Bloomington Base Ball Club must look to their laurels and the Atlantics in their contest with at least one Western club have but little to boast of." Any person missing the game "will wish they had gone."[13]

Brooklyn's reputation justified the buildup. Two modern historians describe the Atlantics as "probably the best base ball club in the United States during the late 1850s and the 1860s." Although not paid directly for their services, the Atlantics were employed by the city of Brooklyn in jobs allowing them plenty of time for practice, games, and long trips. Brooklyn's lineup at Bloomington included one player credited as the original first baseman to play off the bag, another player who invented the bunt, and the pitcher who broke the Cincinnati Red Stockings' winning streak in 1870. Several Atlantics eventually played in the first openly professional league, the National Association of Professional Base Ball Players.[14]

Those taking the *Pantagraph*'s advice had some comfort through mild weather while witnessing the home club's pummeling, 57 to 19. Bloomington players and supporters took solace in scoring more runs than the Chicago Atlantics achieved in their 7–51 drubbing from Brooklyn a few days earlier. Nevertheless, losing to the famous Atlantics was frustrating. Bloomington supporters might have shared the sentiments voiced by the *Greenville Ad-*

vocate in southwestern Illinois. When the Atlantics defeated the St. Louis Unions by a score of 68 to 9, an editor clung to the unrealistic hope that any of Greenville's three local clubs "could do better" than the St. Louis club. "We would like to see some of our Western clubs turn their attention, earnestly, to the game and whip out some of these eastern cubs that seem to be so very successful. We have the muscles and skill in the West to do it." The key, he concluded, was practice.[15]

Although expecting sharp fielding from the Brooklyn club, the *Pantagraph* still registered surprise at "many individual specimens of brilliant playing." At the plate, the Atlantics proved "exceedingly good, most of the nine sending their balls far out into the field." Some of the hits were home runs, and "Mr. Mills," who scored nine times, was never put out. As to its own club, pitcher Patrick Keenan received a reprimand for too many wild pitches leading to runs, demonstrating "that a session of arduous practice was a very desirable thing."[16]

Next came the Buckeye Base Ball Club of Cincinnati, barnstorming its way through several midwestern cities. But the team stepping on the field in those games was not the regular Buckeye club composed of "schoolteachers and ordinary Cincinnatians." Instead, four were professionals imported from the East.[17]

Bloomington backers still nurtured hopes. An 1867 defeat of Rockford's Forest City Club by Bloomington's club combined with Rockford's loss to the touring Buckeyes led the *Pantagraph* to assert that "the Forest Citys cannot call themselves champions until they beat the Bloomingtons." Therefore, even more reason to root for a win over the Buckeyes, who were met at the depot, fed, and shown the town by Bloomington players. The next day's contest, in a familiar refrain, promised to be "one of the best games of ball that has been played this season." Unknown to Bloomington's players and supporters were the abilities two Buckeyes—Charlie Sweasy and Andrew J. Leonard, both starring in 1869 on the first openly professional team, the Cincinnati Red Stockings.[18]

In the Buckeye Club's first at-bat, Leonard tripled and scored as the Ohioans took the lead, steadily increasing it as the afternoon passed, to a 43–17 victory. "It is due to the Buckeyes . . . to say that their playing here places them higher in the rank of fine clubs than was anticipated by many at least," the *Pantagraph* observed. "The result of this game . . . helps to confirm the principle made manifest here, as well as all over the country, whenever the home clubs have come into contact with the trained gymnasts and ball players of clubs that make base ball a business, that nothing but constant practice will ever give them the proficiency necessary to enable them to 'go in and win.'"[19]

Still determined to win, the Bloomington Base Ball Club hosted 1866's national champions, the Union Club of Morrisania (in the Bronx), in August, declared by the *Pantagraph* "the great game of the season." The newspaper played up the visitors' talents and avoided promising a win for the local club or even a close game. Bloomington's mainstays were in the lineup—Cheney, Thomas, and Lackey—but they proved little match for the likes of the Unions, whose roster featured professionals David Solomon Birdsall and George Wright, the latter soon to star for the Cincinnati Red Stockings and the original Boston Red Stockings. (Wright played shortstop in the Bloomington game.) Birdsall, the Unions' catcher, later played for the Washington Nationals.[20]

The Unions "were particularly appealing to women" because of "patriotically dashing uniforms . . . red-trimmed pants, with tri-colored belts . . . white shirts adorned with blue and emblazoned with a U on the front, and blue caps." The Union Club's paid players considered themselves national champions. Among those on its roster at Bloomington was Esteban Enrique "Steve" Bellán, who, in two years, became the first Hispanic major leaguer. Although not "loaded" in the same sense as the Brooklyn Atlantics, the Unions were formidable with Birdsall, Wright, and pitcher Charles H. Pabor. The question was not whether Bloomington would prevail but rather how to hold down the margin of defeat.[21]

"Suffice it to say our boys were beaten badly," the *Pantagraph* admitted after the 57–11 loss. "The Unions are fine players," it continued. "The catcher, Birdsall, stands ahead in that line of anything that has visited this city as yet . . . ditto the short stop, Wright." So ended Bloomington's hopes of contending with the country's top teams in 1868 and its pretensions to superiority in Illinois.[22]

Illustrating the formidable task awaiting small-town amateurs who challenged talented and increasingly semiprofessional or professional clubs is the Monmouth Clippers' 1869 swing through Chicago and Rockford. "Buckle on your armor, boys; puff up your muscles; harden the palms of your hands; doctor the sore fingers; get a good ready, and give them the best you have on hand," urged a Monmouth newspaper. At Chicago, the Clippers played the Amateur Base Ball Club, composed of "four or five of the strongest members of the old [Chicago] Excelsior nine." Although the visitors excelled in hitting, they "were altogether outfielded by the Amateurs," leading the *Monmouth Review* to judge the 31–26 Clipper loss "rather creditable."[23]

At Rockford, the Monmouth team nine suffered an "enormous beat," at the hands of Rockford's Forest City Club, 76 to 1, and later in the summer lost 46 to 2, when the Rockford team visited Monmouth. "It is no disparagement for the Clippers that they were beaten by them," a Monmouth newspaper

FOLEY 3ª BARNES SS BARKER LF SAWYER RF CONE 1ST ADDY C SPALDING P KING CF HASTINGS 2ª

Rockford's famous Forest City Base Ball Club, whose upset of the touring Washington Nationals in 1867 was the talk of the baseball world. In 1869, the team, led by Albert Goodwill Spalding, toured Illinois, crushing local clubs and demonstrating that professionalism was essential for teams wishing to compete at the highest levels. Already essentially professional in 1869, the club openly paid players in 1870 and competed in the first major league, the National Association of Professional Base Ball Players. Courtesy of the Abraham Lincoln Presidential Library and Museum.

explained. The Clippers had "the consolation of knowing that 'the battle is not always to the strong, nor the race to the swift.'"[24]

Historian Peter Morris believes that, between 1868 and 1869, the Rockford team was moving to full professionalism. Rather than salaries for playing baseball, leading players were promised "real jobs at fair pay, with the understanding that the employers would not be opposed to a limited number of lost afternoons," as Horace Buker, another historian of the Forest City Club attests. And on at least one occasion, Forest City players divided game receipts.[25]

Professionalism (the Forest City players were being paid to play baseball, but through an intermediary) hadn't tinged the senior Quincy Occidental Club as it prepared to welcome Forest City in August 1869. Leading up to the August 27 game, newspaper accounts insisted the visitors were "strictly amateur," though "the best amateur nine in the United States." The Forest City Club's arrival on the morning of the 27th followed the standard rituals. Met at the railroad depot, the visitors had dinner at a hotel and then, led by the Occidentals, moved to the fairgrounds. At that point, rituals ceased. The visitors were not simple clerks, merchants, or workers—they were the best players in Illinois. Seven of the nine-man roster—Bob Addy, Charles Roscoe "Ross" Barnes, Joseph Frederick "Fred" Cone, Thomas J. Foley, Winfield "Scott" Hastings, Albert Goodwill Spalding, and Garret C. "Gat" Stires—later played in professional leagues.[26]

The Forest Citys won easily, 43 to 7. "The Forest Citys did some fearful work," a reporter observed, though the loss was no disgrace in light of the beatings that the Rockford team administered to others. Later, a Quincy newspaper took satisfaction in a 103–13 loss suffered by Springfield's Liberty Club (a junior organization): "Our club [referring to the Occidental senior club] have no reason to be ashamed of their record." Recognizing baseball's changing nature at its top levels, the newspaper reported that the Occidental Senior–Forest City game netted gate fees of $149 ($3,202.01 in 2022), with Forest City's players taking three-fourths.[27]

In contrast with the Forest City Club, the Cincinnati Red Stockings did not hide their professionalism. Swinging through Illinois on its national tour, the Red Stockings Club topped Rockford 34 to 13 in July 1869, scoring as many runs in the first at-bat as the Forest Citys made the entire game. But the Rockford club learned from the defeat, specifically to have its catcher, like his Red Stockings counterpart, play close behind the batter, enabling him to snare more foul tips and stymie base stealers. In a return match the same month, the Forest Citys came within a run of defeating the professionals.[28]

Undeterred by the Red Stockings' record—seeing it as a good drawing card—the Quincy Occidentals spent two months that summer promoting the club's stop on its return from California. Newspapers promoted it from early August on and the game attracted interest outside the Quincy area—newspapers in Carthage and Galesburg boosting it.[29]

On October 13, spectators were not disappointed—at least if they came to see the finest baseball team in the country. It took three and a half hours for the Red Stockings to score 51 runs against their hosts' 7. The *Quincy Herald* concluded that the score "is creditable to their [the Occidentals'] proficiency in the game." That evening, as the Occidental players joined their visitors at the Opera House, they reflected on the changing nature of competition. Could aging senior players or even upcoming juniors compete with professional clubs?[30]

An answer came the following season in Bloomington, former home of the once-famous Bloomington Base Ball Club. By 1870, the old club was no more. A "volunteer nine" stepped up to face the Chicago White Stockings, the forerunner of the modern Chicago Cubs. "The White Stockings are professional players who receive from their backers, or rather from their employers in Chicago, a good salary for winning bets, and earning good money for them," the *Bloomington Pantagraph* judged. "The chances are, however, that most of these in any legitimate business or honorable profession, would never rise above mediocrity." As baseball players, the White Stockings proved anything but mediocre, "raining a shower of balls about the amateur players for a space of two hours and a half," on way to a seven-inning, 62–6 victory. "The return game has not been arranged," said the *Chicago Tribune*.[31] There would be none. What was the point?

"There is nothing to censure in ball playing, as an exercise, or a recreation, on occasion, for students or persons of sedentary habits for the glow of pleasure which it inspires when once in a while a spirit of emulation is excited," judged the *Bloomington Pantagraph*. "But professional base ball playing—bah—what is it?"[32]

Though tinged with the sour taste of professionalism, baseball did not disappear. Its vigorous junior level attracted more and more young men. But the old spirit sagged among adult players. "Base ball is being killed by the growing custom of employing professionals to do the hard work and play the matches," wrote *Decatur Magnet* editor James Shoaff in 1868 after the McPhersons, the town's senior club, folded. Other senior clubs—the Springfield Capitals, the Jacksonville Unions, the Cairo Egyptians, Rock Island's Wapellos and Lively Turtles, and countless others—departed between 1868 and 1870. Gone too from local newspapers' columns were long game accounts featuring colorful details beyond the actual game itself, replaced, if at all, by shorter stories. Sometimes a reader simply had a score, nothing indicating the game was more than just another activity like hymn singing or horse auctions. Baseball's honeymoon had ended, its novelty gone, replaced by the harsh realization that practice and high hopes were not enough to gain a community precedence over its neighboring competitors, let alone statewide recognition.[33]

Costs associated with intercity play and equipping a team, though negligible by early twenty-first century standards, reveal the true economic impact in a post–Civil War society in which a dollar was a significant amount of

James A. Shoaff, editor of the *Decatur Magnet* and participant in an uproarious "muffin" game during 1867's Grand Base Ball Tournament of the Western States. Later, he lamented the incursion of professional players. Courtesy of the Abraham Lincoln Presidential Library and Museum.

money. As ambitions for bragging rights with fellow communities or achieving statewide prominence through baseball receded, expenses offered another reason for the adult game's transition to an unorganized recreation.

Charles Darwin might see in this another demonstration of survival of the fittest. Only communities with the funds to support men who did nothing but play baseball could hope to compete for high honors. Men who entered the game in the immediate postwar years were now aging, jobs and families competing for their time as bodies sagged and athletic skills declined. An occasional pickup game on an empty lot might suffice should the urge to hit the ball return. And so, nature took its course, the old yielding to the young until they, too, gave way to a new generation. The shared experience of players and spectators, bound together by ideals, hopes, and rituals became irrelevant. Winning was the goal, the only goal.

Old fields disappeared beneath construction or grew up in weeds; in a generation or two memory of their sporting use vanished. Those who played on them and strode proudly through dusty streets wearing their colorful uniforms and carrying banners and flags sewn by admiring ladies, occasionally came back to life through newspaper memories or in the obituaries of old players and fans. Life moved on, leaving such things quickly forgotten.

GHOSTS

Longest Hit Ever Made on Decatur Diamond
Made by Member of the First Team
Ball Goes through a House
—Headline in *Decatur Review*, June 16, 1918[1]

They haunt newspaper microfilm reels, old city directories sometimes crumbling at the touch, and rarely viewed census reports. These "ghosts" are elusive—only a few appear in detail. One lived into the 1930s, sixty-plus years after he last played. Most died earlier, their days on rough-hewn fields forgotten by history.

A few told their stories before departing. Isaac Archer, a member of Decatur's short-lived McPherson Club, was one. Fifty years after the event, he still gloried in hitting a baseball through a house.

"It went entirely out of bounds," wrote a reporter relaying Archer's memories, "crossing the street at the outer limits of the baseball field, went through the window of a house, out through a rear window or door, and continued its flight for some distance beyond."[2] Sixteen years later, the obituary of Archer, a millwright, omitted his ball playing. Not so with the most distinct ghost of all, Rockford's Albert Goodwill Spalding, a star for the Boston Red Stockings and Chicago White Stockings and the man personally responsible for the Abner Doubleday myth.[3]

Two Egyptians

James T. Cunningham's 150-plus-year-old image, captured in a photographer's studio, stares at us today. A star player for the Centralia Egyptian Base Ball Club, Cunningham's studio portrait preserves a moment of pride as he stands with uniform, bat, and a gilded baseball. At the end of a long life, he drew a brief notice in the *Chicago Tribune*, not for his baseball achievements but because his passing at eighty-nine in 1937 left only two surviving Civil War veterans in Centralia.[4]

Another Egyptian but from Cairo, the irrepressible Sol Silver, scorekeeper and promoter of his city's early baseball efforts, continued to draw attention for his activities and good humor long after he left the game. Local newspaper columns reported a busy life—serving as an agent for steamboats, helping police officers apprehend lawbreakers, aiding an orphan fleeing a yellow fever epidemic, cosponsoring a beautiful baby contest, and raising funds for victims of the Great Chicago Fire.[5]

Politically, he remained an active, loyal Democrat, arranging a visit by his party's gubernatorial nominee in 1880 and, the same year, leading a marching band through the streets of Cairo. Editors delighted in this larger-than-life character. When he failed to participate, as promised, in a balloon ascension, a wit attributed his absence to fear "that he could not cast his 'ANCHOR LINE' [the name of the steamboat company he represented] safely." And confident of a Democratic victory in the 1880 presidential election, Silver scouted offices in Cairo's Custom House, seeking just the right one to occupy when his party took control and rewarded his services.[6]

Entrepreneurial activities paid off, and Silver bought a farm, Villa Ridge, near Mound City, Illinois, where he planted his family and spent the winters. There Silver, descended from Spanish Jews exiled in 1492, died on November 18, 1900. After his funeral services on the farm home's lawn, a lengthy line of carriages formed the procession to the cemetery. Two railroad cars filled with Cairo citizens joined them. "He left a host of friends," a newspaper concluded. Unmentioned was his pioneering role in baseball.[7]

Political and Professional Success

Another Cairo baseballist built an even more colorful life than Silver's. Often a punching bag for the *Cairo Democrat* newspaper, Daniel W. Munn, most prominent among the Munns playing the game there, had the last laugh. After Civil War service as a cavalry colonel, he practiced law in Cairo. Voters elected him to the Illinois State Senate in 1866—to the chagrin of the *Democrat*. A presidential elector in 1868 for U. S. Grant, Munn earned a lucrative position—supervisor of internal revenue for the region that included Illinois, Wisconsin, and Michigan.[8]

The appointment brought relocation to Chicago, where he remained for the rest of his life though he retained property in Cairo as late as 1881. Munn made quite a mark in Chicago between his ceaseless activity for Republican candidates and a successful law practice. It is the latter, however, that jumps from newspaper pages.[9]

Laboring at the usual chores of debt collection, Munn dealt with "wholesale hog stealing" and political bribery on a large scale. "Identified with many important cases," perhaps his most newsworthy was "the notorious Dr. Cream." Thomas Cream practiced medicine in Belvidere, a rural Boone County community. He and the wife of patient Daniel Stitt faced conspiracy to murder charges—Mrs. Stitt for administering a dose of strychnine sufficient, a witness assured the court, to "poison three men." Even Munn's "very brilliant, able and eloquent argument" to the jury did not save Dr. Cream, who was sentenced to life in prison. Fourteen years later, another physician, Mary Shaffer, retained Munn when charged with murdering a patient. Whatever Munn did was successful, as the case drops from the record and Shaffer was practicing a year later.[10]

At seventy-nine, Munn passed away peacefully in his LaGrange home in 1913, the slings and arrows of his Cairo newspaper antagonists as long forgotten as were the days he led the Munn clan on the ball fields of the city between two rivers.[11]

Pana's "Babe Ruth," J. C. McQuigg, enjoyed professional success in the years after his 1867 home run feats. When not practicing law, the native of Country Antrim, Ireland, participated in public debates over banning alcohol sales or converting the city's government to the commission form. An active Republican, he failed in his one attempt for public office. The wounded Civil War veteran's health declined in the last months of 1921, and he passed in early January 1922. All Pana businesses were asked to close during the hour of his funeral. Again, obituary writers were silent on his contributions to baseball.[12]

Decatur's Montgomerys, the Fly Swatter, and the "Father of Base Ball"

Samuel Montgomery was in his early twenties when he joined Decatur's McPherson Base Ball Club. Later, he became a woodworker, laboring at Union Iron Works at a job that eventually took his life. Along with other early local players, he was mentioned in a 1918 article recalling the game's beginnings, though the attention came two years too late for Montgomery. While working his foreman's job at the foundry, he suffered an injury that "affected his mind." His heirs took exception to his settlement with the foundry, attempting to gain a rehearing of his case after his April 1916 death at the state's mental hospital in Jacksonville. Their effort failed.[13]

Success and ripe old age, however, awaited the McPherson's other Montgomery, Robert R., a catcher who "played up close behind the bat." The Union Army veteran went into insurance and real estate after his club disappeared, laying out subdivisions, including today's high-end Montgomery Place. A tinkerer wearied by battling house flies, he retreated to his basement and invented the fly swatter. Correctly, he believed, "there is a fortune in it."[14]

C. M. Allison, who helped W. C. Johns lay out the first regulation field in Decatur, equaled R. R. Montgomery's success. He became "one of the best known and most highly respected of the older generation of Decatur businessmen," observed a local newspaper at his passing in 1926. A banker and industrialist, Allison, who had enlisted in the Union Army at sixteen, helped organize the Decatur Board of Trade.[15]

One player remained associated with the game for life, though his playing days ended in 1868. Published stories on Judge W. C. Johns often referred to the game. Corwin Johns, as he preferred, rose through Republican Party ranks to serve as state's attorney and, later, in the Illinois State Senate until elected a circuit judge in 1903. Promoters of a 1905 game between Decatur and Danville teams asked the judge to throw out the first pitch as "an added attraction," noting that in his day he was "as famous as a pitcher as was Joe McGinnity in modern time." At one time, Johns could "throw a ball further than any other man in Decatur." The newspaper writer expressed confidence that "after a rest of thirty years his good southpaw arm should have all the charley horses worked out of it" for "Judge Johns' . . . farewell appearance as a pitcher."[16]

Unfortunately, three decades' rest proved either too much or too little: Johns's pitch "struck the ground about a foot in front of the plate." Nine years later, when he died unexpectedly, Johns's memorialists recalled two things. He sometimes returned to his chambers to cry after sentencing boys to reform school, and he was "a player of some note. . . . It was he who brought baseball to Decatur."[17]

An Indefatigable Ottawan

It easy to imagine George W. (sometimes with a second W) Blake tending the outfield alongside the Fox River during the summer of 1867 for Ottawa's Shabbona Base Ball Club. On the sidelines and at postgame meals, the seventeen-year-old was surely the life of the party, full of fun and good spirits. Life after his playing days required those traits.[18]

After demonstrating an early aversion to agriculture and displaying academic talents, Blake was admitted to the bar at age nineteen. In 1871 came appointment by his father, the new sheriff, as chief deputy sheriff for the county. The post introduced young Blake to a lifetime mixture of politics, officeholding, and the practice of law. His adventures and misadventures appear frequently in local newspaper columns. For example, while deputy sheriff, he gave a tame squirrel run of the office, taking care to secure "a few thousand dollars represented in notes, bonds, mortgages, etc." in a locked desk drawer. But the squirrel managed to gnaw into the hiding place, shredding the documents. Later, he improvised an early "telephone" system between courthouse offices using fruit cans, "drumhead parchment," and string.[19]

Dubbed "the criminal lawyer of Ottawa," Blake saved a client from the gallows. Yet politics absorbed his energy and attention. He joined Ottawa's city council in 1877, but that body expelled him in less than a year for "collecting the money for a license from a saloon keeper and not turning it over to the treasurer."[20]

Delightful contradictions filled his life. An active member of local temperance groups and the founder of the Red Ribbon Club for, one supposes, highly committed members of the cold-water army, he was, from its inception, the attorney for the LaSalle County Liquor Dealers Association and filled the same role for a time with the state association.[21]

When La Salle County state's attorney died suddenly before the 1888 election, Blake took his place on the ballot and won the race. Two years into his term, county newspapers criticized him for dereliction of duty. The "public interest would have been benefited" by Blake's defeat, according to the *Ottawa Republican*. But the beleaguered prosecutor also had good notices, such as when he personally arrested and later convicted a woman for brutally murdering a man in Ottawa's Allen Park. He did not seek reelection.[22]

Through it all, Blake's political image remained undamaged. A decade later, he gained his party's nomination for state legislature in 1900. On Saturday, October 27, after Blake's long day on the stump ended around 9 p.m., at mid-speech, he asked another on the platform how long he had been speaking. Turning again to the audience, he raised his right hand, pointing his index finger as if preparing to resume, but instead tottered and then fell to the floor and died within minutes. His life, a newspaper judged, demonstrated "a record as a jovial, whole-souled man, seeing the bright side of life, seldom serious." There was no mention of his baseball days.[23]

The Coal Magnate and a US Senator

Consistent success marked Charles A. Starne's life until he died on June 1, 1910, in Springfield after a year-long illness. A second basemen and pitcher for

Alton's Shurtleff Collegiate Club, Starne and his brother, Maurice, also played for Springfield's Athletics. A son of the successful politician and businessman, Alexander Starne, Charles A. Starne grew up in an entrepreneurial household. Alexander, the father, served in elected state offices, gaining wealth through the Capital Horse Railway Company, coal mining, and other ventures.

After baseball, Charles A. Starne focused on coal mining, rising to prominence with Springfield's West End Coal Company and the Barclay Coal and Mining Company. Eulogized by *Fuel Magazine: The Coal Operators National Weekly*, Starne's life provided "a worthy example for any young man to follow. . . . His pleasant and genial manner towards all will be missed." After Starne's death on June 4, 1910, the union representing his workers concurred. His passing, the local resolved, deprived his community of "a faithful citizen, a congenial companion, and an upright conscientious man."[24]

Demonstrating imprecisions already obscuring the game's beginnings, the coal industry magazine claimed Starne played "when the game was first introduced into this country in 1870," at least five years off target.[25]

But another Shurtleff College and Springfield baseballist, like Starne, born into political power and wealth, outstripped most in the game's pioneer generation. F. T. "Fred" Dubois migrated to Idaho in 1880 and immediately struck political gold, not surprising for a son of Jesse K. Dubois, a founder of Illinois's Republican Party and owner of the Capital Horse Railway Company. Both Fred and his brother and fellow baseball player, physician Jesse K. Dubois Jr., found success in the West. While Jesse seems to have concentrated on his practice, Fred plunged into the political world, serving first as US marshal for what was then a territory.[26]

An organizer of Idaho's "Anti-Mormon Party," Fred Dubois led it to victory and was elected territorial delegate for two terms between 1887 and 1890. In Washington, Dubois became "the veritable 'Moses' of Idaho," shepherding its successful campaign for statehood. Afterward, "honored and revered from one end of the State to the other," the new state's legislature sent him to the US Senate.[27]

The free silver issue proved his political undoing—at least temporarily—when Dubois joined the "Silver Republican" faction during the 1896 presidential campaign, supporting the Democratic nominee William Jennings Bryan. The Idaho legislature dumped its "Moses," seeming to end his political career. But four years later, Dubois returned to Washington as a senator, again identifying himself as a Silver Republican. No sooner did he arrive on Capitol Hill than Dubois switched parties, joining the Democrats and attending the party's nominating conventions in 1904 and 1908—perhaps spawning tremors around his father's grave back in Springfield. Not seeking

At his death the only man to represent the same state in the US Senate under both Democratic and Republican affiliations, Fred T. Dubois was born into political prominence and wealth, the son of Jesse K. Dubois, and played baseball in Springfield and at Alton's Shurtleff College. He was considered the Moses of Idaho, as he led its successful campaign for statehood. Courtesy Abraham Lincoln Presidential Library and Museum.

reelection, he remained in Washington, serving on various federal boards and commissions.[28]

Dubois may have hastened his own death in 1930 by spending hours in a poorly ventilated hearing room. An Associated Press story noting his passing appeared in Boston; Oakland, California; Stevens Point, Wisconsin; Greenville, Tennessee; Salem, Oregon; and Bloomington, Illinois—recounting Dubois's "remarkable, interesting, unique and romantic career." Also noted were his "unique distinction" of serving the same state at separate times as a member of the Republican and Democratic parties.[29]

Bloomington's Black Baseballists

Because of the poor, sometimes derogatory, attention paid to black players, it is remarkable that seven of nine players on Bloomington's Independent Club are traceable after baseball. George Brown, described by the local newspaper as "one of the most respected colored citizens of this city," moved from the ball field to the debating and political arenas. He was president of a segregated debating society in Normal, Bloomington's twin city, and judged a student contest at Illinois Normal College (now Illinois State University). In 1880, he was elected a James G. Blaine presidential nominating delegate by fellow Republicans.[30]

Clinton Dudley was working as a maintenance man at the McLean County Jail when a heavy steel door fell on him October 1882. But he recovered and, billed as "Captain Clinton Dudley," joined a minstrel troupe planning a European tour.[31] Remaining active in the game, William Franklin became secretary of the "Good Enough" Baseball Club in 1873. By occupation a domestic servant, his was a strong voice in the black community. When the small village of Bellflower tried to intimidate black residents through anonymous threatening letters, Franklin rallied the opposition. His personal life made the newspapers in 1880, when, returning home from work, he found his wife entertaining another man.[32]

Baseball-playing brothers James and Marion Holly (sometimes spelled "Holley") remained active players into 1873 when both became officers of the new "Good Enough" Club, Marion as president, James as secretary. Both had trades—James a bookbinder and Marion a pressman for two local newspapers. James's life took a troubled turn. First, he was arrested but later found not guilty of stealing a can of sardines from a burning building. Six years later, he was charged with purloining a ham. Somewhat later, he was reported shot and "dangerously wounded," though it turned out the incident was likely a ruse to extricate himself "out of a scrap with a woman of Pontiac." More favorable notice came for his role as "Handy Andy," in a local production.[33]

Marion Holly, too, endured difficulties. During an election in 1876, he and Clinton Dudley's brother, Fuss, "the worse citizen in the Third Ward," fought in a polling place before Fuss fled the scene. Seven years later, the "quite well known" Marion Holly died at thirty-five, leaving a wife and two children, felled by typhoid fever, aggravated by his lingering "long at the shrine of Bacchus." Former teammate Witteor (Victor) James passed away in 1879, beloved in the small village of Heyworth, south of Bloomington. The barber's lingering illness brought aid from his white neighbors, who carried coal and other supplies to his home.[34]

Teamster Frank Thomas of the old Independent Club drove Bloomington's police patrol wagon. He sang in a quartet and served in the all-black McLean Guards militia unit. He was almost a wealthy man, before losing that chance when his wife was denied a reputed $150,000 inheritance from her father, a Chicago hotel owner. After five years' residence in the state's insane asylum at Jacksonville, Thomas died in 1898, age fifty-six, leaving a widow and four children.[35]

The Hustler, the Tobacconist, and the Irishman

His controversial playing career with the Bloomington Base Ball Club set a precedent for Lee Cheney's life. Cheney and trouble seemed to go together. His occupations from saloonkeeper to racing and boxing promoter to inventor sometimes attracted police attention. As a saloonkeeper, Cheney was in court on charges that included selling liquor on Sundays or without a license and operating gambling equipment. He was arrested after a free-for-all fight in the street. Controversy followed him into racing, entangling him in a dispute over a trotting mare and Cheney's involvement in a defunct "jockey club" hinted at fraud.[36]

"It is probable that no one who is acquainted with Mr. Lee Cheney of this city, doubts but that he possesses genuine physical courage and has stamina enough to not much care who knows it," observed the *Bloomington Pantagraph*. Yet even a tough nature failed when an irate Davenport, Iowa, crowd disputed his calls as umpire and he quit.[37]

Death found him alone in his room near downtown Bloomington in the early morning hours of November 2, 1911. At Cheney's passing, details of his disputatious life lived on the edge of the law disappeared. "He was always a friend of the town in which he resided all of his life and greatly thru [sic] his

Lee Cheney, a mainstay of the Bloomington Base Ball Club who later played professionally for Rockford's Forest City Club, nearly broke up the 1867 Decatur tournament by defying national rules prohibiting a player from taking the field on both senior and junior club rosters. After baseball, he led a colorful life, sometimes on the edge of the law. He mentored future Baseball Hall of Famer Charles "Old Hoss" Radbourn. Photograph appeared with Cheney's obituary in the *Bloomington Pantagraph*, November 3, 1911.

efforts was the name of Bloomington spread over the country—especially in the realm of healthful out-door sports." The only mention of baseball was his field management of a local club, the Reds. Missing were his skills and controversies with the Bloomington Base Ball Club, his brief professional career with the Forest City Club of Rockford, and his mentoring of another Bloomington baseball character, future Baseball Hall of Famer, Charles "Old Hoss" Radbourn.[38]

After his 1870 move to Chicago, there is no evidence that George W. Lackey, a founder of the Bloomington Base Ball Club and former president of the Illinois State Base Ball Association, had any further baseball connections. Calling on his Civil War experience, he devoted his spare time to precision military drilling, forming the Lackey Zouaves.[39] He gained reputation as "a drill-master of more than ordinary ability." His unit became the Ellsworth

Zouaves in honor of Lincoln's friend, the late Colonel E. E. Ellsworth. In 1879, Lackey's unit merged into the Illinois National Guard and participated in festivities welcoming former president U. S. Grant to Chicago.[40]

Lackey fell into bankruptcy and his health failed, showing signs of chronic pleurisy and bronchitis about the same time, according to the physician who signed his death certificate. On March 7, 1886, weeks before his forty-fourth birthday, Lackey died in his West Jackson Street residence. His Zouaves participated in his funeral services, five serving as pallbearers. Chicago newspapers took stilted notice of Lackey, referring only to his service in the Civil War and organization of the Zouave unit. His baseball organizing, playing, and umpiring days were not included.[41]

Illinois's pioneer baseball players had postgame lives of various trajectories, some high, others low, most just living obscurely without notice. Still, a particular sadness adheres to lives once offering promise only to spiral downward through a succession of lost opportunities and unexorcised personal demons. Bloomington's star pitcher and first professional player, Patrick J. Keenan, was one.

Born in Ireland on St. Patrick's Day in 1848, Keenan migrated to the United States as a young man, living first in Brooklyn, New York, before arriving in Bloomington by 1866. His daughter, in furnishing information for his death certificate, did not know the name of her paternal grandfather and listed "Mary" as Keenan's mother. A skilled pitcher for the Bloomington Base Ball Club, he was recruited in 1867 by the Chicago Excelsiors and joined them in return for a job. Keenan pitched the Excelsiors to victory in Decatur's Grand Base Ball Tournament of the Western States and umpired the fun-filled muffin game there between local editors and printers. (See chapter 5.) The 1868 season found Keenan back in Bloomington with his old club. But things were not the same, as his skills had faded.[42]

Keenan then started what would be his life's work—the saloon business, usually as a barkeeper. Throughout the 1870s, Keenan appears in city directories employed by, owning, or co-owning a series of saloons, remaining in such jobs until the early twentieth century, a few years before his death.[43]

Both his occupation and personal failings attracted newspaper attention. When Paul Finnan announced he was reopening the old Senate Saloon downtown, he added, "Mr. Patrick Keenan will preside over the bar" doing "ample justice to every caller." Within weeks, Keenan again appeared in newspaper columns after police, suspecting gambling underway in a room above another downtown saloon, launched an early Sunday morning raid, capturing Keenan and three others who faced charges as "inmates of a gambling house." Two years later, while carousing about downtown Bloomington "on a spree," a drunken Keenan was jailed after falling through a drugstore's plate-glass window.[44]

Hints of Keenan's troubles linger between the lines of an obituary for his wife, Agnes, a native of Canada, who died August 14, 1916. She moved to Bloomington in 1870 and two years later married Keenan. Agnes was memorialized as an active member of the local Episcopal church, noted especially for lending "comfort and cheer to those around her" and for exerting a positive influence on those facing "the harder experiences of life." Perhaps Agnes Keenan developed her own tools by coping with similar challenges at home. After suffering paralysis for two years, possibly resulting from a stroke, Keenan died on March 27, 1917, ten days after his sixty-ninth birthday, in his South Center Street home. His only survivor was a daughter, Cora May—"all other close relatives having past [sic] away several years ago."[45]

One wonders whether the bedridden Keenan reflected on the days when he and the Bloomington Base Ball Club challenged—and sometimes beat— the state's best. In 1877, a Chicago newspaper printed an informal list of early professional players by year; "Keenan," without a first name, was listed for 1867—the last time his name appeared in print connected with baseball. Left unmentioned in the article or, decades later, his obituary was the November day in 1867 when Patrick Joseph Keenan bested Albert Goodwill Spalding in an Excelsior Club intrasquad game before Chicago fans crowded around the field, outscoring him 2 to 0 on the basepaths and outpitching the future baseball Hall of Famer in a 24–13 victory. Perhaps the cheers sounded in his memory of a day when he and the game were young, beckoned by a promising future.[46]

Once Keenan and the others enjoyed a clean slate on which to write their dreams in a game for "men of muscle and men who wish to acquire muscle." Today, we imagine their ghosts—playing amid "joking, laughter, and repartee" on fields now paved or abandoned, overgrown tangles of weeds and saplings. So, "blow the cymbals! Beat your tin horns! Sound a loud blast on the squash vine!" Their game begins.[47]

ILLINOIS BASEBALL TEAMS, BY TOWN AND YEAR FOUNDED, 1865-70

As research into early Illinois baseball is ongoing, it is likely that more teams will be found, and therefore the list I offer is incomplete. The dates after team names represent years of existence and appearance in newspaper articles. No dates are provided for teams found in the Protoball website. At the time it was accessed, teams were listed by years in random order.

Town	Team(s)	Source
Abingdon	Abingdon Base Ball Club	Protoball website, https://protoball.org/IL
African Point (Crawford County)	Africans Base Ball Club—1868	*Marshall Messenger*, Sept. 11, 1868
Alexandria	Atlantic Base Ball Club—1869	*Warsaw Bulletin*, Apr. 23, 1869
	Black Hawk Base Ball Club—1868	*Warsaw Bulletin*, Apr. 24, 1868
Algonquin	Algonquin Base Ball Club—1867	https://protoball.org/IL
Alma	Lone Star Base Ball Club—1867, 1868, 1869	*Belleville Democrat*, Sept. 12, 1867, Sept. 3, 1868, July 29, 1869; *Centralia Sentinel*, Oct. 16, 1869
Alton	Shurtleff Collegiate Base Ball Club—1867	*Alton Weekly Telegraph*, Oct. 25, 1867
	Shurtleff Eagle Base Ball Club—1867	*Alton Weekly Telegraph*, Oct. 25, 1867
	Shurtleff Independent Base Ball Club—1867	*Alton Weekly Telegraph*, Oct. 25, 1867
	Bluff City Base Ball Club—1867, 1869	*Alton Weekly Telegraph*, Dec. 13, 1867; *Jersey County Democrat*, Aug. 28, 1869; *Litchfield Monitor*, Sept. 9, 1869

Town	Team(s)	Source
	Wide Awake Base Ball Club—1869, 1870	*Jersey County Democrat*, July 10, 1869; *Edwardsville Intelligencer*, June 9, 1870
Altona	Walnut Base Ball Club—1867, 1870	*Monmouth Atlas*, Aug. 23, 1867; *Monmouth Weekly Review*, June 3, 1870
Amboy	Vigilant Base Ball Club—1867	*Lee County Journal*, Sept. 5, 1867
	Pastime Base Ball Club—1870	*Warren Sentinel*, July 5, 1870, July 7, 1870; *Lee County Journal*, Sept. 1, 1870
	Counter-Jumpers Base Ball Club (Muffin)—1870	*Lee County Journal*, July 14, 1870
Annawan	Black Hawk Base Ball Club—1867	*Bureau County Republican*, July 4, 1867
Apple River	Sherman Base Ball Club—1867, 1870	*Galena Gazette*, Sept. 3, 1867; *Warren Sentinel*, July 26, 1870
Arcola (once known as Okaw)	Pioneer Base Ball Club—1867	*Champaign Union Gazette*, July 10, 1867
Arlington	Arlington Base Ball Club—1867, 1868	*Bureau County Republican*, June 12, 1867, Aug. 22, 1867; https://protoball.org/IL
Ashley	Dead Beat Base Ball Club—1867, 1868	*Nashville Journal*, Sept. 13, 1867; *Centralia Democrat*, July 30, 1868
Atlanta	Atlanta Base Ball Club—1869	*Atlanta Argus*, Aug. 21, 1869
	Lone Star Base Ball Club—1867, 1868	*Bloomington Pantagraph*, Sept. 9, 1867; July 7, 1868
Aurora	Aurora Base Ball Club—1867	*Aurora Beacon*, June 13, 1867
	Antelopes Base Ball Club—1867	*Aurora Beacon*, Aug. 22, 1867
	Plowboys Base Ball Club—1867	*Aurora Beacon*, Aug. 22, 1867
	Clark Seminary Base Ball Club—1867	*Aurora Beacon*, June 6, 1867
	Black Hawk Base Ball Club—1867	*Aurora Beacon*, July 11, 1867; *Aurora Beacon*, July 18, 1867
	Light Weights Base Ball Club (Muffin)—1867	*Aurora Beacon*, July 11, 1867
	Pastimes Base Ball Club—1869	*Aurora Beacon*, Sept. 1, 1869
	Young America Base Ball Club—1869	*Aurora Beacon*, Aug. 25, 1869
Batavia	Eagle Base Ball Club—1867, 1869	*Aurora Beacon*, Nov. 7, 1867; https://protoball.org/IL
	Union Base Ball Club—1867	*Aurora Beacon*, Oct. 24, 1867

Town	Team(s)	Source
Belleville	Eagle Base Ball Club—1868	*Belleville Democrat*, May 21, 1868
	Bluff Base Ball Club—1867, 1868	*Belleville Democrat*, Sept. 19, 1867, July 30, 1868
	White Star Base Ball Club—1869	*Belleville Democrat*, Sept. 9, 1869, Sept. 16, 1869
Belvidere	Mystic Base Ball Club—1865	https://protoball.org/IL; *Rockford Republic*, Apr. 15, 1922
	Belvidere Base Ball Club—1866, 1867	*Belvidere Standard*, May 29, 1866; *Harvard Independent*, Aug. 14, 1867
	Phoenix Base Ball Club—1867	*Belvidere Standard*, Aug. 20, 1867
Blandinsville	Blandinsville Base Ball Club—1867	*Macomb Eagle*, Oct. 5, 1867, Oct. 19, 1867, Nov. 2, 1867
Bloomingdale	Bloomingdale Base Ball Club—1867	https://protoball.org/IL
Bloomington	Railroad Base Ball Club—1865	https://protoball.org/IL
	Lincoln Base Ball Club—1865	https://protoball.org/IL
	Hornet Base Ball Club—1865	https://protoball.org/IL
	Wesleyan Base Ball Club—1865	https://protoball.org/IL
	Gray Eagle Base Ball Club (Black)—1866	*Bloomington Pantagraph*, Aug. 1, 1866
	Independent Base Ball Club (Black)—1867, 1868, 1870	*Bloomington Pantagraph*, Sept. 24, 1867, Aug. 10, 1868; *Illinois State Register*, Aug. 2, 1870
	Bloomington Base Ball Club—1866, 1867, 1868	*Peoria Transcript*, Aug. 27, 1866; *Bloomington Pantagraph*, Apr. 8, 1868, June 27, 1868, July 27, 1868, Aug. 13, 1868, June 15, 1868
	Star Base Ball Club (Junior)—1867, 1868	*Bloomington Pantagraph*, July 16, 1867, July 2, 1868
Bradford	Young America Base Ball Club (Junior)—1870	*Stark County News*, Aug. 20, 1870
Brimfield	Sucker State Base Ball Club—1868	*Peoria Times*, June 27, 1868
	Star of the West Base Ball Club— 1869 (Junior, 12–14 years of age)	*Peoria Transcript*, Sept. 10, 1869
Bristol	Bristol Base Ball Club	*Aurora Beacon*, Aug. 1, 1867
Brooklyn Township (Lee County)	Excelsior Base Ball Club—1870	*Lee County Journal*, Aug. 18, 1870
Bunker Hill	Shakespeare Base Ball Club—1869	*Belleville Democrat*, July 1, 1869
	Star Base Ball Club—1867	*Bunker Hill Gazette*, July 11, 1867; *Bunker Hill Union and Gazette*, Oct. 3, 1867

Town	Team(s)	Source
Bushnell	Orthean Base Ball Club—1867, 1868	*Macomb Eagle*, Aug. 31, 1867; https://protoball.org/IL
Butler	Butler Base Ball Club—1868	*Litchfield Union Monitor*, May 28, 1868, July 9, 1868
Byron	Byron Base Ball Club—1866	https://protoball.org/IL
Cairo	Eclipse Base Ball Club—1867	*Cairo Democrat*, July 23, 1867, Aug. 28, 1867
	Egyptian Base Ball Club—1866	*Cairo Democrat*, July 31, 1866, Aug. 1, 1866, Aug. 15, 1866
	Independent Base Ball Club—1866	*Cairo Democrat*, Aug. 24, 1866
	Magneta Base Ball Club—1866, 1867	*Cairo Democrat*, Sept. 5, 1866, Apr. 11, 1867
	Grasshopper Base Ball Club (Muffin)—1867	*Cairo Democrat*, Sept. 14, 1867
	Caterpillar Base Ball Club (Muffin)—1867	*Cairo Democrat*, Sept. 14, 1867
	Star Base Ball Club (Junior)—1867	*Cairo Democrat*, Sept. 14, 1867
	Champion Base Ball Club (Junior)—1867	*Cairo Democrat*, Sept. 14, 1867
	Clodhopper Base Ball Club (Muffin)—1868	*Cairo Democrat*, Sept. 4, 1868
	Podanger Base Ball Club (Muffin)—1868	*Cairo Democrat*, Sept. 4, 1868
Cambridge	Huss Base Ball Club—1867	https://protoball.org/IL
Camden (from 1848 to 1870, Camden Mills and since then Milan)	Stag Base Ball Club—1867	*Rock Island Union*, June 11, 1867[1]
	Enterprise Base Ball Club—1867	*Rock Island Argus*, July 8, 1867
	Chippewa Base Ball Club (Junior)—1867	*Rock Island Argus*, June 4, 1867
	Black Hawk Base Ball Club	*Rock Island Argus*, June 24, 1867
Campton	Plow Boys Base Ball Club—1868	https://protoball.org/IL
Carbon Cliff	Carbon Cliff Base Ball Club—1867	*Rock Island Argus*, Sept. 2, 1867
Carbondale	Carbondale Base Ball Club—1866, 1867	https://protoball.org/IL; *Carbondale New Era*, May 9, 1867, June 27, 1867
	Shakespeare Base Ball Club—1869	*Belleville Democrat*, Sept. 30, 1869
Carlinville	Active Base Ball Club—1869	*Carlinville Democrat*, May 27, 1869
	National Base Ball Club—1869	*Carlinville Democrat*, May 27, 1869
	Harvesters Base Ball Club—1869, 1870	*Carlinville Democrat*, Aug. 26, 1869; *Illinois State Register*, Aug. 2, 1870

Town	Team(s)	Source
Carlyle	Okaw Base Ball Club—1868	*Centralia Sentinel*, Sept. 24, 1868
	Normal Base Ball Club—1869[2]	*Carlyle Constitution and Union*, June 22, 1869
	Santa Fe Base Ball Club—1869	*Carlyle Constitution and Union*, July 13, 1869
Carrollton	Alert Base Ball Club—1867, 1868	*Jersey County Democrat*, Sept. 13, 1867; 1868—https://protoball.org/IL
	Carrollton Base Ball Club—1867	*Carrollton Gazette*, Oct. 5, 1867
Carthage	Sucker State Base Ball Club—1866, 1867, 1868	*Carthage Gazette*, Sept. 6, 1866, Aug. 22, 1867; *Warsaw Bulletin*, Sept. 20, 1867, July 3, 1868
	Red Jacket Base Ball Club (Junior)—1868	*Carthage Gazette*, June 18, 1868
Caseyville	Silver Moon Base Ball Club—1867	*Belleville Advocate*, Oct. 1, 1867
Centralia	Liberty Base Ball Club—1866	*Centralia Sentinel*, Dec. 20, 1866, May 30, 1867; also see Loomis, "History of Centralia Baseball"
	Egyptian Base Ball Club—1866, 1867, 1868, 1869	*Centralia Sentinel*, May 17, 1866; also see Loomis, "History of Centralia Baseball"
	Empire Base Ball Club (Junior)—1868	*Centralia Sentinel*, Nov. 19, 1868
	Union Base Ball Club—1866, 1868, 1869	*Centralia Sentinel*, Dec. 20, 1866; *Centralia Democrat*, July 30, 1868, Aug. 26, 1869
Champaign	Champaign Base Ball Club—1867	*Champaign Union and Gazette*, Apr. 24, 1867
	Empire Base Ball Club (formerly the Champaign BBC)—1867, 1868	*Champaign Union and Gazette*, July 10, 1867, May 13, 1868
	Heavy Weight Base Ball Club (Muffin)—1867	*Champaign Union and Gazette*, July 3, 1867
	Prairie Base Ball Club—1867	*Champaign Union and Gazette*, Apr. 17, 1867
Chatham	Sheridan Base Ball Club—1866	*Illinois State Register*, Sept. 17, 1866
Chenoa	Lone Star Base Ball Club—1867, 1868	*Peoria Transcript*, July 1, 1867; *Bloomington Pantagraph*, Sept. 29, 1868
Cherry Valley	Maple Leaf Base Ball Club—1869	https://protoball.org/IL

Town	Team(s)	Source
Chicago (partial)	Union Base Ball Club, 1858	Peter Morris, "Excelsiors of Chicago, Prewar," 206–10, in *Base Ball Pioneers, 1850–1870*, Jefferson, NC: McFarland, 2012
	Atlantic Base Ball Club, 1866–69	*Illinois State Journal*, Sept. 13, 1866; Morris, "Excelsiors of Chicago, Postwar," 210–21
	Excelsior Base Ball Club, 1858–60, 1865–68	Morris, "Excelsiors of Chicago, Prewar, 206–10, and "Excelsiors of Chicago, Postwar," 210–21
	Amateur Base Ball Club—1869	*Monmouth Atlas*, Sept. 17, 1869; *Rockford Republic*, June 17, 1922[3]
	Aetna Base Ball Club—1869	*Rockford Republic*, June 17, 1922
	Blue Stockings Base Ball Club (Black)—1870	*Rockford Republic*, July 19, 1922
	Potter Palmer Base Ball Club—1870	*Rockford Republic*, July 19, 1922
	Baltic Base Ball Club—1870	*Chicago Tribune*, Aug. 21, 1870
	Eckford Base Ball Club—1870	*Ottawa Free Trader*, July 2, 1870
	Garden City Base Ball Club—1870	*Ottawa Free Trader*, June 25, 1870
	White Stockings Base Ball Club—1870	*Chicago Tribune*, Oct. 28, 1870; Morris, "Excelsiors of Chicago, Postwar"
Chillicothe	Prairie State Base Ball Club—1867	*Peoria Transcript*, Aug. 30, 1867
Clinton	Eureka Base Ball Club-1867, 1868, 1870	*Clinton Public and General Transcript*, July 11, 1867; *Decatur Republican*, July 2, 1868; *Clinton Public*, May 27, 1870
	Prairie State Base Ball Club (Junior)—1867	*Clinton Public and General Transcript*, June 3, 1867
Clinton County	Farmers Base Ball Club—1868	*Greenville Advocate*, Aug. 21, 1868
Coal Valley	Athletic Base Ball Club—1867	*Rock Island Argus*, June 25, 1867
Colchester	Sucker Base Ball Club—1869	*Macomb Journal*, July 16, 1869
Collinsville	Athletic Base Ball Club—1867	*Belleville Advocate*, Sept. 20, 1867
Columbia	Red, White, and Blue Base Ball Club—1869	https://protoball.org/IL
Crystal Lake	Crystal Lake Base Ball Club—1868	https://protoball.org/IL
Curran	Rurals Base Ball Club—1866	*Illinois State Register*, Sept. 3, 1866
Danby (now Glen Ellyn)	Rustics Base Ball Club—1867	*Peoria National Democrat*, Aug. 23, 1867
Danville	Vermilion Base Ball Club—1866, 1867	*Danville Commercial*, Nov. 15, 1866, June 6, 1867

Town	Team(s)	Source
Dayton	Eagle Base Ball Club—1867	*Ottawa Republican*, Aug. 22, 1867
Decatur	Pastime Base Ball Club—1867	https://protoball.org/IL
	unknown black club—1869	*Decatur Republican*, June 3, 1869; *Bureau County Republican*, June 10, 1869
	Antelope Base Ball Club (Muffin)—1867	*Decatur Republican*, Sept. 5, 1867
	McPherson Base Ball Club—1866, 1867	*Illinois State Journal*, Aug. 20, 1866; *Decatur Republican*, Aug. 8, 1867
	"Ugly Plugs" Base Ball Club (likely a pick-up team)—1867	*Decatur Republican*, Aug. 15, 1867
	Athletic Base Ball Club—1868	*Decatur Republican*, Apr. 23, 1868
	Contest Base Ball Club—1868	https://protoball.org/IL
	Central Base Ball Club (Junior)—1868	*Decatur Republican*, Apr. 23, 1868
Deer Park Township (LaSalle County)	Oak Base Ball Club—1868	*Ottawa Free Trader*, Aug. 8, 1868
De Kalb	De Kalb Base Ball Club—1868	*De Kalb County News*—May 20, 1868
Dixon	Riverside Base Ball Club—1866, 1867	*Sterling Gazette*, Sept. 22, 1866, June 8, 1867; *Rockford Republic*, May 20, 1922
	Swiftfoot Base Ball Club (10–15-year-olds)—1867	*Ogle County Reporter*, July 18, 1867
	Star Base Ball Club—1869	*Dixon Weekly Telegraph*, June 23, 1869
Downers Grove	Downers Grove Base Ball Club—1867	*Aurora Beacon*, Aug. 27, 1867
Dundee	Dundee Base Ball Club—1867	*Aurora Beacon*, Oct. 17, 1867
Du Quoin	Wallapus Base Ball Club—1867	*Du Quoin Tribune*, July 17, 1867
	Independent Sucker Base Ball Club—1867	*Du Quoin Tribune*, July 25, 1867
	Victor Base Ball Club—1867	*Du Quoin Tribune*, Aug. 8, 1867
	Young America Base Ball Club	*Du Quoin Tribune*, Aug. 8, 1867
Dwight	Pony Base Ball Club (Juvenile)—1868	https://protoball.org/IL
Earlville	Earlville Base Ball Club—1868, 1869	*Earlville Gazette*, July 24, 1868; *Bureau County Republican*, Sept. 2, 1869
East St. Louis	St. Clair Base Ball Club—1865, 1866	*East St. Louis Herald*, Oct. 15, 1865, Jan. 21, 1866
	OK Base Ball Club—1865	*East St. Louis Herald*, Aug. 27, 1865

Town	Team(s)	Source
	Elfin Base Ball Club—1866	*East St. Louis Gazette*, Oct. 18, 1866
	Nile Base Ball Club—1866	*East St. Louis Gazette*, Oct. 18, 1866
	Olive Branch Base Ball Club—1866	*East St. Louis Herald*—May 13, 1866
	Defiance Base Ball Club—1868, 1869	*East St. Louis Gazette*, Sept. 19, 1868, July 24, 1869
Edwardsville	Central Base Ball Club—1867	*Belleville Advocate*, Sept. 17, 1867
	Magnolia Base Ball Club—1869, 1870	https://protoball.org/IL; *Edwardsville Intelligencer*, June 9, 1870
Elgin	Young America Base Ball Club—1867	*Aurora Beacon*, July 25, 1867
Elkhart	Elkhart Base Ball Club—1867	*Lincoln Herald*, July 25, 1867
Elmwood	Elmwood Base Ball Club—1868	*Peoria Transcript*, Aug. 25, 1868
El Paso	El Paso Base Ball Club—1867	*Peoria National Democrat*, Oct. 12, 1867
Eureka	Eureka Base Ball Club—1869	*Peoria Transcript*, May 31, 1869
	Independent Base Ball Club—1869	https://protoball.org/IL
Evanston	Favorite Base Ball Club—1865	https://protoball.org/IL
Fairbury	Olympic Base Ball Club—1867	*Chicago Tribune*, Sept. 28, 1867
Fairfield	Snails Base Ball Club—1868	https://protoball.org/IL
	Terrapin Base Ball Club—1868	https://protoball.org/IL
Farm Ridge	Farmers Base Ball Club—1868	*Ottawa Republican*, Aug. 27, 1868
	Oak Base Ball Club—1870	*Ottawa Free Trader*, July 9, 1870
Forrest	Morning Star Base Ball Club—1870	*Ottawa Free Trader*, Aug. 27, 1870
Forsyth	Hit and Go Lightnings Base Ball Club—1867	*Peoria National Democrat*, Sept. 7, 1867
Freedom Township (LaSalle County)	Freedom Base Ball Club—1868	*Earlville Gazette*, July 24, 1868
Freeport	Empire Base Ball Club—1865, 1866	*Rockford Republic*, Mar. 22, 1922; *Freeport Bulletin*, Apr. 12, 1866
	Shaffer Base Ball Club—1866	*Freeport Bulletin*, June 21, 1866
	Star Base Ball Club—1866	*Freeport Bulletin*, Aug. 30, 1866
	Union Base Ball Club (Junior)—1866	*Freeport Bulletin*, Aug. 30, 1866
	Resolute Base Ball Club—1866	*Freeport Bulletin*, Oct. 11, 1866
	Printers Base Ball Club—1867	*Rockford Republic*, May 17, 1922
Fulton	Fulton Base Ball Club—1867	https://protoball.org/IL
Galena	Galena Base Ball Club—1867	*Galena Gazette*, May 28, 1867
	Lead Mine Base Ball Club—1867	*Galena Gazette*, June 4, 1867
	Grant Base Ball Club (Junior)—1867	*Galena Gazette*, June 25, 1867

Town	Team(s)	Source
Galesburg	College City Base Ball Club—1867	*Monmouth Atlas*, May 31, 1867
	Knox Base Ball Club—1867	*Peoria Transcript*, June 17, 1867; *Galesburg Register*, June 20, 1867
	Knox College Junior Base Ball Club—1869	*Galesburg Free Press*, Oct. 25, 1869
	Knox College Freshman Base Ball Club—1869	*Galesburg Free Press*, Oct. 25, 1869
Geneseo	Pioneer Base Ball Club—1866, 1867	*Rock Island Argus*, July 14, 1866, June 7, 1867
	Pioneer Junior Base Ball Club—1867	*Rock Island Argus*, June 28, 1867
	Farmers Base Ball Club—1868	*Sterling Gazette*, Aug. 24, 1867
	Liberty Base Ball Club—1868	*Sterling Gazette*, July 11, 1869
Geneva	Rover Base Ball Club—1867	https://protoball.org/IL
Girard	Girard Base Ball Club—1867	https://protoball.org/IL
Golconda	Mayflower Base Ball Club—1867, 1869	*Metropolis Weekly Times*, Nov. 6, 1867; *Cairo Evening Bulletin*, Aug. 14, 1869
Granville	Granville Base Ball Club—1869	*Bureau County Republican*, Aug. 19, 1869
Greenville	Sucker Base Ball Club—1868	*Greenville Advocate*, Mar. 27, 1868
	Independent Base Ball Club—1869	*Carlyle Constitution and Union*, June 14, 1869; *Greenville Advocate*, July 223, 1869
	Clipper Base Ball Club—1868	*Greenville Advocate*, July 10, 1868
Griggsville	Griggsville Base Ball Club	*Pike County Democrat*, Aug. 20, 1868; https://protoball.org/IL
Hampton	Hampton Base Ball Club—1867	*Rock Island Argus*, July 15, 1867
	Olympic Base Ball Club—1867	*Rock Island Argus*, Sept. 2, 1867
Harvard	Harvard Base Ball Club—1867	*Harvard Independent*, July 17, 1867
	Juvenile Base Ball Club—1867, 1868	*Harvard Independent*, Oct. 2, 1867, July 15, 1868
	Black Hawk Base Ball Club (Junior)—1868	*Harvard Independent*, Aug. 12, 1868
Hennepin	Hennepin Base Ball Club—1868	*Marshall County Republican*, July 9, 1868
Henry	Ristori Base Ball Club—1867	*Marshall County Republican*, Aug. 22, 1867
	Star Base Ball Club—1870	*Ottawa Free Trader*, July 30, 1870
Hillsboro	Hillsboro Base Ball Club—1868	*Litchfield Union and Monitor*, July 23, 1868

Town	Team(s)	Source
Homer	Eureka Base Ball Club—1867	*Danville Commercial*, Nov. 7, 1867
Hudson	Active Base Ball Club—1868	*Bloomington Pantagraph*, June 25, 1868
Hyde Park	Hyde Park Base Ball Club—1867	https://protoball.org/IL
Jacksonville	Hardin Base Ball Club—1866	*Jacksonville Weekly Journal*, May 17, 1866
	Hardin Junior Base Ball Club—1866	*Jacksonville Journal*, Dec. 5, 1866
	Hercules Base Ball Club—1866	*Jacksonville Weekly Journal*, May 17, 1866
	Morgan Base Ball Club—1866	*Jacksonville Journal*, Sept. 3, 1866
	Mohawk Base Ball Club (possibly junior)—1866	*Jacksonville Journal*, Nov. 20, 1866
	Grant Base Ball Club (Junior)—1866, 1867	*Jacksonville Journal*, Nov. 5, 1866, July 26, 1867
	Champion Base Ball Club—1867	*Jacksonville Weekly Sentinel*, Nov. 25, 1867
	Union Base Ball Club—1867	*Jacksonville Journal*, Apr. 27, 1867
	Union Junior Base Ball Club—1867	*Jacksonville Journal*, Sept. 6, 1867
	Alert Base Ball Club (Junior)—1869	*Jacksonville Journal*, July 14, 1869
	Relic Base Ball Club—1869	*Jacksonville Journal*, Aug. 12, 1869
	Olympic Base Ball Club (Junior)—1869	*Jacksonville Journal*, Sept. 3, 1869
	Mutual Base Ball Club (Junior)—1869	*Jacksonville Journal*, Sept. 3, 1868
Jerseyville	Jerseyville Base Ball Club—1867	*Jersey County Democrat*, Sept. 27, 1867
	Athletic Base Ball Club—1869	*Jersey County Democrat*, July 10, 1869
	Independent Base Ball Club—1867	*Jersey County Democrat*, Sept. 13, 1867
	Young America Base Ball Club—1867, 1869	*Jersey County Democrat*, June 28, 1867, July 10, 1869; *Litchfield Union and Monitor*, Sept. 9, 1869
Joliet	Eclectic Base Ball Club—1868	*Ottawa Republican*, Sept. 3, 1868; *Joliet Signal*, Mar. 31, 1868
	Eureka Base Ball Club—1868	https://protoball.org/IL
Jubilee College	Jubilee College Base Ball Club—1867	*Peoria Transcript*, Oct. 10, 1867
	Wild Cats Base Ball Club—1867	*Peoria Transcript*, Oct. 24, 1867

Town	Team(s)	Source
Kankakee	Grove City Base Ball Club—1867, 1868	*Kankakee Gazette*, Oct. 31, 1867, May 21, 1868
	Grove City Junior Base Ball Club—1867	*Kankakee Journal*, Oct. 31, 1867
	Independent Base Ball Club—1868	*Kankakee Gazette*, May 21, 1868
Keithsburg	Keithsburg Base Ball Club—1867	*Oquawka Spectator*, July 4, 1867
	Victoria Base Ball Club—1867	https://protoball.org/IL
Kendall County	Kendall Base Ball Club—1867	*Aurora Beacon*, Aug. 8, 1867
Kewanee	Kewanee Base Ball Club—1867	*Bureau County Republican*, Aug. 15, 1867
	Blue Stockings Base Ball Club—1869	*Stark County News*, Oct. 22, 1869
Kishwaukee	Kishwaukee Base Ball Club—1867	*Harvard Independent*, Oct. 30, 1867
Lacon[4]	Lacon Base Ball Club—1867	*Bureau County Republican*, June 27, 1867
	Lacon City Base Ball Club—1867	*Marshall County Republican*, Aug. 22, 1867
	Defiant Base Ball Club—1867	*Marshall County Republican*, July 11, 1867
La Harpe	Undine Base Ball Club—1868	*Warsaw Bulletin*, Aug. 14, 1868; *Macomb Eagle*, July 11, 1868
	Japonica Base Ball Club—1867	*Macomb Eagle*, Oct. 19, 1867
Lanark	Enterprise Base Ball Club—1867	*Freeport Bulletin*, July 25, 1867
La Salle	Little Vermilion Base Ball Club—1867	*Ottawa Republican*, July 25, 1867
	Blue Stockings Base Ball Club—1870	*Ottawa Free Trader*, Oct. 1, 1870
Lebanon	Lebanon Base Ball Club—1867	*Lebanon Journal*, Apr. 27, 1867
	McKendree College Base Ball Club—1867, 1870	*Carlyle Union Banner*, Apr. 28, 1870; https://protoball.org/IL
Leland	Dirigo Base Ball Club—1867, 1868	*Ottawa Republican*, Aug. 22, 1867; *Earlville Gazette*, Aug. 21, 1868
Lena	Neptune Base Ball Club—1867, 1870	*Warren Sentinel*, Aug. 2, 1870; https://protoball.org/IL
Leroy	Leroy Base Ball Club—1868	*Champaign Gazette and Union*, Aug. 5, 1868
Limerick	Farmers Base Ball Club—1869	*Bureau County Republican*, Sept. 16, 1869

Town	Team(s)	Source
Lincoln	Monitor Base Ball Club—1866	*Jacksonville Journal*, Sept. 17, 1866
	Lincoln Base Ball Club—1867	*Lincoln Herald*, June 13, 1867
	Bachelors Base Ball Club (Muffin)—1867	*Lincoln Monitor*, Oct. 17, 1867
	Benedicts Base Ball Club (Muffin)—1867	*Lincoln Monitor*, Oct. 17, 1867
Litchfield	Prairie Base Ball Club—1866	https://protoball.org/IL
	Litchfield Junior Base Ball Club—1868	*Litchfield Union Monitor*, Aug. 20, 1868
	Union Base Ball Club—1869	*Litchfield Union Monitor*, Sept. 2, 1869
Logansport or Logan Township (Peoria County)	Logan Base Ball Club—1867	*Peoria Transcript*, Aug. 23, 1867
Lostant	Liberty Base Ball Club—1868	*Marshall County Republican and Register*, Sept. 17, 1868
Lysander (old name of Pecatonica Township, Winnebago County)	Clipper Base Ball Club—1866	*Rockford Republic*, Apr. 8, 1922
	Eureka Base Ball Club—1866	*Rockford Republic*, Apr. 8, 1922
Macomb	Excelsior Base Ball Club—1867, 1868	*Macomb Eagle*, Aug. 31, 1867; https://protoball.org/IL
	Union Star Base Ball Club—1867	*Macomb Eagle*, July 6, 1867
Macon	Macon Base Ball Club—1867	*Decatur Republican*, Sept. 12, 1867
Marengo	Star Base Ball Club (Junior)—1867	*Rockford Republic*, May 17, 1922; *Woodstock Sentinel*, Oct. 10, 1867; *Harvard Independent*, July 17, 1867
	Marengo Base Ball Club—1867	*Woodstock Sentinel*, May 30, 1867; *Harvard Independent*, June 26, 1867
	Eagle Base Ball Club—1867	*Harvard Independent*, June 26, 1867
	Forest Base Ball Club—1868	*Rockford Republic*, June 7, 1922
Maroa	Red Hot Base Ball Club—1867	https://protoball.org/IL
	Grand Prairie Base Ball Club—1867	*Maroa Times*, Sept. 19, 1867
Marseilles	Red Jacket Base Ball Club—1868, 1869	*Ottawa Free Trader*, May 16, 1868; 1869; https://protoball.org/IL
	Olympic Base Ball Club—1870	*Ottawa Free Trader*, Oct. 1, 1870
Marshall	Continental Base Ball Club—1867	https://protoball.org/IL
	One Gallows Base Ball Club—1868	*Marshall Messenger*, Oct. 1, 1868

Town	Team(s)	Source
	Rocket Base Ball Club—1869	*Clark County Herald*, July 30, 1869
	Quickstep Base Ball Club—1869	*Clark County Herald*, July 30, 1869; *Marshall Messenger*, July 22, 1869
	Shooting Star Base Ball Club (Junior)—1869	*Marshall Messenger*, July 22, 1869
	White Stockings Base Ball Club—1869	*Marshall Messenger*, July 22, 1869
Martinsville	Martinsville Base Ball Club—1869	*Marshall Messenger*, July 8, 1869
Mascoutah	Mascoutah Base Ball Club—1868	https://protoball.org/IL
	Eclipse Base Ball Club—1869	*Carlyle Union Banner*, May 18, 1869
Mattoon	unknown club—1867	*Pana Gazette*, Oct. 26, 1867
McLean	McLean Base Ball Club—1867, 1868	*Bloomington Pantagraph*, Sept. 9, 1867; *Lincoln Herald*, Oct. 2, 1867; https://protoball.org/IL
Mendota	Prairie Base Ball Club—1867	*Mendota Bulletin*, Aug. 8, 1867
	Mendota Base Ball Club—1869	*Ottawa Republican*, Aug. 19, 1869
Metropolis	Metropolis Base Ball Club—1867	*Metropolis Weekly Times*, Oct. 30, 1867
Minonk	Dexter Base Ball Club—1867	*Peoria National Democrat*, Oct. 12, 1867
	Enterprise Base Ball Club—1868	*Bloomington Pantagraph*, June 25, 1868
Moline	Moline Base Ball Club—1866, 1867	*Rock Island Argus*, July 21, 1866, May 6, 1867
	Wide Awake Base Ball Club—1867	*Rock Island Union*, Apr. 8, 1867[5]
	Active Base Ball Club (Junior)—1867	*Rock Island Argus*, May 27, 1867
	Fort Armstrong Base Ball Club—1867	*Rock Island Argus*, Sept. 5, 1867
	Young America Base Ball Club—1867	*Rock Island Argus*, May 27, 1867
Monmouth	Athletic Base Ball Club—1867	https://protoball.org/IL
	Classic Base Ball Club—1867	*Monmouth Atlas*, May 31, 1867
	Clipper Base Ball Club—1867, 1868, 1869, 1870	*Monmouth Atlas*, Aug. 23, 1867; June 5, 1868, Sept. 17, 1869; *Monmouth Review*, June 3, 1870
	Charter Oak Base Ball Club (Junior)—1868	*Quincy Herald*, July 31, 1868
	Monmouth College Reserve Base Ball Club—1869	https://protoball.org/IL

Town	Team(s)	Source
	Commercial Base Ball Club—1870	*Monmouth Review*, Oct. 14, 1870
	White Stockings Base Ball Club—1870	*Monmouth Review*, Oct. 21, 1870
Morgan	Morgan Base Ball Club—1869	*Carlyle Constitution and Union*, Aug. 10, 1869
Morris	Morris Base Ball Club—1867	*Ottawa Republican*, Aug. 22, 1867
	Illinois Base Ball Club—1867	*Ottawa Republican*, Sept. 19, 1867
Morrison	Achilles Base Ball Club—1867	*Sterling Gazette*, July 27, 1867
Mound City	Monitor Base Ball Club—1866	*Cairo Democrat*, Aug. 12, 1866
Mount Carroll	Hill City Base Ball Club—1869	*Freeport Bulletin*, Sept. 2, 1869
Mount Morris	Logan Base Ball Club—1867, 1870	*Ogle County Republican*, June 13, 1867, July 7, 1870
	Clipper Base Ball Club—1867	*Ogle County Republican*, July 18, 1867
	Diamond Base Ball Club—1867	*Ogle County Republican*, June 27, 1867
Mount Palatine	National Base Ball Club—1868	*Marshall County Republican and Register*, Sept. 17, 1868
Mount Sterling	Mount Sterling Base Ball Club—1867	https://protoball.org/IL
Mount Vernon	Athletae Base Ball Club—1867	*Mount Vernon Free Press*, Sept. 6, 1867
	Star Base Ball Club—1867, 1868	*Mount Vernon Free Press*, Sept. 6, 1867; *Centralia Sentinel*, Oct. 8, 1868
	Star Junior Base Ball Club—1867	*Mount Vernon Free Press*, Sept. 6, 1867
	Great Western Base Ball Club—1869	*Centralia Democrat*, Aug. 26, 1869
	Resolute Base Ball Club—1869	*Mount Vernon Free Press*, Apr. 15, 1869
Mount Zion	Sum Punkins Base Ball Club—1867	*Decatur Republican*, Oct. 24, 1867
Nashville	Nashville Base Ball Club—1866	*Nashville Journal*, Nov. 5, 1866
	Sucker Base Ball Club—1867, 1868	*Nashville Journal*, Aug. 22, 1867; *Centralia Sentinel*, Aug. 13, 1868
Newark	Newark Base Ball Club—1867	https://protoball.org/IL
	XL Base Ball Club—1870	*Ottawa Free Trader*, Oct. 22, 1870
New Rutland	Hickory Base Ball Club—1867	*Marshall County Republican*, Sept. 4, 1867
Nora	Harvest Boys Base Ball Club—1870	*Warren Sentinel*, Aug. 30, 1870

Town	Team(s)	Source
Normal	Normal Base Ball Club—1866, 1868	*Bloomington Pantagraph*, Sept. 29, 1868; https://protoball.org/IL
Northville (LaSalle County)	Shoo Fly Base Ball Club—1870	*Ottawa Free Trader*, Oct. 22, 1870
Nunda	Prairie Farmers Base Ball Club—1868	https://protoball.org/IL
Odin	Odin Base Ball Club—1866	*Centralia Sentinel*, Nov. 8, 1866
O'Fallon	Comet Base Ball Club—1867	https://protoball.org/IL
Ohio Township (Bureau County)	unnamed club—1869	*Bureau County Republican*, Sept. 15, 1869
Onarga	Onarga Base Ball Club—1867	*Grand Prairie Review*, Aug. 31, 1867
	Muffin Base Ball Club—1867	*Grand Prairie Review*, Sept. 28, 1867
	Students' Base Ball Club—1867	*Grand Prairie Review*, Aug. 24, 1867
	Junior Base Ball Club—1867	*Grand Prairie Review*, Aug. 24, 1867
	Eagle Base Ball Club (formerly Juniors)—1867	*Kankakee Gazette*, Nov. 14, 1867
	Muffers Base Ball Club—1868	*Kankakee Gazette*, Oct. 8, 1868
	Hunkidori Base Ball Club—1868	*Grand Prairie Review*, May 16, 1868
Oquawka	Oquawka Base Ball Club—1867	*Oquawka Spectator*, Aug. 15, 1867
Oregon	Social Independents Base Ball Club—1867	*Ogle County Reporter*, June 27, 1867
	Rock River Base Ball Club—1867	*Ogle County Reporter*, June 13, 1867
Ottawa	O.K. Base Ball Club—1867	*Ottawa Republican*, May 9, 1867
	Shabbona Base Ball Club—1867, 1870	*Ottawa Republican*, May 9, 1867; *Illinois State Register*, Aug. 15, 1870; *Ottawa Free Trader*, Aug. 13, 1870
	Athletic Base Ball Club—1867, 1868	*Ottawa Free Trader*, July 27, 1867; *Ottawa Republican*, July 30, 1868
	Avoirdupois Base Ball Club (Muffin)—1867	*Ottawa Republican*, July 25, 1867
	U.S. Base Ball Club of South Ottawa—1867	*Ottawa Free Trader*, Aug. 31, 1867
	Star Base Ball Club (Junior)—1867	*Ottawa Republican*, Aug. 22, 1867
	Young America Base Ball Club (Junior)—1867	*Ottawa Republican*, Aug. 22, 1867
	Shabbona Junior Base Ball Club—1868	*Ottawa Republican*, July 30, 1868
	Niagara Base Ball Club—1868	*Ottawa Republican*, June 11, 1868

Town	Team(s)	Source
	Clifton Base Ball Club (employees of Clifton Hotel)—1870	*Ottawa Free Trader*, June 18, 1870
	Red Legs Base Ball Club (Junior)—1870	*Ottawa Free Trader*, June 18, 1870
	Hefty Base Ball Club—1867	*Ottawa Free Trader,* June 29, 1867
Palmyra	Oriental Base Ball Club—1869	*Quincy Whig and Republican*, June 15, 1869
Pana	Excelsior Base Ball Club—1867, 1868	*Pana Gazette*, May 11, 1867, May 22, 1868
	Athletic Base Ball Club (Junior)—1867	*Pana Gazette*, Sept. 21, 1867
	Wallapus Base Ball Club (Muffin)—1867	*Pana Gazette*, Sept. 28, 1867
Pavilion	Pavilion Base Ball Club—1867	https://protoball.org/IL
Paxton	Blue Jacket Base Ball Club—1867	*Champaign Union and Gazette*, Sept. 18, 1867
	Red Jacket Base Ball Club—1867	*Champaign Union and Gazette*, Aug. 7, 1867, *Grand Prairie Review* (Onarga), Sept. 28, 1867
Payson	Newtown Base Ball Club—1869	*Quincy Herald*, Oct. 7, 1869
Pecatonica	Pecatonica Base Ball Club—1866	*Freeport Bulletin*, June 14, 1866
Pekin	Celestial Base Ball Club—1866, 1868, 1869	*Peoria Transcript*, Sept. 1, 1866, Sept. 4, 1868; *Jacksonville Journal*, July 15, 1869
	Olympic Base Ball Club—1866, 1868	*Peoria Transcript*, Sept. 1, 1866, Sept. 14, 1868
	Pekin Base Ball Club—1869	*Peoria Transcript*, Aug. 3, 1869
Peoria	Olympic Base Ball Club—1865, 1866	*Peoria National Democrat*, Sept. 19, 1865, and Oct. 14, 1866
	Central City Base Ball Club—1866	*Peoria Transcript*, Sept. 25, 1866
	Excelsior Base Ball Club—1866, 1867, 1868, 1869	*Peoria Transcript*, Oct. 18, 1866, June 17, 1867, Sept. 14, 1868, July 12, 1869
	Enterprise Base Ball Club—1866, 1867	*Peoria Transcript*, Oct. 18, 1866, July 20, 1867
	Fort Clark Base Ball Club—1867	*Peoria Transcript*, Aug. 2, 1867
	Peoria High School Base Ball Club—1867	*Peoria Transcript*, July 2, 1867
	Active Base Ball Club—1867	*Peoria Transcript*, Aug. 5, 1867
	Independent Base Ball Club—1867. 1868	*Peoria Transcript*, Aug. 5, 1867, June 15, 1868

Town	Team(s)	Source
	Alert Base Ball Club—1867	*Peoria Transcript*, Oct. 7, 1867
	Crescent Base Ball Club—1867	*Peoria Transcript*, Apr. 27, 1867
	Osceola Base Ball Club—1868	*Peoria Transcript*, Aug. 21, 1868
	Fort Clark Junior Base Ball Club—1868, 1869	*Peoria Transcript*, July 13, 1868, June 11, 1869
	Clipper Base Ball Club—1869	*Peoria Transcript*, July 12, 1869
Perry	Pioneer Base Ball Club—1867	*Pike County Democrat*, Oct. 3, 1867
Peru	Live Oak Base Ball Club—1867, 1868	*Bureau County Republican*, June 12, 1867; *Ottawa Republican*, Aug. 13, 1868
	Peru Base Ball Club—1868	https://protoball.org/IL
Philo	Frontier Base Ball Club—1868	*Champaign Union and Gazette*, July 15, 1868
Pittsfield	Sherman Base Ball Club—1867	*Pike County Democrat*, Oct. 3, 1867
Plano	Union Base Ball Club—1867	*Aurora Beacon*, Aug. 8, 1867
Plattville	Plattville Base Ball Club—1867	*Galena Gazette*, July 2, 1867
Polo	Polo Base Ball Club—1867	https://protoball.org/IL
	Athletes Base Ball Club—1870	*Ogle County Reporter*, July 7, 1870
Pontiac	Greenhorn Base Ball Club—1867	*Chicago Tribune*, Sept. 28, 1867
	Mechanics Base Ball Club—1870	*Ottawa Free Trader*, Aug. 27, 1870
Prairie Creek Township (Logan County)	Independent Base Ball Club—1869	*Atlanta Argus*, Aug. 21, 1869
Princeton	Amateur Base Ball Club—1866, 1867, 1869	*Bureau County Patriot*, Aug. 7, 1866, Apr. 25, 1867, June 24, 1869
Princeville	Lucifer Base Ball Club—1867, 1868	*Peoria Transcript*, Aug. 9, 1867, June 27, 1868
	Alpha Base Ball Club—1868	*Peoria Transcript*, Sept. 10, 1868
Quincy	Quincy Base Ball Club, 1866	*Quincy Herald*, Aug. 15, 1866
	Essex Base Ball Club (Junior)—1866	*Quincy Herald*, Sept. 16, 1866
	Baltic Base Ball Club (likely Junior)—1866	*Quincy Herald*, Sept. 13, 1866
	Mystic Base Ball Club (likely Junior)—1866	*Quincy Herald*, Sept. 4, 1866
	Olympic Base Ball Club—1866	*Quincy Herald*, Sept. 16, 1866
	Occidental Senior Base Ball Club—1866, 1867, 1868, 1869	*Quincy Herald*, July 12, 1866, July 19, 1867, July 3, 1868, July 10, 1868
	Occidental Junior Base Ball Club—1867, 1868, 1869, 1870	*Quincy Herald*, Nov. 17, 1867, Aug. 4, 1868, July 7, 1869; *Illinois State Register*, Aug. 4, 1870

Town	Team(s)	Source
	Dexter Base Ball Club (likely Junior)—1867, 1868, 1869	*Quincy Herald*, Apr. 16, 1867, Sept. 1, 1868, June 30, 1869
	Active Base Ball Club (Junior)—1869	*Quincy Herald*, Aug. 31, 1869
	Atlantic Base Ball Club (Junior)—1869	*Quincy Herald*, Aug. 31, 1869
	Eclipse Base Ball Club (Junior)—1869	*Quincy Whig*, Sept. 4, 1869
	Novelty Base Ball Club (Juveniles)—1869	*Quincy Whig*, Apr. 9, 1869
	Gem City Base Ball Club—1869	*Quincy Herald*, Sept. 16, 1869
	Star Base Ball Club (Juvenile)—1869	*Quincy Herald*, Aug. 4, 1869
Rantoul	Rantoul Base Ball Club—1868	*Champaign Union and Gazette*, Sept. 2, 1868
Richmond	Richmond Base Ball Club—1867	*Harvard Independent*, Aug. 21, 1867
Richview	Grand Republic Base Ball Club—1867	*Mount Vernon Free Press*, Sept. 6, 1867
Riley	Prairie Base Ball Club—1870	*Woodstock Sentinel*, Aug. 25, 1870
Ripley	Sherman Base Ball Club—1867	https://protoball.org/IL
Roberts Township (Henry County)	Farmers Base Ball Club—1867	*Henry County Republican*, Sept. 5, 1867
Robinson	Robinson Base Ball Club—1867	*Robinson Constitution*, June 6, 1867
Rochelle	Clipper Base Ball Club-1866	https://protoball.org/IL
	Independent Base Ball Club—1869	*Dixon Weekly Telegraph*, June 23, 1869
Rockford	Forest City Base Ball Club—1865, 1866, 1867	*Rockford Democrat*, May 31, 1865; *Rockford Republic*, Mar. 15, 1922, Apr. 12, 1922, Apr. 19, 1922
	Sinnissippi Base Ball Club—1865, 1866	*Rockford Republic*, Mar. 15, 1922, Apr. 15, 1922
	Union Base Ball Club (Junior)—1865, 1868	*Rockford Republic*, Mar. 15, 1922, Mar. 29, 1922, Apr. 15, 1922
	Mercantile Base Ball Club—1865	*Rockford Republic*, Mar. 15, 1922
	Pioneer Base Ball Club (Junior)—1865, 1866	*Rockford Republic*, Mar. 15, 1922, Apr. 12, 1922
	Waldo's Nine-1865	*Rockford Republic*, Mar. 18, 1922
	Grand Army of the Republic Base Ball Club—1865	*Rockford Republic*, June 7, 1922
	Rockford Base Ball Club (Black)—1870	*Chicago Tribune*, Aug. 28, 1870; *Rockford Republic*, July 19, 1922

Town	Team(s)	Source
	South Rockford Base Ball Club—1866	*Rockford Republic*, Apr. 15, 1922
	Rock River Base Ball Club—1866, 1867	*Rockford Republic*, Apr. 14, 1922, May 17, 1922
	Forest City Junior Base Ball Club—1867	*Rockford Republic*, Apr. 29, 1922
	Printers Base Ball Club—1867	*Rockford Republic*, May 17, 1922
	East Rockford Base Ball Club—1868	*Rockford Republic*, June 7, 1922,
	West Rockford Base Ball Club—1868	*Rockford Republic*, June 7, 1922
	Engine Number Two Base Ball Club—1868	*Rockford Republic*, June 7, 1922
Rock Island	Wapello Base Ball Club—1866, 1867	*Rock Island Argus*, July 28, 1866, May 8, 1867
	Quick Step Base Ball Club (Junior)—1866, 1867	*Rock Island Argus*, Aug. 9, 1866, May 27, 1867
	Liberty Base Ball Club (Junior)—1866	*Rock Island Argus*, Nov. 12, 1866
	Mohawk Base Ball Club (Junior)—1866	*Rock Island Argus*, Nov. 12, 1866
	Prairie State Base Ball Club (Junior)—1866, 1867	*Rock Island Argus*, Nov. 10, 1866, May 27, 1867
	Spartan (Lively Turtles) Base Ball Club—1867, 1868	*Rock Island Argus*, May 28, 1867, Mar. 24, 1868
	Olympic Base Ball Club (Junior)—1867	*Rock Island Argus*, June 10, 1867
Rockton	Eagle Base Ball Club—1867	https://protoball.org/IL
	Rockton Base Ball Club	*Rockford Republic*, Apr. 15, 1922
Rockville	Rockville Base Ball Club—1868	*Kankakee Gazette*, Sept. 5, 1868
Rome	Farmers Base Ball Club—1867	*Peoria Transcript*, Sept. 30, 1867
Roscoe	Star Base Ball Club	https://protoball.org/IL
Rozetta Township	Rozetta Base Ball Club—1867	*Monmouth Atlas*, Sept. 13, 1867; *Oquawka Spectator*, Oct. 13, 1867
Rushville	Union Base Ball Club—1867	https://protoball.org/IL
Sagetown	Sagetown Base Ball Club—1867	*Oquawka Spectator*, Oct. 24, 1867
Saint Charles	Olympian Base Ball Club—1867	*Aurora Beacon*, Oct. 24, 1867
	Rough and Ready Base Ball Club—1867	*Aurora Beacon*, Sept. 26, 1867
	Active Base Ball Club—1867, 1869	*Aurora Beacon*, Sept. 24, 1867, July 8, 1869

Town	Team(s)	Source
	Prairie Boys Base Ball Club (formerly Olympians)—1868	*Aurora Beacon*, May 14, 1868
	Clipper Base Ball Club—1868	*Aurora Beacon*, Aug. 20, 1868
Salem	Greenhorn Base Ball Club—1868, 1869	*Centralia Democrat*, Aug. 13, 1868; https://protoball.org/IL
Sandwich	Amateur Base Ball Club—1867	*Aurora Beacon*, Sept. 12, 1867
Savoy	Rural Base Ball Club—1868	*Champaign Union and Gazette*, Sept. 30, 1868
	Prairie Base Ball Club—1868	*Champaign Union and Gazette*, Sept. 30, 1868
Seward	Plow Boy Base Ball Club—1866	*Rockford Republic*, Apr. 8, 1922
Shabbona	Lincoln Base Ball Club—1868	*DeKalb County News*, Sept. 16, 1868
Shannon	Prairie Base Ball Club—1867	https://protoball.org/IL
Sheffield	Olympic Base Ball Club—1867	*Bureau County Republican*, June 13, 1867
Sidney	Sidney Base Ball Club—1868	*Champaign Union and Gazette*, Aug. 26, 1868
Sparland	Sparland Base Ball Club—1867	https://protoball.org/IL
Sparta	Sparta Base Ball Cub—1867	*Belleville Advocate*, Sept. 27, 1867
	Asteroid Base Ball Club—1869	*Nashville Journal*, Sept. 23, 1869
Springfield	Hercules Base Ball Club (Junior)—1866, 1867	*Illinois State Journal*, Sept. 17, 1866, Apr. 5, 1867
	Capital Base Ball Club—1866, 1867	*Illinois State Register*, May 16, 1866; *Illinois State Journal*, Aug. 19, 1867
	Olympic Base Ball Club—1866 (merged with Capitals in September 1866)	*Illinois State Register*, May 17, 1866
	Eagle Base Ball Club (Junior)—1866	*Illinois State Register*, May 28, 1866
	Star Base Ball Club (Junior)—1866	*Illinois State Register*, June 1, 1866
	Mystic Base Ball Club—1866	*Illinois State Register*, June 2, 1866
	National Base Ball Club—1866	*Illinois State Journal*, July 19, 1866
	Pioneer Fire Company Base Ball Club—1866	*Illinois State Journal*, July 3, 1866
	Liberty Base Ball Club (Junior)—1866, 1869	*Illinois State Register*, July 11, 1866; *Jacksonville Journal*, July 31, 1869
	Veteran Base Ball Club (Muffin)—1866	*Illinois State Journal*, Aug. 21, 1866
	Dexter Base Ball Club (Black)—1867, 1870	*Rock Island Argus*, Aug. 13, 1867; *Illinois State Register*, Aug. 2, 1870

Town	Team(s)	Source
	Shawnee Base Ball Club (Junior)—1867	*Illinois State Journal*, July 2, 1867
	Grant Base Ball Club (Junior)—1867	*Illinois State Journal*, July 2, 1867
	Active Base Ball Club—1867	*Illinois State Journal*, July 31, 1867
	Empire Base Ball Club—1867	*Illinois State Journal*, July 16, 1867
	Lone Star Base Ball Club (Junior)—1867	*Illinois State Register*, July 11, 1867
	Athletic Base Ball Club-1867	*Illinois State Journal*, July 27, 1867
	Athlete Base Ball Club—1869	*Carlinville Democrat*, July 29, 1869
	Eckford Base Ball Club—1869	*Quincy Whig and Republican*, July 10, 1869
Staunton	unnamed club—1869	*Litchfield Union Monitor*, July 29, 1869
Sterling	Sterling (or Monitor) Base Ball Club—1866, 1867, 1870	*Sterling Gazette*, Sept. 22, 1866, June 8, 1867; *Chicago Tribune*, Aug. 21, 1870
	Eagle Base Ball Club (Junior)—1867	*Sterling Gazette*, July 20, 1867
Stillman Valley	Plow Boys Base Ball Club—1870	*Ogle County Reporter*, July 7, 1870
Sugar Creek	Independent Base Ball Club—1869	*Carlyle Constitution and Union*, Aug. 10, 1869
Summerfield	St. Clair Base Ball Club—1869	*Carlyle Constitution and Union*, Aug. 3, 1869
Sycamore	Crescent Base Ball Club—1867, 1868	*Sycamore True Republican*, Apr. 15, 1868; *Rockford Republic*, June 7, 1922; https://protoball.org/IL
Taylorville	unnamed club—1867	*Pana Gazette*, Sept. 21, 1867
Tennessee	Clipper Base Ball Club—1869	*Macomb Journal*, July 16, 1869
Thomson	Thomson Base Ball Club—1867	*Sterling Gazette*, June 22, 1867
Tiskilwa	Valley Base Ball Club—1867	*Bureau County Republican*, Sept. 5, 1867
Toulon	Mollie Starks Base Ball Club—1868, 1869	*Peoria Transcript*, Aug. 26, 1868; *Stark County News*, Oct. 22, 1869
	Greenhorn Base Ball Club—1869	*Stark County News*, Oct. 15, 1869
	Old Fogy Base Ball Club—1869	*Stark County News*, Oct. 15, 1869
	Reckless Base Ball Club (Junior)—1870	*Stark County News*, Aug. 20, 1870
Trenton	Athletic Base Ball Club—1868, 1869, 1870	*Greenville Advocate*, July 3, 1868, July 16, 1869; *Carlyle Union Banner*, Apr. 28, 1870
Union	Union Base Ball Club—1868	https://protoball.org/IL

Town	Team(s)	Source
Urbana	Urbana Base Ball Club—1867	https://protoball.org/IL
	Continental Base Ball Club—1868	*Champaign Union and Gazette*, June 3, 1868
	Pioneer Base Ball Club—1868	*Champaign Union and Gazette*, July 15, 1868
Utica	Grant Base Ball Club—1868	https://protoball.org/IL
Vandalia	Active Base Ball Club—1867	*Pana Gazette*, Sept. 14, 1867
	Champion Base Ball Club—1867	*Pana Gazette*, Sept. 14, 1867
	Old Capitol Base Ball Club—1869	*Greenville Advocate*, May 21, 1868
Vermont	Vermont Base Ball Club—1868	*Macomb Eagle*, Aug. 8, 1868
	Dashaway Base Ball Club—1868	https://protoball.org/IL
Virginia	Virginia Base Ball Club—1869	*Petersburg Democrat*, Sept. 11, 1869
Walshville	unnamed club—1869	*Litchfield Union Monitor*, July 29, 1869
Warren	Warren Base Ball Club—1867	*Warren Sentinel*, May 2, 1867
	Prairie City Base Ball Club—1870	*Lee County Journal*, July 7, 1870
Warsaw	Mutual Base Ball Cub—1867, 1868	*Warsaw Bulletin*, Sept. 6, 1867, July 3, 1868
	Neptune Base Ball Club—1867	*Warsaw Bulletin*, Sept. 6, 1867
	Young America Base Ball Club (Junior)—1868	*Warsaw Bulletin*, Apr. 24, 1868
	Mutual Base Ball Club (Junior)—1868, 1869	*Quincy Herald*, Aug. 22, 1868, Aug. 15, 1869
	Rounders Base Ball Club—1869	*Warsaw Bulletin*, Sept. 17, 1869
Waterloo	Monroe Star Base Ball Club—1869	https://protoball.org/IL
Watseka	Watseka Base Ball Club—1867	*Iroquois Republican*, Aug. 14, 1867
	Comet Base Ball Club—1868	*Grand Prairie Review*, June 27, 1868
Waukegan	Lake Shore Base Ball Club—1867	*Waukegan Gazette*, May 25, 1867
	Waukegan Base Ball Club—1867	*Waukegan Gazette*, May 25, 1867
	Dexter Base Ball Club—1867	*Waukegan Gazette*, June 15, 1867
	Acme Base Ball Club—1867	*Waukegan Gazette*, June 22, 1867
	Star Base Ball Club—1867	*Waukegan Gazette*, June 22, 1867
Wayne	Dexter Base Ball Club—1867	https://protoball.org/IL
Webster	Yellow Jacket Base Ball Club Junior—1868	*Carthage Gazette*, Aug. 20, 1868
Wenona	Wenona Base Ball Club—1867	*Marshall County Republican*, Sept. 5, 1867
	Henry Marshall Base Ball Club—1867	*Marshall County Republican*, Aug. 1, 1867

Town	Team(s)	Source
Westfield	Star Base Ball Club—1868	*Marshall Messenger*, Oct. 1, 1868
Wheaton	Athletic Base Ball Club—1867	*Aurora Beacon*, July 25, 1867
	Schoolboy Base Ball Club—1869	*Aurora Beacon*, June 10, 1869
Wilmington	Tempest Club—1867	*Kankakee Gazette*, Nov. 14, 1867
Winchester	Central Base Ball Club—1867	*Jacksonville Journal*, Aug. 6, 1867
Winnebago	Farmers Base Ball Club—1866	*Freeport Bulletin*, Oct. 19, 1866
	Bummers Base Ball Club—1866	*Rockford Republic*, Apr. 8, 1922
	Winnebago Base Ball Club—1867	*Ogle County Reporter*, June 27, 1867
Woodstock	Falstaff Base Ball Club—1867	https://protoball.org/IL
	Woodstock Base Ball Club—1867	*Woodstock Sentinel*, May 30, 1867
Wyanet	Star Base Ball Club—1867	*Bureau County Republican*, July 12, 1867
	Tempest Base Ball Club—1867	*Kankakee Gazette*, Nov. 14, 1867
Yorkville	Yorkville Base Ball Cub—1867	*Aurora Beacon*, Aug. 22, 1867
Young America (now Kirkwood)	Dexter Base Ball Club—1867	*Monmouth Atlas*, Aug. 30, 1867
	Star Base Ball Club (Junior)—1870	*Monmouth Review*, Oct. 21, 1870

BLOOMINGTON'S FIFTH WARD SCHOOL-GROUNDS NEIGHBORHOOD

Residents of the Fifth Ward School-grounds neighborhood, with occupations and addresses:

Thomas A. Adams, carpenter, 908 N. Lee
T. R. Ambrose, machinist, 802 N. Oak
Christopher Baneke, no occupation listed, 806 N. Oak
George Brown, fireman, 912 N. Lee
Richard Carle, machinist, 912 N. Lee
Duncan Carmichael, carpenter, 916 N. Oak
John Copley, machinist, 802 N. Oak
John Cubs, machinist, 912 N. Lee
Joseph Donovan, laborer, 901 N. Oak
James Duffey II, no occupation listed, 809 N. Lee
Eli Dunn, carpenter, 912 N. Lee
Daniel Dye, carpenter, 802 N. Oak
A. F. Eggelston, machinist, 916 N. Lee
O. Gassett, carpenter, 914 N. Oak
George Gorhan, engineer, 914 N. Oak
Joseph Hackett, fireman, 802 N. Oak
A. M. Hannaford, fireman, 812 N. Oak
John Hayes, blacksmith, 1106 N. Lee
Henry Hullison, machinist, 802 N. Oak
Andrew Johnson, brakeman, 906 N. Oak
J. L. Kenyon, Kenyon & Sons (grocer), 1181 N. West
Thomas Kigher, engineer, 911 N. Oak

John Kirby, blacksmith, 908 N. Oak
William Lapton, machinist, 912 N. Lee
Burton Lyons, brakeman, 906 N. Oak
John Major, druggist, 901 N. West
David Mann, mechanic, 912 N. Oak
William McClure, carpenter, 802 N. Lee
David McGill, carpenter, 807 N. Lee
C. McGrew, patent rights dealer, 1216 N. Lee
Robert S. McIntyre, county clerk, 612 N. Lee
Henry McKoon, molder, 802 N. Oak
March McLockland, miner, 802 N. Oak
George R. Means, lumberman, 1105 N. Oak
John O'Neil, laborer, 1203 N. Oak
C. W. Parke, machinist, corner of West and Chestnut
Alpheus Pike, lumber dealer, 303 W. Chestnut
Edward M. Pike, sheriff, 303 W. Chestnut
H. W. Pike, stock dealer, 303 W. Chestnut
Noah H. Pike, lumber dealer, 303 W. Chestnut
L. C. Read, carpenter, 812 N. Lee
O. T. Reeves, real estate agent, 316 W. Chestnut
Hamilton Ripley, brakeman, 812 N. Oak
___ Sanford, planer, 802 N. Oak (first name not given)
John C. Schutte, machinist, 1207 N. Oak
___ Scott, carpenter, 802 N. Oak (first name not given)
John Seller, machinist, 802 N. Oak St.
John Settler, engineer, 910 N. Oak
Jeremiah Shaw, fireman, 906 N. Oak
Thomas J. Shelbourne, engineer, 916 N. Oak
Michael Shonnessy, laborer, 807 N. West
Joseph Shough, carpenter, 808 N. Oak
Miss Spaine, teacher, 810 N. Lee
Henry Speen, machinist, 907 N. Oak
W. H. Stennett, Dunn and Stennett (homeopathic physician), 807 N. West
James Sullivan, laborer, 912 N. Lee
Patrick Sullivan, engine driver, 814 N. Oak

Source: *Holland's Bloomington City Directory—1868–69* (Chicago: Western, 1869).

ILLINOIS BASEBALL PLAYERS, BY TOWN AND TEAM, 1865-70

The players listed in this appendix are those who appeared in reports of games or in news stories that contained club rosters. This appendix is incomplete, as it does not list players on the Forest City Club of Rockford and the Excelsior Chicago Club, who are listed in other publications. Occupations were determined from city directories (see the Bibliography), US census tables, and news reports.

Research by Peter Morris has produced information on several players on Illinois clubs during this era who are not listed here, including the Excelsiors of Chicago, the Byron Base Ball Club, the Forest City Club of Rockford, and the Pecatonica Base Ball Club. See Morris et al., eds., *Base Ball Pioneers*: for the Excelsiors, see 217–20; for the Byron Club, see 221–23; for Rockford's Forest City Club, see 229–34; and for Pecatonica, see 237–39.

Town & Team	Player	Occupation
Alton		
Shurtleff Collegiate Base Ball Club[1]	Dubois, F. T.	student
	Dubois, J. K.	student
	Starne, Charles A. (Alex)	student
Bloomington		
Bloomington Base Ball Club[2]	Cheney, Lee	clerk
	Ewing, Henry A.	professional
	Hardacre, George W.	professional

Town & Team	Player	Occupation
	Keenan, Patrick J.[3]	unknown
	Lackey, George W.	business owner
	McCart, Robert W.	professional
	Moore, James P.	business owner
	Roe, Charters S.	clerk
	Rex, George	business owner
	Rood, E. H.	business owner[4]
	Thomas, Lewis B.	business owner
Independent Base Ball Club (African American)[5]	Brown, George	unknown[6]
	Downs, David	no occupation
	Dudley, Clinton	unknown
	Franklin, William	servant
	Holley (Holly), James	bookbinder
	Holley, Marion	pressman
	Thomas, Frank	teamster
	Witteor (Victor), James	barber
Cairo		
Caterpillar Base Ball Club[7]	Abell, Joseph	business owner
	Clancy, John	unknown
	Dunning, Dr. C. W.	doctor
	Halliday, S. B.	business owner
	Sweeney, Antony	business owner
	Whitaker, A. R.	business owner
	Williams, Isaac "Ike"	business owner
Clodhopper Base Ball Club[8]	Dunning, M. L.	clerk
	Hall, C. R.	deputy collector and US commissioner
	Munn, J. M.	assistant postmaster
	Reynolds, Joseph W.[9]	barkeeper
	Van Velsor, Henry	clerk
Eclipse Base Ball Club[10]	Arrick, James C.[11]	clerk
Egyptian Base Ball Club[12]	Gossman, John H.C[13]	barkeeper
	Hely, John P.	civil engineer
	Hilt, Louis	barber
	Sweeney, Anthony	clerk
	Young, Martin V.	insurance agent

Town & Team	Player	Occupation
Grasshopper Base Ball Club[14]	Bross, F.	police magistrate
	Cushing, George T.	unknown
	Fitzgerald, Pat	saloon and restaurant worker
	Harrell, Moses B.	newspaper editor
	Hunsaker, Nicholas	police magistrate
	McKenzie, Joseph	lumber dealer
	Oberly, John H.	newspaper owner and editor
	Schutter, William H.	business owner
	Smyth, Bernard	business owner
	Smyth, Robert	business owner
	Wilson, Samuel[15]	unknown
Magneta Base Ball Club[16]	De Vaus, John	barkeeper
	Devere, John	billiard tender
	Fretty, Joseph	barkeeper
	Veirun, Joseph	clerk
Independent Base Ball Club[17]	Kerney, W. B.	business owner
	Munn, Benjamin M.	attorney
	Munn, Daniel W.	professional and state senator
	Munn, James W.	assistant postmaster[18]
	Wilcox, Jewett	business owner
Podanger Base Ball Club[19]	Cunningham, R. A.	clerk
	Grear, J. B.	clerk
	Pilcher, William	business owner
	Saup, Peter	clerk
	Spaulding, H. E.	postal clerk[20]
	White, Captain J. C.	assistant US assessor
Centralia		
Liberty Base Ball Club[21]	Condit, Henry[22]	unknown
	Condit, Zack	business owner
	Hay, Bill[23]	unknown
	Fletcher, Frank[24]	unknown
	Johnson, Bill[25]	unknown
	Johnson, Free[26]	unknown
Egyptian Base Ball Club[27]	Cunningham, James	business owner
	Cunningham, James T.	unknown
	Cunningham, Tom[28]	town constable

Town & Team	Player	Occupation
	Nelson, Richard	professional
	Pittenger, George L.	grocer
	Van Cleve, Horace	clerk
	Welden, Golden	engineer
	White, William H. "Billy"	restauranteur
	Wilson, James M.	railroad section hand
Union Base Ball Club[29]	Randall, A. J.	insurance agent
Champaign		
Empire Base Ball Club (originally Champaign Base Ball Club)[30]	Arnold, Grant	business owner
	Bailey, D. (Dave) [31]	uncertain
	Conklin, Joe E.	business owner
	Eppstein, Max[32]	business owner
	Gilen, John	farmer
	Hill, J. W.[33]	census taker
	Houston, P. C.	clerk
	Jefferson (first name unknown)[34]	uncertain
	Pierce (first name unknown)[35]	unknown
	Pollock, J. W.	grocer
	Scott (first name unknown)[36]	ticket agent
	Seger, Ed T.	clerk
	Tulleys, L.	attorney
Prairie Base Ball Club[37]	Guy, H. G.	clerk
	Maxwell, W. S.	business owner
	Scroggs, George	newspaper publisher
	Van Horn, P.	unknown
Heavyweight Base Ball Club[38]	Dallenbaugh, J.	butcher
Danville		
Vermilion Base Ball Club, 1866, 1867[39]	J. G. Kingsbury	editor
	C. G. Harris	occupation unknown
	D. A. Childs	occupation unknown
	Horace H. Redford	occupation unknown

Town & Team	Player	Occupation
Decatur		
Antelope Base Ball Club[40]	Keck, Adam[41]	tavern owner
	Libby, G. L.	physician
McPherson Base Ball Club[42]	Allison, C. M.	clerk
	Archer, Isaac T.[43]	painter
	Bramble, Ed[44]	clerk
	Gill, Levi (Lee)[45]	grocer
	Hinkle, Thomas	uncertain
	Johns, W. C.[46]	student
	Montgomery, R. R. (Robert)	insurance agent
Ugly Plug Base Ball Club[47]	Kaufman, Mathias	student
Earlville		
Earlville Base Ball Club[48]	Buckingham, John	wagonmaker's apprentice
	Signor, George	unknown
	Snow, Ed	laborer
Galesburg		
College City Base Ball Club[49]	Burt, Theodore A.	railroad engineer
	Knowles, H. (Howard)	student
	Leeper, Charles	unknown
	O'Neil, Frank	railroad brakeman
	Reed, Jud	student
	Sheik, Charles	railroad conductor
	Woods, William	clerk
Knox Base Ball Club[50]	Castle, A. A.	unknown
	Hayner, H. C.	clerk
Jacksonville		
Hardin Base Ball Club[51]	Barr, S. O.	salesman
	Case, General H.	attorney
	Dunlap, William	merchant
	Greenleaf, E. L.	grocer
	Ironmonger, J. J.	unknown
	King, John W.[52]	unknown
	Marsh, L. N.	billiard hall worker
	McConnel, George M.[53]	clerk
	Mitchell, J. M.	occupation unknown

Town & Team	Player	Occupation
	Smith, W. H.	merchant
	Stevenson, R. E.	perfume merchant
Hercules Base Ball Club[54]	Bailey, G. W.	college professor
	Brown, A. (Abel)	occupation unknown
	Green, O. S.	stock dealer
Champion (later Union) Base Ball Club[55]	King, Jonathan	occupation unknown
	Smith, D. B.	clerk
	Smith, W. H.	student
	Ten Eyck, Charles H. [56]	express company agent
Moline		
Moline Base Ball Club[57]	Kuncknel, John	business owner
	Sayles, Henry G.	clerk
	Velie, S. H. [58]	occupation unknown
Young America Base Ball Club[59]	Cleland, George	molder
	Gould, Frank	unknown
	Gould, Fred	unknown
Monmouth		
Classic Base Ball Club[60]	George Mitchell	foreman
	Stewart, W. K.	student, attorney
	Templeton, David C.	school principal, traveling agent
Clipper Base Ball Club[61]	Leeper, Jeremiah	blacksmith
Mount Vernon		
Star Base Ball Club[62]	Bogan, Joseph L.	unknown
Ottawa		
Avordupois [sic; likely also known as "Hefty"] Base Ball Club[63]	Caton, John D.[64]	business owner
	Dean, Josiah W.	livery stable worker
	DeLano, Lucien B.	master mason
	Dewey, E. W.	attorney
	Godfrey, Dr. H. M.	physician
	Hunsberger, S. H.	implement dealer
	Parry (Parrey), Samuel	brick mason
	Terry, Rev. Patrick	pastor

Town & Team	Player	Occupation
OK Base Ball Club[65]	McKinley (McKinlay), Thomas[66]	attorney
	Newkirk, George	painter
	Phelps, Thomas W.	bookkeeper
Shabbona Base Ball Club[67]	Blake, G. W.	schoolteacher, attorney, and politician
	Hall, P. A.	clerk
	Perkins, L.	dry goods clerk
	Smith, E. H.	cigar manufacturing worker
	Stone, J. D.	shoemaker
	Withrow, J. J.	grain buyer
	Wood, A. L.	bookkeeper
Pana		
Excelsior Base Ball Club[68]	McMillen, A. C.	attorney
	McQuigg, J. C.	professional
	Owen, Erastus	merchant
	Paddock, O. H.[69]	agricultural implement and coal dealer
Philo		
Frontier Base Ball Club[70]	Daugherty (Dougherty), John	farmer
	Moore, John	farmer
	Radebaugh, John	farmer
	Radebaugh, Peter	farmer
Quincy		
Quincy Base Ball Club (Occidental Senior Base Ball Club)[71]	Adams, James E.	forwarding clerk
	Bradley, Frank	cashier
	Bull, C.H.	bank cashier
	Bushnell, W.B.	occupation unknown
	Castle, A. (Alfred L.)	clerk
	Castle, C. (Chauncy)	clerk
	Castle, S. (Jay Seymour)	clerk
	Grubb, A. O. (Armistead)	clerk
	Osborn, E. H. (Edward Halsey)	clerk
	Schermerhorn, Frank	businessperson
	Selleck, E. C.	clerk
	Wood, John Jr.[72]	businessperson

Town & Team	Player	Occupation
Rantoul		
Rantoul Base Ball Cub[73]	Bannister, J.	farmer
	Brown, John	laborer
	Phillips, A.B.	farmer
Rock Island		
Lively Turtles Base Ball Club[74]	Andrews, Charles W.	tanner
	Buford, James	bank cashier
	Buford, Louis M.	manufacturer
	Burwell, L. C.	business owner
	Copp, James M.	postmaster and livery stable owner
	Fleming, J. E.	telegraph operator
	Gregg, Joseph K.	clerk
	Jackson, J.B.	bookkeeper
	Jones, Milton[75]	occupation unknown
	Kirkpatrick, I.N.	printer
	Lamont, George	meat market owner
Quicksteps Base Ball Club[76]	Bell, Charlie[77]	unknown
	Dart, Stuart[78]	grocery clerk
	Gregg, Spencer	occupation unknown
Springfield		
Athletic Base Ball Club[79]	Burch, R. S.	clerk
	Conkling, James	grocery clerk
	Hickox, Silas W.	miller
	Ives, J. G. Jr.	business owner
	Starne, Maurice	law student
Capital Base Ball Club[80]	Cook, Hamilton F.	salesperson
	Mather, T. C.	attorney
	Pearson, R. N.	government clerk
	Roberts, Edward	government clerk
	Seaman, Charles H.	clerk
	Strickland, Edward P.	captain, clerk?
	Whittemore, F. K.	government clerk
Lone Star Base Ball Club[81]	Kane (Kain), C. P	unknown

NOTES

Prologue

1. Alexis de Tocqueville, *Democracy in America*, vols. 1 and 2, ed. J. P. Mayer, trans. George Lawrence (New York: Harper and Row, 1988), 513.

2. *Quincy Herald*, October 12, 1869, October 14, 1869.

3. For a brief discussion of the Cincinnati club and its impact, see Harold Seymour, *Baseball: The Early Years* (New York: Oxford University Press, 1960), 56–58. (Although she did not get credit at the time, the late Seymour's wife, Dorothy Zander Seymour, is generally acknowledged as coauthor of the book.) A fictional account of the Red Stocking's 1869 season and national tour is in Darryl Brock, *If I Never Get Back: A Novel* (Frog Books, 2007).

4. "Local Matters," *Decatur Magnet*, November 6, 1868.

5. *Quincy Herald*, July 12, 1866, July 9, 1868, July 10, 1868.

6. *Quincy Herald*, September 13, 1868.

7. *Quincy Herald*, June 4, 1869.

8. *Quincy Herald*, July 6, 1869, and July 7, 1869.

9. *Quincy Whig and Republican*, August 30, 1869; Alstyne's Prairie was located near the intersection of Vine and College streets (Carl Landrum, ed., *Quincy: A Pictorial History* (St. Louis: G. Gradley, 1990), 135. It was apparently a quarter section of land not particularly attractive, referred to as "an eye-sore" in *Quincy Herald*, April 17, 1869.

10. The $5,314.50 figure is based on the purchasing power of a US dollar according to the Consumer Price Index; for instance, what $1 would buy in 1869 (Consumer Price Index Inflation Calculator, "$250 in 1869 Is Worth $5,314.50 Today," https://www.in2013dollars.com/us/inflation/1869?amount=250.

11. *Quincy Herald*, September 23, 1869, October 8, 1869, October 9, 1869; for notice of the game outside Quincy, see *Galesburg Free Press*, October 8, 1869, and *Carthage Gazette*, September 30, 1869, and October 21, 1869.

12. *Quincy Herald*, October 14, 1869. An account in the *Quincy Whig and Republican*, October 14, 1869, contains less detail but the same essentials.

13. A match between the Occidental Junior and Senior clubs was announced for November 4, 1869, but it was rained out. There are no accounts in subsequent newspapers that the game was ever played or that the Occidental Seniors turned out for the 1870 season (*Quincy Herald*, November 3, 1869, and November 5, 1869).

14. The figures for organized clubs are taken from two calculations. First, the author's extensive search through extant Illinois newspapers during the period which yield 536 clubs between 1865 and 1869 and another 43 in 1870. The Protoball website (http://protoball.org/IL) finds slightly more than 150 teams during the first period and an additional 337 in 1870. The total of 1,067 organized clubs between 1865 and 1870 is achieved by combining the two lists. The Protoball list appears to be based on searches of online newspaper files, a source which at the time of this writing leaves out significant areas of the state. Another note about the final figures: it is highly likely that there were even more clubs during this time. Clubs are "lost" because there were either no surviving newspaper issues on film from that time or their activities were not covered or mentioned by surviving papers. A large portion of southern Illinois from the Indiana border to the center of the state falls into the latter category. Additionally, the "known" list may grow as researchers find clubs missed in searches by the author and Protoball contributors.

15. Peter Morris, *But Didn't We Have Fun? An Informal History of Baseball's Pioneer Era, 1843–1870* (Chicago: Ivan R. Dee, 2008), 64–66.

16. John Thorn, *Baseball in the Garden of Eden: The Secret History of the Early Game* (New York: Simon and Schuster, 2011), is the best source for the evolution of the game. The ancient roots of ball-and-bat games are covered in David Block, *Baseball before We Knew It: A Search for the Roots of the Game* (Lincoln: University of Nebraska Press, 2005), especially the summary on 154–62. Warren Goldstein addresses the wildfire-like growth of the game outside the New York area in his book *Playing for Keeps: A History of Early Baseball*, 20th Anniversary Edition (Ithaca, NY: Cornell University Press, 2009. For early Illinois teams, see the Protoball website, http://protoball.org/IL.

17. For Alton clubs, see *Porter's Spirit of the Times*, July 17, 1858, 309; for Freeport, see *Freeport Bulletin*, May 24, 1866. The *Freeport Bulletin* article notes that "for the last four or five years our city has been noted for the number and excellence of its ball clubs and ball players." For the Freeport Empire vs. St. Louis Empire game's significance, see Jeffrey Kittle, "Empires," in *Base Ball Pioneers, 1850–1870: The Clubs and Players Who Spread the Sport Nationwide*, ed. Peter Morris, William J. Ryczek, Jan Finkel, Leonard Levin, and Richard Malatzky (Jefferson, NC: McFarland, 2012), 300.

18. Alexis de Tocqueville, *Democracy in America*, ed. J. P. Mayer, trans. George Lawrence (New York: Harper and Row, 1988). De Tocqueville's original two volumes were published in 1835 and 1840, respectively.

19. Information on the spread of baseball in the Midwest and Illinois can be found

in James M. Egan Jr., *Baseball on the Western Reserve: The Early Game in Cleveland and Northeast Ohio, Year by Year and Town by Town* (Jefferson, NC: McFarland, 2008), quote on 1; Mark E. Eberle, *Kansas Baseball, 1868–1941* (Lawrence: University Press of Kansas, 2017). In his prologue, Eberle describes his book as a result of his search for old ballparks and playing fields in Kansas and, once much of that information was in hand, of a desire for "additional context" (xxii). See also John Liepa, "Baseball Mania Strikes Iowa," *Iowa Heritage* 87, no. 1 (Spring 2006), 3–6; Peter Morris, *Baseball Fever: Early Baseball in Michigan* (Ann Arbor: University of Michigan Press, 2003), quote on 4. Morris is a prolific and skilled historian of early baseball in the United States. See especially his *But Didn't We Have Fun?* For clubs in Byron, Chicago, Pecatonica, and Rockford during the 1865–70 era, see Morris et al., *Base Ball Pioneers.* Especially relevant are Morris's chapters "Excelsiors of Chicago, Prewar," 206–9; "Excelsiors of Chicago, Postwar," 210–20; "Byron (Illinois) Base Ball Club," 221–23; "Forest City Club of Rockford," 224–33; and "Pecatonica Base Ball Club," 235–38. For Chicago baseball during this period, see Stephen Freedman, "The Baseball Fad in Chicago, 1865–1870: An Exploration of the Role of Sport in the Nineteenth Century City, " *Journal of Sports History* 5, no. 2 (Summer 1978): 42–64; and Robert Pruter, "Youth Baseball in Chicago, 1868–1890: Not Always Sand Lot Ball," *Journal of Sports History* 26, no. 1 (Spring 1999): 1–28. The best, and perhaps only, history of a community's involvement with baseball during the early period is Steve Loomis, "Egyptian Summer," an unpublished manuscript in the Centralia Area Historical Museum, Centralia, Illinois.

20. John Keiser, *Building for the Centuries: Illinois 1865 to 1898*, vol. 4, *The Sesquicentennial History of Illinois* (Urbana: University of Illinois Press, 1977), xii, xiii, 2.

21. For Tom's eulogy, see *Quincy Whig and Republican*, August 16, 1869. Dogs running at large was a problem throughout the state. Nearly every surviving newspaper examined contained stories and warnings about the problem. For cows in the streets and public places, see for example, *Jacksonville Journal*, August 28, 1868, and *Jacksonville Weekly Sentinel*, June 13, 1867. For Danville's hog stampede, see *Danville Commercial*, December 24, 1868. Like dogs, hogs were complained of frequently in newsprint though not as consistently as stray dogs: *Belleville Advocate*, October 4, 1867, and *Joliet Signal*, April 16, 1867. For description of Frank Douglas, the prostitute, sometimes called "Frankie," see *Cairo Democrat*, May 30, 1866. And for bear steaks, see *Cairo Democrat*, October 26, 1866.

First Inning. Baseball Fever and Pioneers

1. *Pike County Democrat* (Pittsfield, Illinois), September 6, 1866.

2. Ibid. For Jesse K. Dubois, see "Biography—Dubois File," Sangamon Valley Collection, Lincoln Library, Springfield, Illinois [hereafter, Sangamon Collection]; and Joseph Wallace, *Past and Present of the City of Springfield and Sangamon County* (Chicago: S. J. Clarke, 1904), 57–58. For Capital Street Railway, see "Transportation History," *Illinois State Journal-Register*, January 26, 1947, and "Street Car History," *Illi-*

nois State Journal, November 8, 1931, both clippings in "Street Railroads—Springfield," Sangamon Collection. For Alexander Starne, see Interstate Publishing Company, *History of Sangamon County* (Chicago: Interstate, 1881), 719; for Milton Hay, see Wallace, *Past and Present*, 47; for Ozias Mather Hatch, see Wallace, *Past and Present*, 1477.

3. *Chicago Tribune*, August 19, 1867; *Peoria Transcript*, August 21, 1866; *Peoria National Democrat*, June 15, 1866; *Peoria Transcript*, September 27, 1866; "Stickler" was a Peoria bookseller and stationer, see *Peoria Transcript*, September 27, 1866; *Quincy Herald*, July 26, 1866; *Sterling Gazette*, Juley 28, 1866; *Cairo Democrat*, October 13, 1866.

4. *Alton Weekly Telegraph*, October 4, 1867; *Illinois State Journal*, March 2, 1867; *Lee County Journal*, April 6, 1867; *Bureau County Republican* (Princeton), July 4, 1867; *Lee County Journal*, June 1, 1867.

5. *Pana Gazette*, July 13, 1867; *Iroquois Republican* (Watseka), August 14, 1867; *Belleville Advocate*, August 9, 1867; *Decatur Republican*, September 5, 1867; *Woodstock Sentinel*, August 5, 1869.

6. *Galena Gazette*, October 10, 1865; *Belleville Advocate*, November 15, 1867; *Illinois State Journal*, August 24, 1867.

7. *Warsaw Bulletin*, October 4, 1867.

8. For examples of baseball's perceived importance, see the *New York Sun* quoted in the *Illinois State Journal*, September 19, 1867; Rev. C. H. Everett's sermon in praise of the game in Seymour and Seymour, *Baseball*, 45; and the *Washington Chronicle* quoted in the *Illinois State Journal*, April 2, 1867.

9. *Chicago Times*, December 20, 1866, quoted in Freedman, "Baseball Fad," 44. See also *Chicago Tribune*, July 26, 1867.

10. *Peoria National Democrat*, June 3, 1866; "W. K. Beans—School Column," *Aurora Beacon*, October 31, 1867.

11. *Sterling Gazette*, November 3, 1866. See also *Champaign Union and Gazette*, March 21, 1867.

12. *Illinois State Journal*, June 2, 1866, June 16, 1866; *Illinois State Register*, July 10, 1866; *Jacksonville Journal*, April 18, 1866; *Cairo Democrat*, November 3, 1866. For a baseball club that was drawing some newspaper interest, see *Galena Gazette*, May 13, 1866, August 21, 1866, September 4, 1866, October 2, 1866. George B. Kirsch, who studied cricket in the United States in the mid-nineteenth century, notes it "remained distinctly marginal to the recreational life of the vast majority of Americans." Cricket's lengthy games and slow pace of play reduced its allure in a bustling US society. Attempts to "Americanize" the game by picking up the pace of play and other alterations were resisted by English immigrants, who controlled the game. Economic reasons also played a role. Cricket "required more care for its grounds and was more expensive to play." Americans also felt alienated by the British associations of the game (George B. Kirsch, *Baseball and Cricket: The Creation of American Team Sports, 1838–72* [Urbana: University of Illinois Press, 2007], 262, 106–7).

13. *Jacksonville Weekly Sentinel*, July 26, 1866; *Carlyle Constitution and Union*, April 27, 1869; *Danville Times*, April 14, 1869; *Bureau County Patriot* (Princeton), June 4, 1867; *Peoria National Democrat*, August 8, 1867; *Peoria Transcript*, August 25, 1866; *Bureau County Patriot* (Princeton), July 23, 1867.

14. *Du Quoin Tribune and Recorder*, March 13, 1869; *Lincoln Herald*, March 25, 1869; *Centralia Democrat*, April 1, 1869; *Litchfield Union and Monitor*, April 1, 1869; *Peoria Transcript*, April 3, 1869; *Galena Gazette*, May 18, 1869; *Macomb Journal*, July 2, 1869; *Peoria Transcript*, April 9, 1869; *Ottawa Free Trader*, April 10, 1869; *Rock Island Argus*, May 12, 1869; *Sterling Gazette*, September 21, 1869; *Carthage Gazette*, May 13, 1869; *Chebanse Herald*, June 4, 1869; *Peoria Transcript*, August 20, 1869; *Bureau County Republican* (Princeton), June 17, 1869.

15. *Decatur Review*, June 28, 1914; also quoted in Morris, *But Didn't We Have Fun?*, 42; Johns was credited as the father of the game in Decatur in *Decatur Herald*, June 13, 1909. For the team name, see Michael Benson, *Ballparks of North America* (Jefferson, NC: McFarland, 1989), 130.

16. For a history of the Johns family and Lincoln connection, see Jane Johns, *Personal Recollections of Early Decatur, Abraham Lincoln, Richard Oglesby and the Civil War*, ed. Howard C. Schaub (Decatur, IL: Stephen Decatur Chapter, National Society Daughters of the American Revolution, 1912), 11–13, 21, 59, 82, 95; *Decatur Review*, October 30, 1904; "Judge W. C. Johns," *Journal of the Illinois State Historical Society* 7, no. 2 (July 1914): 130–35. For Corwin's speech on the militia general, see Thomas Corwin, "Speech of Mr. Thomas Corwin of Ohio in Reply to General Crary's Attack on General Harrison, Delivered in the House of Representatives, February 14, 1840" (Washington: Gales and Seaton, 1840), 1–16, quotes on p. 6; also see Peter Morris, "Corwin Johns," *Society for American Baseball Research*, http://sabr.org/bioproi/person/c48808d8.

17. *Decatur Herald*, June 13, 1909.

18. Ibid.

19. "Out Door Sports and Base Ball," *Peoria National Democrat*, June 15, 1866, (quote), June 6, 1866, July 17, 1866, July 18, 1866.

20. *Peoria National Democrat*, August 3, 1866, and August 4, 1866.

21. *Peoria National Democrat*, September 1, 1866; August 14, 1866; *Peoria Transcript*, August 14, 1866, August 24, 1866.

22. *Peoria Transcript*, November 1, 1866, September 10, 1866.

23. *Peoria National Democrat*, June 15, 1866.

24. *Cairo Democrat*, August 1, 1866; *Edwards' City Directory to the City of Cairo for 1868* (St. Louis: Edwards, 1868), 86.

25. *Cairo Democrat*, July 31, 1866; August 1, 1866. For Silver as "eloquent auctioneer," see *Cairo Democrat*, October 14, 1866; for his enterprises, *Cairo Democrat*, September 18, 1866, November 19, 1865; for Silver as candidate for local office, *Cairo Democrat*, August 26, 1866; October 30, 1866; for his theatrical venture, *Cairo Democrat*, October 23, 1866; for his fishing trip, *Cairo Democrat*, June 1, 1866.

26. Peter Morris, "Forest City Club of Rockford," in Morris et al., eds., *Base Ball Pioneers*, 224–35, 224, 233; "Last Rites for Hiram Waldo," *Chicago Tribune*, April 29, 1912. Also see Horace Buker, Cradle of Baseball series, *Rockford Republic*, March 15, 1922. Buker's series in the *Rockford Republic* extended for several months in 1922.

27. *Bloomington Pantagraph*, June 20, 1857; October 20, 1857. See also "Captain George W. Lackey," *Chicago Inter Ocean*, March 8, 1886.

28. Lackey's service was mentioned in his obituary, *Chicago Inter Ocean*, March 8, 1886. For brief histories of the 68th and 145th Illinois Volunteer Infantries, see *Illinois in the Civil War*, https://civilwar.illinoisgenweb.org/history/068.html, and https://civilwar.illinoisgenweb.org/history/145.html. For Zouave units in the Civil War, see *Regiments of the Civil War*, https://www.civilwar.org/learn/articles/regiments-civil-war. Brent Nosworthy in *The Bloody Crucible of Courage: Fighting Methods and Combat Experience of the Civil War* (New York: Carroll and Graf, 2003), 98–101, writes that the French Zouave units "captured the imagination of the American public" in the years leading up to the Civil War. The catalyst for acceptance as volunteer infantry units came in 1860 when Colonel E. E. Ellsworth of Chicago formed a unit and took it on a tour of the Northeast and Midwest, demonstrating its skill at drilling. Unlike traditional infantry, who stood, fired, and reloaded, Zouaves lay on the ground, fired, rolled over on their backs to reload (offering a smaller target), and then rolled back on their stomachs to fire again. One demonstration by Ellsworth's unit drew ten thousand spectators in New York.

29. For the location of Lackey's store, see *Bloomington City Directory and McLean County Gazetteer* (Chicago: Baily and Hair, 1866), 147 [hereafter cited as *Bloomington 1866 City Directory*], and *Holland's Bloomington City Directory for 1868–69* (Chicago: Western, 1868), 108 [hereafter cited as *Holland's Directory*].

30. *Bloomington Pantagraph*, May 25, 1865.

31. For examples of Lackey's position on the field, see *Bloomington Pantagraph*, September 13, 1866; June 27, 1868; and July 27, 1868; August 25, 1866. For examples of games in which Lackey played shortstop or third base, see *Bloomington Pantagraph*, June 15, 1868, and June 16, 1868. Lackey also played shortstop in the game reported on July 27. Henry Chadwick, *Haney's Base Ball Book of Reference for 1867* (Bedford, MA: Applewood), 123–24, describes requirements for catchers. Lackey served as captain for the Bloomington Base Ball Club in 1866 (*Chicago Times*, September 12, 1866, which notes that Lackey donated thirteen balls for use in a tournament at Bloomington). A good overview of the evolution of the catcher's position can be found in Peter Morris, *Catcher: How the Man behind the Plate Became an American Folk Hero* (Chicago: Ivan R. Dee, 2009), esp. 27–58.

32. *Bloomington Pantagraph*, April 23, 1867; October 27, 1868. For the Illinois State Base Ball Association Convention, see *Illinois State Journal*, July 29, 1867, and *Bloomington Pantagraph*, July 30, 1867.

Second Inning. Organizing Clubs, Funding, Travel, and the Game's Rituals

1. Chadwick, *Haney's Base Ball Book*, 74.

2. Andrew J. Schiff, *"The Father of Baseball": A Biography of Henry Chadwick* (Jefferson, NC: McFarland, 2008), 6; Jules Tygiel, "The Mortar of Which Baseball Is Held Together: Henry Chadwick and the Invention of Baseball Statistics," in *Past Time: Baseball as History* (New York: Oxford, 2008), 15–16; Chadwick, *Haney's Base Ball Book*, 71–72.

3. *Illinois State Register*, May 16, 1866, June 6, 1866; *Cairo Democrat*, July 31, 1866, August 1, 1866; *Aurora Beacon*, July 11, 1867. For Knickerbocker, see *Aurora Beacon*, July 25, 1867.

4. *Aurora Beacon*, July 11, 1867.

5. *Maroa Times*, September 6, 1867; September 13, 1867; *Jacksonville Journal*, April 19, 1866, April 20, 1866; April 21, 1866. Other surviving accounts of club organization can be found in *Jersey County Democrat* (Jerseyville), June 28, 1867; *Oquawka Spectator*, August 8, 1867, August 15, 1867; *East St. Louis Herald*, October 15, 1865; and *Centralia Sentinel*, May 17, 1866.

6. *Bureau County Patriot* (Princeton), July 30, 1867.

7. Morris, *But Didn't We Have Fun?*, 130–31.

8. Ibid., 126–27.

9. *Illinois State Journal*, September 18, 1867.

10. *Waukegan Gazette*, May 25, 1867.

11. *Lee County Journal* (Amboy), July 28, 1870; *Peoria Transcript*, July 28, 1866, August 10, 1866. George Gilbert is identified as a hatter with Gilbert Brothers in the *Peoria Transcript*, September 5, 1866.

12. *Carthage Gazette*, July 2, 1868; *Illinois State Journal*, May 31, 1866; *Jacksonville Journal*, May 18, 1866; *Aurora Beacon*, June 13, 1867; *Jacksonville Journal*, November 5, 1866; *Rock Island Argus*, August 4, 1866.

13. *Illinois State Register*, July 28, 1866; *Illinois State Journal*, June 27, 1866.

14. *Marshall County Republican* (Henry), August 22, 1867; *Ottawa Republican*, August 13, 1868.

15. *Lee County Journal* (Amboy), July 14, 1870.

16. *Grand Prairie Review* (Onarga), August 3, 1867, September 28, 1867.

17. *Ottawa Republican*, August 19, 1869.

18. *Jacksonville Journal*, August 22, 1866.

19. Morris, *But Didn't We Have Fun?*, 130; *East St. Louis Gazette*, November 29, 1866; *East St. Louis Herald*, January 21, 1866.

20. *Cairo Democrat*, December 4, 1866; December 21, 1866; *DeKalb County News*, May 27, 1868, May 20, 1868; *Nashville Journal*, September 11, 1868; *Lincoln Herald*, October 31, 1867; June 27, 1867.

21. *Centralia Sentinel*, June 6, 1867, October 31, 1867, November 7, 1867, December 10, 1868, September 30, 1869, October 12, 1869, October 14, 1869.

22. *Belleville Advocate*, August 17, 1866; *Freeport Bulletin*, June 14, 1866; *East St. Louis Gazette*, August 8, 1867; *Belleville Democrat*, July 29, 1869, September 9, 1869; *Danville Commercial*, August 15, 1867; *Centralia Sentinel*, June 24, 1869. The figure of $19.75 has been used for the value of the 1867 dollar as of June 6, 2022.

23. Keiser, *Building for the Centuries*, 152–53. For the railroad map, see the Prologue.

24. *Chicago Tribune*, July 20, 1867; July 25, 1867.

25. *Rock Island Argus*, July 2, 1867, June 5, 1867; *Quincy Whig and Republican*, July 28, 1869; *Quincy Herald*, July 28, 1868. A value of $19.75 for the 1867 dollar has been used, as of June 6, 2022.

26. *Monmouth Atlas*, July 31, 1868.

27. *Peoria Transcript*, July 11, 1867; *Aurora Beacon*, August 22, 1867. For other examples, see *Monmouth Review*, July 15, 1870; *Monmouth Atlas*, May 29, 1868, June 25, 1869; *Jacksonville Journal*, August 20, 1869, August 16, 1869; *Galesburg Register*, May 23, 1867; *Champaign Gazette and Union*, August 28, 1867. For projected 2022 costs of the 1867 discount tickets, a value of $19.75 for the 1867 dollar has been used, as of June 6, 2022.

28. *Peoria Transcript*, August 4, 1868; *Peoria National Democrat*, August 4, 1868; *Peoria Transcript*, May 31, 1867; *Quincy Whig and Republican*, July 3, 1868, August 13, 1869. For other examples, see *Quincy Herald*, May 22, 1869.

29. *Quincy Herald*, May 21, 1869, June 5, 1868. A value of $21.49 for the 1869 dollar has been used, as of June 6, 2022.

30. *Cairo Democrat*, October 27, 1866.

31. *Quincy Herald*, August 30, 1866, August 31, 1866; *Jacksonville Journal*, August 27, 1869.

32. *Jacksonville Journal*, August 6, 1867; *Aurora Beacon*, October 24, 1867.

33. Goldstein, *Playing for Keeps*, 19–20; Morris, *But Didn't We Have Fun?*, 130.

34. *Danville Commercial*, November 15, 1866, December 20, 1866, March 5, 1868, March 12, 1868.

35. Chadwick, *Haney's Base Ball Book*, 74; *Grand Prairie Review* (Onarga), August 3, 1867.

36. *Illinois State Journal*, September 11, 1866.

37. Ibid., October 13, 1866.

38. Morris, *But Didn't We Have Fun?*, 101, 122; Goldstein, *Playing for Keeps*, 18–19.

39. Morris, *But Didn't We Have Fun?*, 120–21.

40. For a few examples of good and bad treatment by opponents, see *Aurora Beacon*, August 29 and October 31, 1867, and *Edwardsville Intelligencer*, June 9, 1870.

41. *Quincy Herald*, August 15, 1866.

42. For examples, see *Lee County Journal* (Amboy), July 7, 1870; *Rock Island Argus*, June 25, 1867; *Freeport Bulletin*, July 8, 1869; *Harvard Independent*, July 17, 1867; *Jacksonville Journal*, August 21, 1867; *Kankakee Gazette*, November 14, 1867.

43. *Cairo Democrat*, October 28, 1866.

44. Ibid.

45. *Aurora Beacon*, August 8, 1867, August 29, 1867. A value of $19.75 for the 1867 dollar has been used, as of June 6, 2022.

46. *Rock Island Argus*, June 25, 1867; *Harvard Independent*, July 17, 1867; *Kankakee Gazette*, November 14, 1867.

47. *Bureau County Republican* (Princeton), June 20, 1867; *Champaign Union and Gazette*, July 10, 1867; *Aurora Beacon*, November 7, 1867; *Warsaw Bulletin*, June 26, 1868, August 14, 1867; *Sterling Gazette*, June 1, 1867; *Illinois State Register*, August 10, 1866.

48. *Centralia Democrat*, July 30, 1868; *Rock Island Argus*, June 7, 1867.

49. *Rock Island Argus*, June 17, 1867; *Illinois State Register*, August 18, 1866.

50. Letter signed "Fair Play" in *Aurora Beacon*, August 29, 1867; *Edwardsville Intelligencer*, June 9, 1870.

Third Inning. Playing Fields, Gambling, and Injuries

1. Letter to the editor, "A Member of the Bloomington Base Ball Club," *Bloomington Pantagraph*, May 29, 1867.

2. "A Member of the Bloomington Base Ball Club." Problems related to obtaining and retaining playing fields were also discussed in Robert D. Sampson, "Fields of Battle: The Problem of Base Ball Playing Space in Post–Civil War Illinois," *Journal of the Illinois State Historical Society* 110 (Fall–Winter 2017): 283–304.

3. Morris, *But Didn't We Have Fun?*, 30, 34–36, 93–100.

4. Peter Morris, *Level Playing Fields: How the Groundskeeping Murphy Brothers Shaped Baseball* (Lincoln: University of Nebraska Press, 2007), 21. John Clifford, who attended the 1866 tournament, was quoted in Michael Benson, *Ballparks of North America: A Comprehensive Historical Reference to Baseball Grounds, Yards, and Stadiums, 1845 to Present* (Jefferson, NC: McFarland, 1989), 343; Horace Buker, Cradle of Baseball series, *Rockford Republic*, April 19, 1922.

5. *Kankakee Gazette*, September 3, 1868; *Aurora Beacon*, August 29, 1867.

6. *Danville Commercial*, June 6, 1867; *Waukegan Gazette*, June 5, 1867; *Aurora Beacon*, August 1, 1867; *Belleville Democrat*, November 28, 1867; *Cairo Democrat*, August 10, 1866; *East St. Louis Gazette*, September 19, 1868; *Freeport Bulletin*, August 30, 1866; *Harvard Independent*, July 10, 1867. For Eureka, see *Clinton Public and Central Transcript*, August 1, 1867.

7. Carl Landrum, *Quincy: A Pictorial History* (St. Louis: G. Bradley, 1990), 135; *Quincy Herald*, April 17, 1869, September 22, 1866, October 12, 1869, October 14, 1869, October 21, 1866.

8. For founding of the McPherson Club and its field, see *Decatur Review*, June 28, 1914 (also quoted in Morris, *But Didn't We Have Fun?*, 42). For the McPherson Club name, see Benson, *Ballparks*, 130; *Illinois State Journal*, August 20, 1866. For the field near the railroad intersection and its stands, see Decatur *Republican*, August, 8, 1867; *Pana Gazette*, August 17, 1867; *Republican* August 22, 1867; *Illinois State Journal*, September 12, 1867, September 23, 1867.

9. *Decatur Weekly Republican*, October 10, 1867; *Jacksonville Journal*, June 17, 1868, September 6, 1869, September 30, 1869.

10. *DeWitt Register* (Clinton), July 31, 1868.

11. *Peoria Transcript*, July 20, 1868; *Peoria National Democrat*, August 8 and October 16, 1866, and August 29, 1867.

12. *Carrollton Gazette*, October 26, 1867; *Danville Commercial*, September 19, 1867; *Quincy Whig and Republican*, September 8, 1869, *Quincy Herald*, August 5, 1868, August 20, 1868; *Peoria Transcript*, July 20, 1868; *Peoria National Democrat*, August 8, 1866, August 29, 1867, October 16, 1866.

13. *Cairo Democrat*, October 30, 1867; *Chicago Tribune*, November 1, 1870.

14. *Bloomington Pantagraph*, April 24, 1867, May 6, 1867.

15. Location of the Fifth Ward School is found in *1874 Atlas of McLean County* (Chicago: Warner and Beers, 1874), n.p. Today Bent School is on the southern portion of the site and houses occupy the northern portion.

16. For neighborhood occupations, see appendix B.

17. *Bloomington Pantagraph*, May 14, 1867, May 16, 1867.

18. *Bloomington Pantagraph*, May 22, 1867. For details on the Bloomington Base Ball Club's members and their occupations, see *Pantagraph*, May 25, 1865; and, for George W. Lackey, see *Bloomington City Directory; Holland's Directory for 1868–69*. For Henry A. Ewing, see Newton Bateman, *Historical Encyclopedia of Illinois and History of McLean County* (Chicago: Munsell, 1908), 845; *Bloomington 1866 City Directory*, 121; *Holland's Directory*, 80, 212. For Charter Roe, see *Bloomington 1866 City Directory*, 174, 194; *Holland's Directory*, 142. Club players that could be found include attorney Robert McCart (*Holland's Directory*, 208; Bateman, *Historical Encyclopedia*); attorney George W. Hardacre (*Bloomington 1866 City Directory*, 131; *Holland's Directory*, 92); marble dealer James P. Moore (*Bloomington 1866 City Directory*, 161); insurance agent Lewis B. Thomas (*Bloomington 1866 City Directory*, 182; *Holland's Directory*, 157); grain and coal merchant and future Bloomington mayor E. H. Rood (*Bloomington 1866 City Directory*, 151, 152, 174; *Holland's Directory*, 32); photographer George Rex (*Bloomington 1866 City Directory*, 128, 173, 177; *Holland's Directory*, 140.

19. *Bloomington Pantagraph*, May 25, 1867.

20. Ibid.

21. Ibid. For Bloomington's battle against Sunday recreation, see Bill Kemp, "Sunday Movies Come to Bloomington in 1928," *Bloomington Pantagraph*, April 14, 2013.

22. *Bloomington Pantagraph*, May 29, 1867.

23. *Bloomington Pantagraph*, August 14, 1867; for the counter letter, see August 17, 1867.

24. *Bloomington Pantagraph*, September 2, 1867, September 2, 1868. For the dollar value, see https://www.in2013dollars.com/us/inflation/1868?amount=0.75.

25. For Dubois, see "Jesse K. Dubois" in Joseph Wallace, *Past and Present of the City of Springfield and Sangamon County* (S. J. Clark, 1904), 57–58, and "Biography—Dubois" File, Sangamon Valley Collection, Lincoln Library, Springfield. For Capital Horse Railway Company organization, see "Street Car History," *Illinois State Journal*, November 8, 1931.

26. Alexander Starne was superintendent of Capital Railway ("Street Car History," *Illinois State Journal*, November 8, 1931). For Starne's background, see *1881 History of Sangamon County, Illinois* (Chicago: Interstate, 1881), 719.

27. *Illinois State Register*, May 19, 1866.

28. Ibid., May 21, 1866, For Pioneer Base Ball Club, see *Illinois State Journal*, August 6, 1866; August 15, 1866.

29. *Illinois State Register*, September 10, 1866; *Illinois State Journal*, June 16, 1866; October 16, 1866; *Illinois State Register*, August 27, 1866; *Illinois State Journal*, December 5, 1866.

30. *Illinois State Journal*, July 2, 1866; *Illinois State Register*, July 3, 1867; *Illinois State Journal*, July 3, 1867. The tournament included the Capital Club, the Athletic Club of Springfield, the St. Louis Union Club, and teams from Bloomington and Jacksonville. See *Illinois State Journal*, July 3, 1867.

31. *Illinois State Register*, July 3, 1867, and July 5, 1867.

32. *Illinois State Register*, May 17, 1866; May 18, 1866; May 24, 1866; May 22, 1866; *Illinois State Journal*, June 12, 1866. James Brown, who resided at the corner of Market and New Streets, was identified as a city alderman in *Sangamon County Gazetteer* (Springfield: n.p., 1866), 68; *Illinois State Journal*, June 14, 1866.

33. *Illinois State Register*, May 29, 1866; *Illinois State Journal*, June 6, 1866, and May 30, 1866. For the history of the Home for the Friendless and Iles's relation to it, see Carolyn Doyle, "Home for the Friendless," *Illinois State Journal-Register*, August 1, 1982; Chris Dettro, "Friendless No More," *Illinois State Journal-Register*, January 20, 2006, both in "Springfield, Illinois—Charities—Home for the Friendless," Sangamon Valley Collection, Lincoln Library, Springfield; *Sangamon County Gazetteer* (Springfield: n.p., 1866), 136. Examples of National Base Ball Club games at the Capital grounds can be found in *Illinois State Journal*, July 17, 1866, and July 10, 1866; *Illinois State Register*, July 10, 1866. For Pascal P. Enos, see *Sangamon County Gazetteer and City Directory of Springfield and Jacksonville* (Springfield: John C. W. Bailey, 1866, 99). For the Eagle Club, see *Illinois State Journal*, May 28, 1866; July 2, 1866; *Illinois State Register*, May 28, 1866. For the Star Club, see *Illinois State Register*, June 1, 1866; *Illinois State Journal*, June 1, 1866; June 18, 1866; June 25, 1866.

34. One of Alexander Starne's sons, Charles A. Starne, who became a prominent coal industry leader, was described in an obituary as "one of the early players of base ball." See "Death of Charles A. Starne," in *Fuel Magazine: The Coal Operators National Weekly*, June 24, 1910, 419. In 1867, while students at Shurtleff College, Starne and two of Dubois's sons, F. Dubois and K. Dubois, were starters on college clubs (*Alton Weekly Telegraph*, November 1, 1867, and November 22, 1867.

35. *Nashville Journal*, July 10, 1868.

36. Ibid., July 24, 1868. For Vernor's possible connection to Nashville's Sucker Base Ball Club, see box scores of Sucker Club games in *Nashville Journal*, August 22, 1867, and September 13, 1867, and *Centralia Sentinel*, August 13, 1868. In the *Centralia Sentinel* and *Nashville Journal* article of September 13, 1867, Vernor is mentioned only by his last name. The August 22, 1867, article in the Nashville newspaper identifies a player as "A. Vernor." It is possible that there was more than one Vernor on the Sucker nine, but the one identified as "A. Vernor" was the only one of that name in the lineup that day. The 2022 valuation of the bail amounts uses $20.58 for the value of a dollar in 1868.

37. *Quincy Whig and Republican*, August 18, 1869; *Quincy Herald*, August 18, 1869, and August 19, 1869.

38. *Ottawa Republican*, September 5, 1867; Warren Goldstein, *Playing for Keeps: A History of Early Baseball* (Ithaca, NY: Cornell University Press, 1989), 90.

39. John Thorn, *Baseball in the Garden of Eden: The Secret History of the Early Game* (New York: Simon and Schuster, 2011), xiii; 65, 86–87, 89, 286.

40. *Cairo Democrat*, March 31, 1868.

41. *Illinois State Journal*, August 20, 1867. See Henry Condit interview in *Centralia Sentinel*, July 2, 1925, quoted in Loomis, "Egyptian Summer," 10.

42. *Macomb Eagle*, August 1, 1868; *Quincy Herald*, July 30, 1869; *Carthage Gazette*, "Letter from Quincy Correspondent," August 26, 1869.

43. *Ottawa Free Trader*, July 30, 1870.

44. *Chicago Tribune*, July 29, 1867. For suspicions that the games involving the Forest City, National, and Excelsior Clubs were fixed, see Horace Buker, Cradle of Baseball series, *Rockford Republic*, April 26, 1922. Buker wrote, "Naturally the victory of the prairie boys [Forest City] and the defeat of the Excelsiors caused a financial disaster to many betting men and a controversy raged in the Chicago papers, the Tribune and the Republican charging that the Forest City game was framed."

45. *Danville Commercial*, August 29, 1867; *Woodstock Sentinel*, May 21, 1868.

46. *Ottawa Republican*, September 5, 1867.

47. For differing views of the 1919 World Series scandal, see Eliot Asinof, *Eight Men Out and the 1919 World Series* (New York: Holt Paperbacks, 2000, and Tim Hornbaker, *Turning the Black Sox White: The Misunderstood Legacy of Charles A. Comiskey* (New York: Sports Publishing, 2014). Asinof's book, once considered a classic and later made into a motion picture, tarred White Sox owner Charles A. Comiskey as a tight-fisted mogul who exploited his players, leading some to seek more money by conspiring with gamblers to throw the World Series. Hornbaker's book, using Asinof's notes (or more correctly, the lack of them) persuasively argues that the 1919 Sox included some of the best-paid players in the game, undercutting Asinof's main argument.

48. *Illinois State Register* (Springfield), November 12, 1866 (reprinted two days later in the *Quincy Herald*, November 14, 1866); *Peoria Transcript*, September 26, 1867; *Rock Island Argus and Union*, August 30, 1867.

49. *Ottawa Republican*, September 26, 1867; *Rock Island Argus*, September 20, 1866; *Aurora Beacon*, May 20, 1869; *Cairo Times*, November 1, 1868; *Centralia Sentinel*, October 22, 1868; *Carlinville Democrat*, August 26, 1869.

50. *Champaign Gazette and Union*, August 21, 1867; *Galena Gazette*, August 7, 1866, the incident with the Bloomington player was also reprinted in *Belvidere Standard*, July 31, 1866; *Rock Island Union*, June 11, 1867, located in files of Rock Island County Historical Society, Moline, Illinois.

51. *Bloomington Pantagraph*, July 23, 1867. This article may have appeared in Decatur, but attempts to locate it in surviving local newspapers have failed.

52. *Illinois State Journal*, August 31, 1867; *Quincy Whig and Republican*, October 14, 1869.

53. *Woodstock Sentinel*, November 10, 1870; *Bloomington Pantagraph*, September 26, 1870; *Clinton Public*, November 17, 1870; *Chicago Tribune*, May 23, 1870.

54. *Chicago Tribune*, August 16, 1867; *Ottawa Free Trader*, October 26, 1867.

55. For "Base Ball" poem, see *Quincy Herald*, July 24, 1868, and *Decatur Republican*, June 25, 1869.

56. *Quincy Herald*, July 24, 1868. The poem also appeared in the *Decatur Republican*, June 25, 1869.

57. *Mount Vernon Free Press*, October 25, 1867, September 6, 1867.

58. *Mount Vernon Free Press*, October 25, 1867.

59. Ibid.

Fourth Inning. The Game and Its Players

1. Chadwick, *Haney's Base Ball Book*, 123. Chadwick, a *New York Clipper* sportswriter, was a dominant force in shaping baseball reporting, its rules, and its perception by players and spectators.

2. Jimmy Breslin, *Can't Anybody Here Play This Game?* (New York: Ballantine, 1971), quote on 39.

3. Chadwick, *Haney's Base Ball Book*, 123.

4. *Jacksonville Journal*, November 21, 1866.

5. Ibid.

6. Ibid.

7. *Aurora Beacon*, July 8, 1870, 1869; *Greenville Advocate*, June 19, 1868.

8. *Ottawa Republican*, July 2, 1868.

9. *Peoria Transcript*, August 14, 1866.

10. Ibid.

11. This account by a *Chicago Times* correspondent was reprinted in the *Weekly Jacksonville Sentinel*, September 20, 1866.

12. *Champaign Union and Gazette*, August 7, 1868.

13. *Quincy Whig and Republican*, July 30, 1869.

14. *Decatur Review*, June 16, 1918.

15. Peter Morris, *A Game of Inches: The Story behind the Innovations That Shaped Baseball* (Chicago: Ivan R. Dee, 2010), 28.

16. *Sporting News*, November 9, 1895; Jeffrey Kittle, "Empires," in Morris et al., *Baseball Pioneers*, 300.

17. *Bloomington Pantagraph*, September 27, 1867.

18. *Decatur Review*, June 16, 1918. The player was Isaac T. Archer of the Decatur McPherson Base Ball Club in an 1867 game against the Centralia Egyptians.

19. Chadwick, *Haney's Base Ball Book*, 123–24; Horace Buker, Cradle of Baseball series, *Rockford Republic*, March 18, 1922, March 22, 1922.

20. Peter Morris, "Excelsiors of Chicago, Postwar," 210–21, "Byron (Illinois) Base Ball Club," 221–23, "Forest City Club of Rockford," 224–35, and "Pecatonica Base Ball Club," 235–39, in Morris et al., eds., *Base Ball Pioneers*.

21. The full list is in appendix C. Information that follows is taken from that list.

22. *Holland's Classified Business Directory of Rock Island and Moline* (Chicago: Western, 1868), 40. For William H. Dart, see *Danville Commercial*, August 1, 1867; for the Cunninghams, see Loomis, "Egyptian Summer," 2–3. A photograph of James T. Cunningham's is in George E. Ross, *Centralia, Illinois: A Pictorial History* (St. Louis: G. Bradley, 1992), 70.

23. *Cairo Democrat*, January 17, 1867, February 1, 1867, October 5, 1865, and October 3, 1866.

24. *Cairo City Directory for 1866* (Cairo: Cairo Democrat Company, n.d.), 111.

25. *Alton Weekly Telegraph*, November 1, 1867, and November 22, 1867, list the Dubois brothers and Starne as players. Starne's early involvement with the game is mentioned in his obituary in *Fuel Magazine: The Coal Operators National Weekly*, June 21, 1910, 419. For the Dubois brothers' father, Jesse K. Dubois, see "Biography—Dubois File," Sangamon Valley Collection, Springfield Lincoln Library. For Alexander Starne, Charles Starne's father, see *1881 History of Sangamon County* (Chicago: Interstate, 1881), 719.

26. See appendix C.

27. Ibid.

28. 1870 Christian County Census, 132. For source of "Babe Ruth" quote, see *Decatur Review*, July 17, 1921, and Dorothy Jordan, "The Old Home Town," *Decatur Review*, July 17, 1921. Jordan is also quoted in Morris, *"But Didn't We Have Fun?,"* 208. For Archer's claim, see *Decatur Review*, June 16, 1918.

29. *Bloomington 1866 City Directory*, 109; *Holland's Directory*, 65. For Cheney's war record, see *Bloomington Pantagraph*, November 3, 1911. Cheney's part in a controversy over the use of ineligible players is covered in chapter 7.

30. Newton Bateman, *Historical Encyclopedia of Illinois and History of McLean County*, (Chicago: Munsell, 1908), 2: 845. Also see *Bloomington 1866 City Directory*, 194, 121; *Holland's City Directory*, 69. For the Roes, see *Bloomington 1866 City Directory*, 174, 194, *Holland's City Directory*, 36, 142. For Rood, see Bateman, *Historical Encyclopedia of Illinois*, 2: 895–96; *Bloomington 1866 City Directory*, 151–52, 174; *Holland's City Directory*, 32.

31. For Cheney's and Keenan's occupations, see appendix C. Cheney eventually played for the professional Forest City Club of Rockford in the first professional league, the National Association. See Morris, "Forest City Club of Rockford," in Morris et al., eds., *Base Ball Pioneers*, 230. Keenan was lured to the Excelsiors in the summer of 1867 after that club's embarrassing loss to the Washington Nationals (*Bloomington Pantagraph*, September 11, 1867).

Fifth Inning. Sharing the Fun

1. "Brick Pomeroy as a Base Ballist," *Rock Island Argus*, July 25, 1867; also see *Jacksonville Weekly Sentinel*, August 8, 1867.

2. *Illinois State Register*, June 28, 1866; *Bureau County Patriot* (Princeton), August 7, 1866.

3. *East St. Louis Gazette*, September 6, 1866; *Illinois State Journal*, July 7, 1866; *Chicago Tribune*, November 14, 1868.

4. *Bureau County Patriot* (Princeton), October 12, 1869, July 11, 1867.

5. "A Serious Rival of Base Ball—Mumble Peg," *Woodstock Sentinel*, August 1, 1867.

6. *Macomb Journal*, July 16, 1869.

7. Ibid.

8. *Peoria Transcript*, July 25, 1867.

9. Ibid.

10. Ibid.

11. *Ottawa Free Trader*, August 13, 1870.

12. *Peoria National Democrat*, November 2, 1866.

13. *Du Quoin Tribune*, September 5, 1867.

14. Franklin J. Meine, "Pomeroy, Marcus Mills," *Dictionary of American Biography*, ed. Dumas Malone (New York: Charles Scribner's Sons, 1935).

15. Brick Pomeroy, "Brick Pomeroy as a Base Ballist," *Rock Island Argus*, July 25, 1867.

16. Ibid.

17. Ibid.

18. Ibid.

19. Ibid.

20. Morris, *But Didn't We Have Fun?*, 59. Morris's full discussion of the relation of the muffin game to the increase in baseball's competitiveness and professionalization can be found on 213–25.

21. Ibid., 216–17.

22. *DeWitt Register* (Clinton), July 31, 1868.

23. *Cairo Democrat*, September 14, 1867.

24. Ibid.

25. *Cairo Democrat*, September 18, 1867.

26. *Cairo Democrat*, September 17, 1867, September 18, 1867. No account of the September 21, 1867, rematch survives.

27. *Cairo Democrat*, September 20, 1867.

28. *Cairo Democrat*, September 24, 1867.

29. *Ottawa Free Trader*, June 29, 1867.

30. *Ottawa Republican*, July 4, 1867, July 25, 1867, August 8, 1867.

31. *Ottawa Free Trader*, August 13, 1870.

32. *Ottawa Free Trader*, August 3, 1867; *Jacksonville Journal*, August 1, 1867; *Champaign Union and Gazette*, July 31, 1867.

33. *Sterling Gazette*, July 27, 1867; *Pana Gazette*, August 31, 1867, September 28, 1867.

34. *Mound City Journal*, July 21, 1866; *Jacksonville Journal*, September 1, 1869, September 2, 1869.

35. *DeKalb County News*, July 24, 1867.

36. Ibid.

37. *Jacksonville Journal*, August 4, 1869.

38. Ibid.

39. *Stark County News* (Toulon), October 15, 1869.

40. *Illinois State Journal*, August 21, 1866, August 22, 1866; *Illinois State Register*, August 28, 1866, August 16, 1866.

41. *Quincy Herald*, July 7, 1866.

42. *Danville Commercial*, September 6, 1867.

43. *Cairo Democrat*, October 6, 1866; *Bloomington Pantagraph*, April 25, 1867, May 2, 1867, May 15, 1867; *Woodstock Sentinel*, October 10, 1867.

44. *Lincoln Herald*, August 29, 1867, October 10, 1867, October 17, 1867.

45. *Champaign Gazette and Union*, September 4, 1867.

46. *Monmouth Review*, July 15, 1870, August 19, 1870.

47. *Monmouth Review*, August 19, 1870.

48. Ibid.

49. *Chicago Tribune*, August 22, 1867; *Lee County Journal*, August 4, 1870, September 22, 1870; *Monmouth Review*, September 9, 1870; *Rock Island Argus*, August 26, 1867; *Champaign Gazette and Union*, September 11, 1867.

50. *Bloomington Pantagraph*, July 28, 1868.

51. Ibid., July 29, 1868, July 30, 1868.

52. *Monmouth Review*, July 15, 1870, July 22, 1870.

53. *Rock Island Argus*, August 22, 1867, August 23, 1867.

54. *Bloomington Pantagraph*, August 3, 1868, August 4, 1868, August 5, 1868, August 6, 1868.

55. *Chicago Tribune*, August 8, 1867, August 22, 1867.

56. *Ottawa Free Trader*, July 25, 1868.

57. Ibid.

58. *Illinois State Journal*, September 23, 1867; *Decatur Republican*, September 26, 1867.

Sixth Inning. Barriers of Race and Gender

1. *Chicago Tribune*, August 24, 1870.

2. *Jacksonville Journal*, August 8, 1868.

3. "The Exclusion of African Americans from the NABBP (1867)," in *Early Innings: A Documentary History of Baseball, 1825–1908*, ed. and comp. Dean A. Sullivan (Lincoln: University of Nebraska Press), 68–69.

4. For a full discussion of drawing the color line in the early game, see Ryan A. Swanson, *When Baseball Went White: Reconstruction, Reconciliation, and Dreams of a National Pastime* (Lincoln: University of Nebraska Press, 2014), esp. 69–90.

5. Ibid., vii, viii–ix.

6. Ibid., 3, 18–19.

7. Ibid., 69–73, 75–80.

8. Ibid., 100–102.

9. *Jacksonville Journal*, August 24, 1866; *Ottawa Free Trader*, August 13, 1870; *Quincy Herald*, October 11, 1868.

10. *Bloomington Pantagraph*, August 1, 1866.

11. *Bloomington Pantagraph*, September 24, 1867 (one of only two instances that the author has found in surviving Illinois newspapers from this era in which black players were named), August 10, 1868; *Illinois State Register*, August 8, 1870. For

other references to the championship series, see *Illinois State Register*, August 2, 1870, August 5, 1870.

12. Horace Buker, Cradle of Baseball series, *Rockford Republic*, July 19, 1922; *Chicago Tribune*, "Base Ball from a Colored Point of View: Match Game between American Clubs of African Descent," August 28, 1870.

13. *Chicago Tribune*, "Base Ball from a Colored Point of View."

14. Leslie A. Heaphy, ed., *Black Baseball and Chicago: Essays on the Players, Teams and Games* (Jefferson, NC: McFarland, 2006), 7, 8.

15. *Chicago Tribune*, "Base Ball from a Colored Point of View."

16. For the Blue Stockings club's plans to enter the tournament for the senior amateur championship of the city and a $100 prize for first place, see *New York Clipper*, September 3, 1870; *Chicago Tribune*, September 17, 1870, August 24, 1870.

17. Heaphy, *Black Baseball*, 8–9; *Chicago Times*, September 28, 1870, September 23, 1870, September 21, 1870. For Johnson's complaint, also see *New York Clipper*, September 24, 1870.

18. *Chicago Times*, September 25, 1870, September 28, 1870; Heaphy, *Black Baseball*, 9.

19. *Bureau County Republican* (Princeton), June 10, 1869; *Decatur Weekly Republican*, June 3, 1869; quote, May 12, 1870.

20. Debra A. Shattuck, *Bloomer Girls: Women Baseball Pioneers* (Urbana: University of Illinois Press, 2017), 18, 19.

21. Swanson, *When Baseball Went White*, xiii.

22. *Ottawa Free Trader*, August 13, 1870; *Cairo Democrat*, August 14, 1867.

23. *Pana Gazette*, November 9, 1867.

24. Shattuck, *Bloomer Girls*, 53–54; also see Pruter, "Youth Baseball in Chicago," 5–6. For the Northwestern Female College team, see *Chicago Times*, October 11 and 24, 1870, and for the Rockford game, see *Chicago Tribune*, August 17, 1870, both quoted in Kirsch, *Baseball and Cricket*, 136.

25. *Centralia Sentinel*, October 15, 1869, October 16, 1869.

Seventh Inning. Trouble in Baseball's Eden

1. *Illinois State Journal*, September 20, 1867.

2. For examples of the pretournament coverage, see *Cairo Democrat*, August 30, 1867; *Quincy Herald*, August 31, 1867; *Peoria National Democrat*, September 1, 1867; *Bloomington Pantagraph*, August 30, 1867; *Illinois State Journal*, August 31, 1867, September 6, 1867; *Illinois State Register*, September 12, 1867. The *Illinois State Journal* sent a correspondent to Decatur to cover the event.

3. *Bloomington Pantagraph*, August 3, 1867, August 30, 1867. For a fuller account of the Bloomington-Chicago rivalry, see Robert D. Sampson, "'The Spirit of Discord Arose': The Birth Pangs of Base Ball in Central Illinois, 1866–1868," *Journal of Illinois History* 15 (Winter 2012): 247–68, esp. 252–55, 259; *Bloomington Pantagraph*, September 9, 1867, September 11, 1867.

4. *Decatur Republican*, September 19, 1867. For Keenan's role at Decatur, see *Illinois State Journal*, September 23, 1867.

5. Chadwick, *Haney's Base Ball Book*, 23–24; *Illinois State Journal*, September 19, 1867; *Decatur Republican*, September 19, 1867.

6. *Decatur Republican*, September 19, 1867.

7. Ibid.; *Illinois State Journal*, September 19, 1867; *Bloomington Pantagraph*, September 21, 1867; *Illinois State Journal*, September 20, 1867.

8. *Centralia Sentinel*, November 1, 1866, November 8, 1866. Wilke's reference is in November 1 issue.

9. *Centralia Sentinel*, November 8, 1866; *Cairo Democrat*, July 20, 1867.

10. Loomis, "Egyptian Summer," 15–16.

11. Ibid. The rules referred to, covering when a game could be ended and guidelines calling an end of play on account of darkness, are in Chadwick, *Haney's Base Ball Book*, 25, 54–57.

12. Loomis, "Egyptian Summer," 16–17.

13. *Centralia Democrat*, October 1, 1868, October 8, 1868; *Centralia Sentinel*, October 1, 1868.

14. *Centralia Sentinel*, October 15, 1868, October 22, 1868.

15. *Centralia Sentinel*, October 22, 1868.

16. *Centralia Democrat*, October 22, 1868; *Centralia Sentinel*, October 29, 1868. The figure of $20.58 has been used for the value of the 1868 dollar as of June 6, 2022.

17. *Centralia Sentinel*, October 29, 1868; Loomis, "Egyptian Summer," 10.

18. See box score in *Centralia Sentinel*, October 29, 1868.

19. *Rock Island Argus*, August 22, 1867.

20. *Litchfield Union Monitor*, "Butler Items," July 29, 1869; *Sterling Gazette*, October 26, 1867; *Earlville Gazette*, August 21, 1868, August 28, 1868.

21. *Marshall County Republican* (Henry), September 5, 1867.

22. *Illinois State Journal*, August 20, 1867.

23. Ibid.

24. Ibid., August 20, 1867.

25. Ibid., August 21, 1867.

26. Ibid., August 22, 1867.

27. Kirsch, *Baseball and Cricket*, 143–44.

28. Chadwick, *Haney's Base Ball Book*, 72.

29. *Ottawa Free Trader*, August 27, 1870.

30. *Quincy Herald*, August 17, 1869. The figure of $21.49 has been used for the value of the 1869 dollar as of June 6, 2022.

31. Ibid., August 18, 1869; *Illinois State Journal*, August 20, 1869.

32. *Quincy Whig and Republican*, August 18, 1869; *Quincy Herald*, August 18, 1869; *Illinois State Journal*, August 20, 1869. The figure of $21.49 has been used for the value of the 1869 dollar as of June 6, 2022.

33. *Quincy Whig and Republican*, August 18, 1868; *Quincy Herald*, August 18, 1869.

34. *Quincy Herald*, August 17, 1869; *Illinois State Journal,* August 20, 1869.

35. *Quincy Herald*, August 18, 1869.

36. For account of the game, see *Rock Island Argus*, July 5, 1867. Umpire Edward Hughes responded to those questioning his decision in the *Argus* of July 8, 1867; the *Geneseo Republic*'s comments are in the *Argus* July 13, 1867; the *New York Clipper's* final decision and reactions of the *Geneseo Republic* are in the *Argus*, July 26, 1867.

37. *Rock Island Argus*, August 22, 1867.

38. *Carlyle Constitution and Union*, July 13, 1869.

39. For the Aurora-Dundee incident, see *Aurora Beacon*, October 17, 1867, and for "Mr. Gould" incident, same paper, August 8, 1867; for allegations of favoritism against umpire of Monmouth-Princeton contest, see *Bureau County Republican* (Princeton), September 16, 1869; for Moline-Davenport dispute, see *Rock Island Argus*, June 28, 1867, and *Bloomington Pantagraph*, July 10, 1868.

40. *Mount Vernon Free Press*, September 6, 1867; *Ottawa Free Trader*, August 31, 1867; *Belleville Advocate*, September 17, 1867; *Quincy Herald*, July 30, 1868.

41. *Carrollton Gazette*, October 12, 1867.

42. *Pike County Democrat* (Pittsfield), August 29, 1867; *Bureau County Patriot* (Princeton), July 20, 1869; *Oquawka Spectator*, September 5, 1867.

43. *Centralia Sentinel*, September 3, 1868; *Champaign Gazette and Union*, October 30, 1867; *Illinois Democrat* (Urbana), March 28, 1868; *Greenville Advocate*, July 23, 1869.

44. *Quincy Herald*, September 3, 1868; *Rock Island Argus*, April 16, 1867; *Illinois State Register,* October 14, 1867.

45. *Sterling Gazette*, August 4, 1866; *Warren Sentinel*, September 5, 1867; *Grand Prairie Review* (Onarga), October 12, 1867; *Warsaw Bulletin*, October 11, 1867, November 1, 1867.

46. *Jacksonville Journal*, August 25, 1869, August 28, 1869.

47. *Cairo Democrat*, July 26, 1867, August 29, 1867.

48. *Cairo Democrat*, September 3, 1867; "Why They Beat Us," *Cairo Democrat*, September 11, 1867.

49. *Cairo Democrat*, September 16, 1867, September 27, 1867 (first quotation), September 28, 1867 (second quotation).

50. For Jacksonville's need for practice, see *Jacksonville Journal*, May 5, 1866, May 9, 1866, July 15, 1869, August 11, 1869; for "systematic practice," see *Woodstock Sentinel*, August 25, 1870; for the shortcomings of Rock Island's Lively Turtles Club, see *Rock Island Argus*, June 20, 1867; "want of practice" on the part of Quincy's Occidental Club is in *Quincy Herald*, July 9, 1868; for Harvard's need for practice, see *Harvard Independent*, July 17, 1867; the failure of Decatur's Central Club was noted in *Decatur Republican*, July 9, 1868.

51. *Quincy Herald*, September 13, 1868; *Ottawa Republican*, September 19, 1867; *Peoria Transcript*, September 7, 1866, September 22, 1866.

52. Quoted in Horace Buker, Cradle of Base Ball series, *Rockford Republic*, May 31, 1922.

53. *Woodstock Sentinel*, August 25, 1870; *Rock Island Argus*, July 18, 1867.

Eighth Inning: Representative Teams

1. *Freeport Bulletin*, August 1, 1867, reprinted from the *Chicago Times*.

2. J. H. G. Brinkerhoff, *Brinkerhoff's History of Marion County, Illinois* (Indianapolis: B. F. Bowen, 1909), 142, 192; Loomis, "Egyptian Summer," 1; *Centralia Sentinel*, October 31, 1867, August 20, 1866, September 27, 1866, October 14, 1869.

3. For background on the Liberty Club, see Loomis, "Egyptian Summer," 1–2, and Harold Gerlach, "Local Enthusiasm for Baseball Ran High in Those Early Days," *Centralia Evening Sentinel*, Golden Jubilee Edition, Centralia Area Historical Museum Archives.

4. *Centralia Sentinel*, June 21, 1866, July 12, 1866, August 16, 1866, August 23, 1866.

5. *Centralia Sentinel*, July 11, 1867; *Bunker Hill Union Gazette*, July 11, 1867.

6. *Centralia Sentinel*, September 5, 1867; *Nashville* (IL) *Journal*, September 13, 1867; *Illinois State Journal*, September 21, 1867; *Centralia Sentinel*, September 25, 1867, October 24, 1867. Confusing the finish of Centralia in the Decatur tournament are conflicting reports in the *Illinois State Journal*, September 23, 1867, and the *Centralia Sentinel*, September 25, 1867. As can best be reconstructed, Centralia's club was put in the senior division, where it lost to the Chicago Excelsiors, who then defeated Springfield's Capital club on the tourney's last day. Centralia may have been awarded second place for having a better record overall than Springfield. The disappointments and disputes marring the Decatur tourney and its aftermath was discussed in detail in chapter 7. The figure of $19.75 has been used for the value of the 1867 dollar as of June 6, 2022.

7. Loomis, "Egyptian Summer," 10–11.

8. *Centralia Democrat*, July 30, 1868, August 27, 1868; *Centralia Sentinel*, August 27, 1868, August 13, 1868, September 2, 1868. For coverage of the Egyptian-Union game, also see *Centralia Democrat*, September 3, 1868.

9. *Centralia Sentinel*, October 29, 1868, September 24, 1868, December 10, 1868. Henry Condit said of the $50 prize that it "looked like a million to us. . . . What a time we had with that fifty dollars!"—quoted in Loomis, "Egyptian Summer," 11. The figure of $19.75 has been used for the value of the 1867 dollar as of June 6, 2022.

10. *Centralia Democrat*, April 1, 1869, April 9, 1869.

11. *Centralia Democrat*, September 22, 1870, September 29, 1870.

12. Loomis, "Egyptian Summer," 11.

13. Peter Morris, "Excelsiors of Chicago, Postwar," in Morris et al., *Base Ball Pioneers*, 211–12.

14. Morris, "Excelsiors of Chicago, Prewar," 206–9; Bessie Louise Pierce, in *A History of Chicago* (New York: Alfred A. Knopf, 1940), finds four teams in the city by 1860, 2: 470.

15. Horace Buker, Cradle of Baseball series, *Rockford Republic*, March 25, 1922; also covered in Morris, "Excelsiors of Chicago, Postwar," 210; Freedman, "Baseball Fad in Chicago," 58.

16. Morris, "Excelsiors of Chicago, Postwar," 210–11. The figure of $19.75 has been used for the value of the 1866 dollar as of June 6, 2022.

17. Sampson, "Spirit of Discord," 253–55.

18. Morris, "Excelsiors of Chicago, Postwar," 211–13.

19. Ibid., 212–13.

20. Morris, "Excelsiors of Chicago, Postwar," 213. For an example of coverage, see *Jacksonville Journal*, July 1, 1867, July 24, 1867, July 20, 1867. Interest in the match was such that the day of the Nationals-Excelsior game, the *Rock Island Argus* squeezed the score of the first two innings into the edition before its deadline on July 27, 1867; earlier, the same paper ran a notice that the Chicago, Rock Island, and Pacific Railroad would carry passengers to the tournament "for $8.75 round trip" ($172.81 in 2022).

21. For a contemporary account of the game, see Henry Chadwick, "The Forest City Club Upsets the Nationals of Washington, D.C.," in *Early Innings: A Documentary History of Baseball, 1825–1908*, ed. Dean A. Sullivan, 62–66 (Lincoln, NE: University of Nebraska Press, 1995). Morris, "Excelsiors of Chicago, Postwar," covers the game on 213. For other contemporary accounts, see *Belvidere Standard*, July 30, 1867, and *Chicago Tribune*, July 26, 1867.

22. *Warsaw Bulletin*, August 2, 1867. For the gambling charge, see Morris, "Excelsiors of Chicago, Postwar," 213; *Chicago Tribune*, August 3, 1867; *Waukegan Gazette*, July 27, 1867; *Danville Commercial*, August 1, 1867; *Bloomington Pantagraph*, August 3, 1867; and "The Great Match Game at Chicago," *Illinois State Journal,* July 30, 1867.

23. "Base Ball in Dudalville," *Peoria Transcript*, July 30, 1867.

24. *Freeport Bulletin*, August 1, 1867.

25. For the origins of the Pecatonica horn and the legendary status it achieved, becoming a sort of apocryphal story about incompetent rural teams, see Morris, *But Didn't We Have Fun?*, 114–15, 118–19; Morris, "Pecatonica Base Ball Club," in Morris et al., eds., *Base Ball Pioneers*, 235–39; Morris, "Excelsior Club of Chicago, Postwar," 213–14; and *Jacksonville Journal*, August 13, 1867. For more on the tin horn and the Forest City Club's role, see Buker, Cradle of Baseball series, *Rockford Republic*, April 8, 1922; May 10, 1922; May 6, 1922; *Chicago Tribune*, August 9, 1867. Stephen Nissenbaum, in *The Battle for Christmas: A Cultural History of America's Most Cherished Holiday* (New York: Vintage, 1996), 130, places "tin horns" in a fuller context. Although a Christmas gift for children, the horns were associated with noise and disorder and "later banned in the city of Philadelphia." Therefore, the gift of a tin horn placed the marks of childishness and disruptive behavior on the recipient, shedding light on the joy with which Pecatonica returned the symbol of its humiliation.

26. Morris, "Excelsiors of Chicago, Postwar," 214; *Bloomington Pantagraph*, September 11, 1867. For fuller account of Bloomington reaction to Keenan's signing, see Sampson, "Spirit of Discord," 259.

27. Morris, "Excelsiors of Chicago, Postwar," 214.

28. Ibid., 215.

29. Ibid., 215–16. For the quote, see *Chicago Tribune*, July 22, 1868. For "muffin nine," see *Chicago Times*, August 4, 1868.

30. Morris, "Excelsiors of Chicago, Postwar," 216–17.

31. Ibid., 217; Freedman, "Baseball Fad in Chicago," 54, 60. For *Chicago Tribune* quote, see issue of November 7, 1868; for *Chicago Times* quote, see issue of June 13, 1869.

32. For hogs, see *Danville Commercial*, December 24, 1868; for the fire company, May 16, 1867. The Lincoln Fire Company No. 1 roster included D. A. Childs and H. Redford. Horace H. Redford was also vice president of the Vermilion Base Ball Club and D. A. Childs was a captain of one team in the intrasquad game (*Danville Commercial*, October 11, 1866, November 15, 1866).

33. *Danville Commercial*, November 15, 1866. For Kingsbury's role at the newspaper, see *Danville Commercial*, November 14, 1867, September 17, 1868.

34. *Danville Commercial*, April 25, 1867, July 11, 1867, August 1, 1867.

35. *Champaign Union and Gazette*, September 1, 1867, September 4, 1867.

36. *Champaign Gazette and Union*, September 25, 1867; *Danville Commercial*, October 3, 1867, October 10, 1867; *Champaign Gazette and Union*, November 6, 1867.

37. *Danville Commercial*, November 7, 1867.

38. Dorothy Jordan, "The Old Home Town," *Decatur Review*, July 17, 1921; also quoted in Morris, *But Didn't We Have Fun?*," 208.

39. *Pana Gazette*, July 6, 1867, July 20, 1867, July 27, 1867, August 3, 1867.

40. *Pana Gazette*, August 10, 1867.

41. *Pana Gazette*, August 17, 1867; *Decatur Weekly Republican*, August 22, 1867.

42. *Pana Gazette*, August 31, 1867.

43. *Pana Gazette*, September 14, 1867; September 21, 1867; *Decatur Weekly Republican*, September 19, 1867. For a full account of the Decatur tournament debacle, see Sampson, "Spirit of Discord," esp. 247–48, 260–68.

44. *Pana Gazette*, September 21, 1867, October 5, 1867, October 26, 1867.

45. *Pana Gazette*, November 16, 1867, May 22, 1868.

46. Jordan, "Old Home Town."

47. Quote is from *Ottawa Republican*, May 9, 1867 (emphasis in original). See also *Ottawa Free Trader*, May 18, 1867; *Ottawa Republican*, May 23, 1867. After a few months of play, the Shabbonas' tenure on the Fox River site was secured when the property's owner, Col. William R. W. Cushman, "granted the club complete control of the ball ground" (*Ottawa Republican*, August 22, 1867).

48. *Ottawa Free Trader*, June 1, 1867, June 29, 1867, June 15, 1867, June 29, 1867.

49. *Ottawa Republican*, July 11, 1867. Also see *Ottawa Free Trader*, July 27, 1867. *The Black Crook*, sometimes termed the first Broadway musical, toured several Illinois towns and cities in summer 1867. Somewhat risqué by the standards of the time, it featured tights-clad young women dancing and parading about the stage (Pete Hamill, *Downtown: My Manhattan* [New York: Back Bay, 2004], 123–24). Ottawa was not the only town featuring a game with the Black Crook troupe. The actors and crew also played games in Dubuque and Oquawka, a small town on the Mississippi

River. A junior club from Young America declared themselves the "Black Crooks" and played two games with a Monmouth club (*Rock Island Argus*, August 7, 1867; *Oquawka Spectator*, October 17, 1867; *Monmouth Atlas*, October 4, 1867, October 11, 1867).

50. *Ottawa Republican*, July 11, 1867. Also see *Ottawa Free Trader*, July 27, 1867; *Chicago Tribune*, August 20, 1867.

51. *Ottawa Free Trader*, September 7, 1867; *Ottawa Republican*, September 19, 1867.

52. *Ottawa Free Trader*, September 28, 1867.

53. *Ottawa Republican*, October 17, 1867; *Ottawa Free Trader*, November 2, 1867.

54. For skating rink, see *Ottawa Free Trader*, November 16, 1867.

55. *Ottawa Free Trader*, March 7, 1868, March 14, 1868, May 16, 1868; *Ottawa Republican*, June 25, 1868.

56. *Ottawa Free Trader*, May 23, 1868, May 30, 1868, June 27, 1868; *Ottawa Republican*, July 2, 1868. An article early in the 1868 season claimed the Shabbona Base Ball Club had played thirteen match games in 1867, outscoring their opponents 648 to 514. Victories were recorded over clubs from Ottawa, LaSalle, Dayton, Wheaton (Athletics), and the Black Crook theatrical troupe (*Ottawa Free Trader*, May 16, 1868).

57. *Ottawa Free Trader*, August 8, 1868, August 27, 1868. The chronology here is complicated by the fact that the second game is combined in an article mentioning both the second and the third games. For Shabbona meeting to determine future of the club, see *Ottawa Republican*, September 3, 1868; results of the second and third games (the latter won 39 to 11 by the Shabbonas) are in *Ottawa Free Trader*, September 24, 1868.

58. *Ottawa Free Trader*, August 8, 1868, May 16, 1868.

59. *Ottawa Free Trader*, September 18, 1869. For advertisements, see *Ottawa Free Trader*, April 17, 1869, May 29, 1869, July 3, 1869, July 24, 1869, and July 31, 1869. Organization of a new club in Earlville was reported in the issue of May 22, 1869. Leland's Dirigio Base Ball Club was mentioned and somewhat unfavorably compared to a new croquet club in the issue of August 7, 1869. For the Morris game, see October 2, 1869.

60. *Ottawa Free Trader*, June 25, 1870. A later article, on July 30, 1870, noted, "This club has been in existence two or three years, in name, but not in a complete organization before this season."

61. An account of the game can be found in *Ottawa Free Trader*, July 2, 1870. The "country greenhorn team" quote comes from the same newspaper, July 30, 1870.

62. *Ottawa Free Trader*, July 30, 1870.

63. *Ottawa Free Trader*, August 13, 1870.

64. Ibid.

65. *Ottawa Free Trader*, August 27, 1870.

66. Ibid.

67. *Chicago Times*, September 25, 1870.

68. *Ottawa Free Trader*, August 27, 1870, October 1, 1870.

Ninth Inning. The Thrill Departs

1. *Bloomington Pantagraph*, October 28, 1870.

2. *Rock Island Union*, June 15, 1868.

3. *Cairo Democrat*, May 30, 1868.

4. *Carlyle Constitution and Union*, June 8, 1869, June 14, 1869, June 22, 1869, July 13, 1869.

5. *Bureau County Patriot*, July 20, 1869, August 24, 1869, August 31, 1869; *Bureau County Republican*, June 24, 1869, July 22, 1869, July 15, 1869, September 2, 1869. For Freeport, see *Freeport Bulletin*, August 12, 1869, September 2, 1869.

6. *Jacksonville Journal*, July 15, 1869, July 22, 1869, July 28, 1869, July 30, 1869.

7. *Aurora Beacon*, May 13, 1869, August 25, 1869.

8. *Quincy Herald*, June 4, 1869.

9. Morris, *But Didn't We Have Fun?* 9, 136, 46, 166; Seymour and Seymour, *Baseball*, 43, 48, 51.

10. For Thomas Fitzgerald's resignation letter, see Richard Hershberger, "Athletic Base Ball Club," in *Base Ball Founders: The Clubs, Players and Cities of the Northeast That Established the Game*, edited by Peter Morris, William J. Ryczek, Jan Finkel, Leonard Levin, and Richard Malatzky (Jefferson, NC: McFarland, 2013), 235. Background on the Athletics players who took the field in Bloomington is drawn from Hershberger's chapter. For Al Reach, a left-handed second baseman, see 239–40; for John Dickson McBride, who pitched that day, 239; for catcher John Radcliffe, 239; for Isaac Wilkins, shortstop, 240; for Wes "Icicle" Fistler, first baseman, 237–38; for third baseman Tom Berry, 237; for Ned Cuthbert, left fielder, 237; for John "Count" Sensenderfer, center fielder, 240; and for right fielder Harry Schafer, 240.

11. *Bloomington Pantagraph*, June 10, 1868, June 11, 1868, June 15, 1868.

12. *Bloomington Pantagraph*, June 16, 1868; *Quincy Whig and Republican*, June 23, 1868.

13. *Bloomington Pantagraph*, June 25, 1868, June 26, 1868.

14. Craig B. Waff and William J. Ryczek, "Atlantic Base Ball Club," in Morris et al., *Base Ball Founders*, 117. Information on players is taken from the Waff and Ryczek chapter. Shortstop Dicky Pearce is credited with inventing the bunt (133) and left fielder John Chapman was viewed as the "best left fielder in the country" (129–30). First baseman Joseph Start is now believed to be the first at his position to play off the base (refuting the earlier credit assigned to Charles Comiskey), 134–35. Pitcher George Zettlein was the one who broke the Reds' winning streak (135–36). Other players in the lineup that day were Charles J. Smith, third base (134); right fielder Thomas J. Pratt (133–34); catcher Charles Mills (132); second baseman Frederick William Hotchkiss Crane (130); and Robert V. Ferguson (130).

15. *Bloomington Pantagraph*, June 25, 1868, June 27, 1868; *Greenville Advocate*, July 3, 1868.

16. *Bloomington Pantagraph*, June 27, 1868.

17. David Ball, "Buckeyes of Cincinnati," in Morris et al., *Base Ball Pioneers*, 142.

18. *Bloomington Pantagraph*, July 24, 1868, July 25, 1868; Ball, "Buckeyes of Cincinnati," 144; and Ball, "Cincinnati Base Ball Club ('Red Stockings'), in Morris et al., *Base Ball Pioneers*, 156. For Sweasy and Leonard on the Buckeyes, see Thorn, *Baseball in the Garden of Eden*, 143. For Sweasy on the Red Stockings, see Ball, "Cincinnati Base Ball Club," 157–58.

19. *Bloomington Pantagraph*, July 27, 1868.

20. *Bloomington Pantagraph*, August 11, 1868, August 13, 1868, August 14, 1868. For Wright, see Ball, "Cincinnati Base Ball Club," 158. For Birdsall, see Peter Morris, "Nationals of Washington," in Morris, *Base Ball Pioneers*, 276.

21. Aaron W. Miller, "Union Base Ball Club of Morrisania," in Morris et al., *Base Ball Founders*, 93; for the use of paid players, see 94; for Esteban Enrique "Steve" Bellán, see Peter Morris, "Unions of Lansingburgh (Troy 'Haymakers')," in Morris et al., *Base Ball Pioneers*, 62, and Miller, "Union Base Ball Club of Morrisania," 95. Union players in Bloomington that day, in addition to Birdsall, Pabor, and Wright, are taken from Miller's chapter, including second baseman Henry C. Austin (95); center fielder Alfred D. Martin, who would play major league baseball (96); Ed Shelly, third baseman (96); and two other players, "Goldie" and Smith, for whom no further information could be found (97).

22. *Bloomington Pantagraph*, August 14, 1868.

23. *Monmouth Review*, May 15, 1869, July 2, 1869; *Monmouth Atlas*, July 2, 1869. The five former members of the defunct Chicago Excelsior Club on the Amateur roster that day were Goodrich, Stearns, Kennedy, Sweet, and Grant (Peter Morris, "Excelsiors of Chicago, Postwar," in Morris et al., *Base Ball Pioneers*, 220). Horace Buker, an early historian of the Rockford Forest City Club, terms the Chicago Amateurs "the remains of the once lordly Excelsiors" (Horace Buker, Cradle of Baseball series, *Rockford Republic*, June 17, 1922).

24. *Monmouth Atlas*, July 9, 1869, September 3, 1869.

25. Peter Morris, "Forest City Club of Rockford," in Morris et al., *Base Ball Pioneers*, 225; for Horace Buker, see his article in the *Rockford Republic*, April 22, 1922.

26. References to the amateur status of the Forest City Club can be found in *Quincy Whig and Republican*, August 25, 1869; *Quincy Herald*, August 26, 1869, and August 27, 1869. For the professional futures of Addy, Barnes, Cone, Foley, Hastings, and Spalding, see Morris, "Forest City Club," 229, 229–30, 230, 230–31, 232, respectively; for Stires, see Peter Morris, "Byron (Illinois) Base Ball Club," in Morris et al., *Base Ball Pioneers*, 223.

27. *Quincy Herald*, August 28, 1869, September 3, 1869. Touring downstate Illinois that summer, the Forest City Club won "with ridiculous ease" games likely against Jacksonville's Alert Base Ball Club and the Liberty Club of Springfield, in addition to the two best St. Louis clubs (Buker, Cradle of Baseball series, *Rockford Republic*, June 24, 1922). A value of $21.49 has been used for an equivalent of 1869 dollar as of June 6, 2022.

28. Buker, Cradle of Baseball series, *Rockford Republic*, June 21, 1922.

29. *Quincy Herald*, August 4, 1869, September 23, 1869, September 29, 1869, Oc-

tober 2, 1869, October 8, 1869, October 9, 1869; *Quincy Whig and Republican*, August 5, 1869, September 14, 1869, and September 22, 1869; *Galesburg Free Press*, October 8, 1869; *Carthage Gazette*, October 21, 1869.

30. *Quincy Herald*, October 14, 1869.

31. *Chicago Tribune*, October 28, 1870.

32. *Bloomington Pantagraph*, October 23, 1870.

33. *Decatur Magnet*, November 6, 1868.

Epilogue

1. *Decatur Review*, June 16, 1918.

2. Ibid. In 2019, the author and a friend, Decatur historian R. Lee Slider, inspected the site of the baseball field in question, locating it in what today is a thick patch of brush and saplings to the northwest of the old Great Western Railway Depot (currently the Wabash Depot antique store). The site of the house struck by the ball in Archer's account remains, though the house is not there. The uncertain location of the 1867 home plate, compounded by the overgrown condition of the former ball field, makes it impossible to measure how far the hit might have gone. It is not impossible, however, that the event Archer recalled or at least some similar event occurred. Archer is listed on the McPherson Club's roster as playing in at least one game (*Decatur Weekly Republican*, August 8, 1867), though the player is listed as "J. G. Archer," perhaps a misprint.

3. For Isaac Archer's obituary, see *Decatur Review*, December 19, 1934. For Spalding's career, see Morris, "Forest City Club of Rockford," 232; Spalding's career and tactics, as well as his role in the Doubleday myth, are brilliantly presented in Thorn, *Baseball in the Garden of Eden*. Every facet of Spalding's long career is covered with concision and clarity by Thorn.

4. *Chicago Tribune*, April 23, 1937.

5. *Cairo Bulletin*, April 22, 1880, June 24, 1878, July 30, 1871, October 11, 1871, October 22, 1882, November 13, 1878, November 18, 1879.

6. *Cairo Bulletin*, June 27, 1880, August 31, 1882, September 26, 1880, October 10, 1884.

7. *Cairo Bulletin*, December 2, 1879; birth and death dates from "Find a Grave" website, https://www.findagrave.com. For details of Silver's life and burial, see *St. Louis Republic*, November 24, 1900, and the *Jewish Voice* (St. Louis, Missouri), November 29, 1900.

8. Background information on Munn can be found in his obituary, *Chicago Tribune*, September 18, 1913; for his role in the 1860 Republican convention in Decatur, see *Chicago Inter Ocean*, May 10, 1900; for his role as a Grant elector, see *Mattoon Weekly Journal*, July 5, 1902. The latter story is an old electoral ticket perhaps pasted into a news column to fill space.

9. *Cairo Bulletin*, April 6, 1881, September 7, 1881. For examples of Munn's political

activities, see *Chicago Tribune*, March 19, 1886, March 22, 1885, June 14, 1884, August 29, 1886, October 18, 1890, October 27, 1886, and *Chicago Inter Ocean*, March 30, 1890.

10. For the "wholesale hog stealing" case, see *Chicago Inter Ocean*, September 8, 1887; for Munn's "defense of the boodlers" and subsequent efforts to receive his fees, see *Inter Ocean*, November 4, 1887, and *Chicago Tribune*, September 18, 1913; for Dr. Cream's background, see *Chicago Tribune*, June 19, 1881, June 29, 1881, September 22, 1881, September 23, 1881, September 24, 1881, October 19, 1881; for the Mary Shaffer case, see *Inter Ocean*, August 21, 1895, and *Chicago Tribune*, May 31, 1896.

11. *Chicago Tribune*, September 18, 1913.

12. Decatur *Herald*, February 13, 1913, March 23, 1916, January 4, 1922, January 5, 1922; *Decatur Review*, January 2, 1922, January 4, 1922.

13. For Samuel Montgomery, see *Decatur Republican*, February 17, 1897; *Decatur Review*, April 17, 1916, July 16, 1918; *Decatur Herald*, July 13, 1916.

14. For R. R. Montgomery, see *Decatur Herald*, June 13, 1909, March 8, 1930; for flyswatter, see *Decatur Review*, July 1, 1900, and O. T. Banton, *History of Macon County* (Decatur: Macon County Historical Society, 1976), 229; *Decatur Herald*, March 28, 1896, May 3, 1898, November 21, 1889.

15. *Decatur Herald*, September 6, 1926; *Decatur Republican*, April 30, 1887.

16. For W. C. Johns's political and judicial career, see "Judge W. C. Johns," *Journal of the Illinois State Historical Society* 7, no. 2 (July 1914): 130–35; Peter Morris, "Corwin Johns," Society for American Baseball Research, http://sabr.org/bioproj/person/c48808d8; *Decatur Review*, August 11, 1905.

17. *Decatur Review*, August 13, 1905, June 26, 1914, June 28, 1914.

18. For Blake's position, see *Ottawa Free Trader*, May 18, 1867, and *Peoria National Democrat*, June 22, 1867.

19. *Streator Times*, October 29, 1900; for squirrel incident and "telephone," see *Ottawa Free Trader*, December 30, 1871, May 11, 1878.

20. *Streator Free Press*, December 15, 1877. For a client's gift of a revolver to Blake, see *Streator Free Press*, March 2, 1900. The client did not go free, however, and received a twenty-year term in the state penitentiary (*Ottawa Free Trader*, March 17, 1877, February 8, 1879; *Streator Free Press*, January 5, 1878; *Ottawa Free Trader*, September 22, 1882, October 13, 1888).

21. *Ottawa Free Trader*, April 6, 1878, May 18, 1878, June 1, 1878; *Streator Times*, October 29, 1900; *Streator Free Press*, June 8, 1894.

22. For Blake's nomination, see *Ottawa Free Trader*, October 13, 1888. The *Ottawa Free Trader*, in its January 18, 1890, edition, carried excerpts from several newspapers calling for Blake's political scalp. Blake made the arrest on the steps of the Clifton Hotel, where the coroner was conducting an inquest into the murder and robbery of David Moore (*Ottawa Free Trader*, June 28, 1890; *Streator Times*, October 29, 1900).

23. *Streator Times*, July 24, 1900, October 29, 1900; *Streator Free Press*, November 2, 1900.

24. *Fuel Magazine*, June 24, 1910, 419.

25. Ibid.

26. "Fred Thomas Dubois (1851–1930), *Biographical Directory of the United States Congress*, http://bioguide.congress.gov/scripts/biodisplay.pl?index=d000509; Fred's brother, J. K., was described as a "leading physician in Boise City," *Wood River Times* (Haily, Idaho), June 18, 1891.

27. *Idaho Semi-weekly World* (Idaho City), September 7, 1888; *Wood River Times* (Haily, Idaho), June 18, 1891.

28. *McPherson Opinion* (McPherson, Kansas), February 4, 1897; "Dubois, Fred Thomas," *Biographical Dictionary of the United States Congress*, https://bioguide.congress .gov/search/bio/D000509; *Bloomington Pantagraph*, February 14, 1930; also see *Greeneville Democrat-Sun* (Greenville, Tennessee), February 15, 1930.

29. *Boston Globe*, February 14, 1930; *Oakland* (California) *Tribune*, February 14, 1930; *Stevens Point* (Wisconsin) *Journal*, February 14, 1930; *Salem* (Oregon) *Capital Journal*, February 14, 1930; *Bloomington* (Illinois) *Pantagraph*, February 14, 1930; *Salt Lake Tribune* (Salt Lake City, Utah), February 12, 1930; *Brooklyn Times Union*, February 18, 1930; *Marshall* (Indiana) *Evening Chronicle*, February 14, 1930; *Ogden* (Utah) *Standard-Examiner*, February 14, 1930; *Greenville* (Tennessee) *Democrat*, February 15, 1930.

30. For the information on Bloomington's African American ballplayers, the author is indebted to Bill Kemp, head of the McLean County Historical Society and Museum's library, and volunteer Terri Clemens for their skilled, persistent, and invaluable help. See "The Dark Side of Politics," a story about "a grand rally" of African American Republicans, also attended by whites, which Brown chaired (*Bloomington Pantagraph*, October 26, 1878). For the debating society, see *Bloomington Pantagraph*, February 24, 1876; for judging the debate contest, see *Bloomington Pantagraph*, December 28, 1887; for his election as delegate, see *Bloomington Pantagraph*, April 26, 1880.

31. *Bloomington Pantagraph*, October 14, 1882, and January 25, 1883.

32. *Bloomington Pantagraph*, April 24, 1873. For his role in the protest meeting, see *Bloomington Pantagraph*, February 7, 1885. *Bloomington Pantagraph*, April 12, 1880, recounts his domestic situation. Franklin is identified as a servant in *Tenth Census of United States 1880*, roll 230, page 243d. Enumeration District 163.

33. *Bloomington Pantagraph*, August 24, 1873, July 4, 1923. James's and Marion's occupations are in *Holland's Bloomington City Directory, 1870–71*, 126; for James, see also *Bloomington Pantagraph*, December 23, 1871, October 18, 1875, May 26, 1876, May 31, 1876, September 11, 1877, April 4, 1878.

34. *Bloomington Pantagraph*, April 18, 1876, July 12, 1883. For James, see *Bloomington Pantagraph*, November 6, 1879, December 2, 1879, December 29, 1879, December 25, 1879.

35. *Bloomington Pantagraph*, July 18, 1872, February 8, 1878, December 25, 1879, June 3, 1882, July 25, 1898.

36. Cheney's obituary reviews his multioccupation career: *Bloomington Pantagraph*, November 3, 1911; for gambling and liquor charges and the change of venue, see *Bloomington Pantagraph*, September 29, 1879, September 30, 1879, November 8,

1879, November 25, 1879, November 26, 1879. For the fraud charges, see *Bloomington Pantagraph*, February 27, 1879, August 14, 1883. For the trotting mare dispute, see *Bloomington Pantagraph*, September 5, 1879, February 14, 1880; for the jockey club article, see *Bloomington Pantagraph*, July 16, 1882; he also faced a larceny charge; see *Bloomington Pantagraph*, February 19, 1875.

37. *Bloomington Pantagraph*, June 15, 1883, September 12, 1883, March 30, 1886, May 23, 1888.

38. *Bloomington Pantagraph*, November 3, 1911. Peter Morris identifies Cheney as seeing "sporadic duty" with the Forest City Club in 1869 and as a "close friend" of future Hall of Fame member Charles Radbourn (Morris, "Forest City Club of Rockford," 230). For the career of Charles Radbourn, who won fifty-nine games in 1884 for the National League's Providence Grays, see Edward Achorn, *Fifty-Nine in '84: Old Hoss Radbourn, Barehanded Baseball and the Greatest Season a Pitcher Ever Had* (New York: Harper-Collins, 2010).

39. Lackey's move to Chicago is noted as occurring in 1870 on his death certificate (Physician's Certificate of Death, State of Illinois, Cook County, dated March 7, 1886, Cook County Vital Records, Chicago, Illinois). His role in the founding of the Bloomington Base Ball Club can be found in *Bloomington Pantagraph*, May 25, 1865; for his election as president of the Illinois State Base Ball Association, see *Illinois State Journal*, July 29, 1867; *Chicago Inter Ocean*, March 8, 1886; for Zouaves, see Brent Nosworthy, *The Bloody Crucible of Courage: Fighting Methods and Combat Experience in the Civil War* (New York: Carroll and Graff, 2003), 98–101.

40. *Chicago Inter Ocean*, February 19, 1880, March 8, 1886; *Chicago Tribune*, July 15, 1877, November 3, 1879, November 16, 1879; *Bloomington Pantagraph*, August 10, 1881.

41. *Chicago Tribune*, December 12, 1880; *Chicago Inter Ocean*, January 20, 1881; Lackey death certificate. For reactions of the Zouave unit, see *Chicago Tribune*, March 9, 1886, and *Chicago Inter Ocean*, March 9, 1886. See also obituaries of Lackey in *Chicago Tribune*, March 8, 1886, and *Chicago Inter Ocean*, March 8, 1886.

42. Patrick Joseph Keenan, Certificate of Death, March 26, 1917, State of Illinois Archives; *Bloomington Pantagraph*, March 27, 1917. The *Bloomington Pantagraph*'s anger was reprinted by the *Illinois State Journal*, September 20, 1867. See also Morris, "Excelsiors of Chicago, Postwar," in Morris et al., *Base Ball Pioneers*, 215. For Keenan's role at the Decatur tournament, see *Illinois State Journal*, September 23, 1867.

43. *Holland's Bloomington City Directory for 1870–71*, lists him as a bartender (133), and the *Bloomington City Directory for 1872–75*, 218, indicates Keenan was proprietor of the Senate Saloon; see *Gould's City Directory for 1875–76* (Bloomington: David B. Gould, 1875), 118–19; *Gould's City Directory 1876–77* (Bloomington: David B. Gould, 1877), 113. For Keenan's retirement listing, see *Bloomington and Normal City Directory for 1915* (Bloomington: Pantagraph Printing, n.d.), 859.

44. *Bloomington Pantagraph*, May 10, 1881, June 20, 1881, April 19, 1883.

45. *Bloomington Pantagraph*, August 15, 1916, March 27, 1917; Patrick Joseph Keenan, death certificate.

46. *Chicago Tribune*, October 31, 1867, November 3, 1867, December 30, 1877.

47. *Oquawka Spectator*, August 8, 1867; *Jacksonville Weekly Sentinel*, May 4, 1866; *Illinois State Register*, August 18, 1866; *Peoria Transcript*, September 14, 1867.

Appendix A. Illinois Baseball Teams, by Town and Year Founded, 1865–70

1. Found in Rock Island County Historical Society files, Moline, Illinois.

2. Apparently contained several members of old Okaw club.

3. Article identifies team as remnant of the Chicago Excelsiors.

4. It is possible that team names were confused by newspaper editors as game reports and other information apparently were often contributed by citizens. Therefore, it is possible that the Lacon and Lacon City clubs are one and the same and perhaps the Defiant is the same club as well. Teams would sometimes change names during a season. The entry on the Empire Base Ball Club shows an example.

5. Found in Rock Island County Historical Society files, Moline, Illinois.

Appendix C. Illinois Baseball Players, by Town and Team, 1865–70

1. *Alton Weekly Telegraph*, November 1, 1867; November 22, 1867; *Fuel Magazine: The Coal Operators National Weekly*, June 21, 1910, 419.

2. *Bloomington City Directory and McLean County Gazetteer* (Chicago: Bailey and Hair, 1866), 66, 109, 131, 142, 151, 152, 161, 174, 194; *Holland's Bloomington City Directory for 1868–69* (Chicago: Western, 1868), 65, 69, 92, 108, 128, 140, 142, 208.

3. Patrick Joseph Keenan does not appear in city directories during the 1860s so his occupation during his playing days remains a mystery. He appears in later city directors as a saloon owner or bartender. (*Bloomington City Directory, 1872–73* [Bloomington: Edward Arntzen, 1872], 218).

4. Rood was also mayor of Bloomington (*Holland's Bloomington City Directory, 1868–69*, 32, and *Historical Encyclopedia of Illinois and History of McLean County*, ed. Ezra M. Prince and John H. Burman [Chicago: Munsell, 1908], 2: 895–96).

5. *Gould's Bloomington and Normal Directory of 1873* (Bloomington: Leader, 1873), 61; *Tenth Census of the United States, 1880*, roll 230, p. 243d. Enumeration District 164; *Holland's Bloomington City Directory, 1870–71*, 126; *Bloomington Pantagraph*, December 2, 1879, December 25, 1879, December 29, 1879.

6. Several references to Brown in the *Bloomington Pantagraph* through the 1860s, 1870s, and 1880s fail to name his occupation.

7. *Edwards' Annual Directory to the City of Cairo for 1868* (no place: Edwards), 41, 50, 54, 61, 89, 95 [hereafter, *Cairo Directory 1868*].

8. *Cairo Directory 1868*, 54, 61, 76, 83, 91, 97.

9. Reynolds may also have played for the Magneta Base Ball Club.

10. *Cairo Directory 1868*, 42.

11. Arrick may also have played for the Podanger Base Ball Club but will not be listed with that club.

12. *Cairo Directory 1866*, 90, 130; *Cairo Directory 1868*, 59, 63, 91, 130.

13. Gossman, who also may have played with the Podanger Base Ball Club, was a barkeeper in an enterprise that also sold stoves, tinware, hardware, and cigarettes (*Cairo Directory 1868*, 59).

14. *Cairo Directory 1868*, 47, 53, 57, 62, 66, 77, 78, 85, 87.

15. *Cairo Directory 1868*, 97, lists a Samuel and a Samuel E. Wilson at the same address. Samuel owned a boat supply firm. No occupation is listed for Samuel E., who is likely the player. He also played for the Podanger Base Ball Club but will not be listed with that organization.

16. *Cairo Directory 1866*, 72, 82, 97, 133, 139; *Cairo Directory 1868*, 58, 69.

17. *Cairo Directory 1866*, 11, 97, 100, 111, 137; *Cairo Directory 1868*, 69, 76, 95.

18. At that time, likely a political appointment.

19. *Cairo Directory 1868*, 53, 59, 61, 71, 75, 80, 95.

20. Likely a political appointment.

21. Loomis, "Egyptian Summer," 3, 4.

22. Henry Condit also played for the Egyptian Base Ball Club.

23. Hay also played for the Egyptians.

24. Fletcher also played for the Egyptians.

25. Bill Johnson also played for the Egyptians.

26. Free Johnson also played for the Egyptians and Union Base Ball Club.

27. Loomis, "Egyptian Summer," 2, 3, 4; Ross, *Centralia Illinois*, 22, 39; *Centralia Sentinel*, August 13, 1868.

28. Possibly related to the father and son, James and James T. Cunningham.

29. Loomis, "Egyptian Summer," 4.

30. J. S. Lothrop's *Champaign County Directory, 1870–71* (Chicago: Rand, McNally, 1871), 197, 198, 204, 207, 208, 212, 222 [hereafter cited as *Lothrop's Directory*].

31. *Lothrop's Directory* also lists D. Bailey, Champaign Township supervisor, and David J. Bailey, a farmer. D. S. Bailey, a telegraph operator, seems the most likely ballplayer.

32. For at least one game, Eppstein was the team's scorer. The "popular clothing house" of "R .M. Eppstein and Bros." burned in 1868 but was rebuilt (*Champaign Gazette and Union*, July 22, 1868. The same newspaper reported on August 5, 1868, that "Max Eppstein" had just returned from New York City, where he was "purchasing goods."

33. Hill as served as the first president of the Champaign (Empire) Base Ball Club.

34. *Lothrop's Directory*, 212, offers four possibilities: H. Jefferson, a livery stable keeper; J. W. Jefferson, a farmer; William Jefferson, owner of a livery stable; and John Jefferson, a laborer.

35. Edwin Pierce, as the only "Pierce" in *Lothrop's Directory*, 222, may be the "Pierce" named in newspaper accounts of the Empire Club.

36. *Lothrop's Directory*, 225, lists an N. E. Scott as a general ticket agent. He seems more likely than Charles Scott, a dentist, the only two Scotts in the directory.

37. *Lothrop's Directory*, 210, 216, 225, 229.

38. *Lothrop's Directory*, 205.

39. *Danville Commercial*, October 11, 1866, November 14, 1867, and November 15, 1866.

40. *Decatur Weekly Republican*, March 5, 1868, September 23, 1869.

41. *Decatur Weekly Republican*, March 5, 1868, identifies Keck as the keeper of an illegal tavern.

42. *City Directory of Decatur, Illinois, 1871–72* (Decatur, IL: Wiggins, n.d.), 112, 126, 143 [hereafter cited as *Wiggins Directory*]; *Decatur Weekly Republican*, August 8, 1867, Dec. 31, 1868; *Decatur Review*, June 26, 1914, June 16, 1918, 15; *1870 Macon County, Illinois, Census*, vol. 2, *Decatur and Decatur Township* (Decatur: Decatur Genealogical Society, 1997), archived in Local History Room, Decatur Public Library; *Decatur Herald*, June 13 and 16, 1909. Also see Morris, *But Didn't We Have Fun?*, 42; US Census of 1860, vol. 1, 17–18.

43. Isaac Theodore is likely the "J. G. Archer" listed in a team line-up in the *Decatur Weekly Republican*, August 8, 1867.

44. *Wiggins Directory*, 86, lists Bramble in a partnership with his father, Onius, in a book and stationery store.

45. An advertisement in the *Decatur Weekly Republican*, November 7, 1867, indicates Gill is a marble monument dealer.

46. Johns laid out the first baseball field in Decatur and played for the McPhersons that year and in 1867.

47. *Wiggins Directory*, 130.

48. LaSalle County US Census for 1860, transcribed by the LaSalle County Genealogical Guild, Illinois Room, Riddick Public Library District, Ottawa, Illinois, 54; LaSalle County US Census for 1870, transcribed by the LaSalle County Genealogy Guild, Illinois Room, Riddick Public Library District, Ottawa, Illinois, 112.

49. *Annawalt and Lawrence's Galesburg City Director—1867–68* (Burlington, IA: Annawalt and Lawrence, 1867), 50, 91, 94, 107, 114, 118, 131 [hereafter cited as *A and L Directory*].

50. *A and L's Directory*, 52, 79,

51. *Holland's Jacksonville City Directory, 1871–1872* (Chicago: Western, 1871), copy in Abraham Lincoln Presidential Library, Springfield, IL, 69 [hereafter cited as *Holland's Jacksonville City Directory*]; *Nixon's Jacksonville Directory for 1868–1869* (repr., Jacksonville Area Genealogical Society, 1991), copy at Abraham Lincoln Presidential Library, Springfield, IL, 53, 67, 82, 85, 89, 91, 93, 103 [hereafter cited as *Nixon's Jacksonville Directory*]; *Jacksonville Journal*, October 17, 1866, October 16, 1868.

52. Aside from box scores, King gained only two notices in local newspapers, the first in *Jacksonville Journal*, October 31, 1866, on the occasion of his dog's death: "The purp [*sic*] has gone to rest/By Parsons surely blessed/By Kings, while living fed/ Let

none despise him dead." The second, in *Jacksonville Journal*, August 27, 1869, noted that King, "One of the old nine" had quit playing and begun umpiring.

53. McConnel was the son of the powerful Democratic officeholder and party leader Murray McConnel.

54. *Holland's Jacksonville City Directory*, 68, 73, 97.

55. *Holland's Jacksonville City Directory*, 111, 127, 139; *Jacksonville Journal*, April 27, 1866,

56. According to the *Jacksonville Journal*, May 1, 1869, and June 21, 1869, Ten Eyck left the city, moving to Kansas to enter the banking business.

57. *Holland's Classified Business Directory for Rock Island and Moline* (Chicago: Western, 1868), 175, 186, 191, and plate 162 [hereafter cited as *Holland's Moline Directory*].

58. *Moline Directory*, 191 and plate 162 list no occupation for Velie but indicate a connection with Deere and Co. and the Moline Plow Works.

59. *Holland's Moline Directory*, 160, 166, 167.

60. *Hawley's Monmouth City Directory for 1874–75* (Jacksonville, IL: J. J. Ironmonger, 1874), 81, 99. [hereafter cited as *Monmouth Directory for 1874–75*]. *Monmouth Atlas*, June 7, 1867, April 3, 1868.

61. *Monmouth Directory for 1874–75*, 74.

62. *Mount Vernon Free Press*, October 25, 1867.

63. *Holland's Ottawa City Directory for 1869–70* (Chicago: Western, 1869), 14, 21, 69, 74, 75, 85, 93. [hereafter cited as *Holland's Ottawa Directory*].

64. Caton was a retired justice of the Illinois Supreme Court (*History of LaSalle County, Illinois,* vol. 1 (Chicago: Interstate, 1886), 568–69 [hereafter cited as *History of LaSalle County*].

65. *Ottawa Republican*, May 9, 1867, and *Ottawa Free Trader*, May 18, 1867; *1870 US Census*, population schedules, Ottawa, IL, Roll: M593_244, 586B, Family History Library Film: 545743, accessed at Ancestry.com, *1870 U.S. Census*, NARA microfilm publication M593, 1,761 rolls (Washington, DC: National Archives and Records Administration, n.d.); *Holland's Ottawa Directory*, 63, 109, 113.

66. Thomas McKinley also played for the Ottawa *Free Trader Base Ball Club*.

67. *Holland's Ottawa Directory*, 63, 88, 112, 123, 124, 133, 187; *Ottawa Republican-Times, Ottawa: Old and New, A Complete History of Ottawa, Illinois, 1829–1914* (Ottawa, IL: Republican-Times, 1912–1914), 116 [hereafter cited as *Ottawa: Old and New*].

68. Transcription of 1870 US Census for Christian County, Illinois History and Lincoln Collections, University of Illinois Library, Urbana, 116, 118, 132 [hereafter cited as 1870 Christian County Census]; Dorothy D. Drennan and Helen B. Broverman, *Illinois Sesquicentennial Edition of Christian County History* (Jacksonville, IL: Production, 1968), 199, 200; Dorothy Jordan, "The Old Home Town," *Decatur Review*. July 17, 1921. Jordan is also quoted in Morris, *"But Didn't We Have Fun?,"* 208.

69. Paddock was president of the club in 1868.

70. *Lothrop's Directory*, 255, 268, 269.

71. *Root's Quincy City Directory for 1866* (Quincy, IL: Quincy Whig and Republican, 1866), in Abraham Lincoln Presidential Library, 10, 16, 21, 30, 35, 37, 40, 74, 137, 151, 157, 163 [hereafter cited as *Root's Quincy Directory*]. *Quincy City Directory and Reference Book for 1871–1872* (Quincy, IL: Addison L. Langdon and Edward Arntzen, 1871), 39, 42. Hereafter cited as *Quincy City Directory*

72. John Wood Jr., son of former Governor John Wood, was likely affiliated with his father's milling business.

73. *Lothrop's Directory*, 274, 276; Champaign County, 1860 US Federal Census of Champaign County, Illinois, in Champaign County Genealogical Society, 1988, 153.

74. *Holland's Moline Directory*, 26, 33, 34, 38, 45, 49, 56, 59, 61.

75. A man, possibly Milton's father, is listed as the proprietor of the *Rock Island Argus*. (*Holland's Moline Directory*, 40).

76. *Holland's Moline Directory*, 28, 40, 49.

77. Charlie Bell may be the son of William Bell, a carpenter.

78. Stuart was an employee of W. H. Dart, who was secretary of the Illinois Base Ball Association.

79. *Springfield City Directory and Business Mirror for 1866* (Springfield, IL: Bronson and Nixon, 1865), 137 [hereafter cited as *Springfield Directory 1866*]; *Holland's Springfield City Directory for 1868–69* (Chicago: Western, 1868), 64, 72, 103, 108, 159 [hereafter cited as *Holland's Springfield Directory 1868*].

80. *Springfield Directory 1866*, 165, 181, 206, 219; *Holland's Springfield City for 1868*, 10, 127, 138, 152, 161.

81. *Springfield City Directory 1866*, 141.

BIBLIOGRAPHY

Censuses

Illinois, State of. 1870 Census, vol. 3, Decatur and Decatur Township. On file with Decatur Genealogical Society, transcribed and published, 1994, Local History Room, Decatur Public Library, Decatur, Illinois.

US Census. 1860 Census of Champaign County, Illinois. On file with Champaign County Genealogical Society, 1988.

US Census. 1870 Census of Christian County, Illinois. Typed copy on file with Illinois History and Lincoln Collections, University of Illinois Library, Urbana.

US Census. 1860 Census of LaSalle County, vol. 1, Ottawa. On file with LaSalle County Genealogy Guild, transcribed and published, 1993, Illinois Room, Riddick Public Library District, Ottawa, Illinois.

US Census. 1870 Census of LaSalle County, vol. 1, Ottawa. On file with LaSalle County Genealogy Society, undated, Illinois Room, Riddick Public Library District, Ottawa, Illinois.

City Directories

Annawalt and Lawrence's Galesburg City Directory, 1867. Burlington, IA: Annawalt and Lawrence, 1867.

Bloomington City Directory, 1872–73. Bloomington, IL: Edward Arntzen, 1872.

Bloomington City Directory and McLean County Gazetteer. Chicago: Bailey and Hair, 1866.

Bloomington and Normal Illinois City Directory for 1915. Chas. M. Samson, compiler, Bloomington, IL: Pantagraph Printing, n.d.

Cairo City Directory for 1866. Cairo, IL: Cairo Democrat Company.

Cairo City Directory for 1868. Cairo, IL: Edwards, 1868.

City Directory of Decatur, Illinois, 1871–72. Decatur, IL: Wiggins, n.d.

Dewey's Galesburg City Directory, 1868. Galesburg: J. Dewey, 1868.

Edwards' Annual Directory to the City of Cairo for 1868. St. Louis: Edwards, 1868.

Gould's Bloomington and Normal Directory of 1873. Bloomington, IL: Leader, 1873.

Gould's City Directory for 1876–77, Bloomington, IL: David B. Gould, 1877.

Hawley's Monmouth City Directory, 1874–1875. Jacksonville, IL: J. J. Ironmonger, 1874.

Holland's Bloomington City Directory for 1868–69. Chicago: Western, 1868.

Holland's Bloomington City Directory, 1870–71. Chicago: Western, 1870.

Holland's Classified Business Directory of Rock Island and Moline. Chicago: Western, 1868.

Holland's Galesburg City Directory, 1870–71. Chicago: Western, 1870.

Holland's Jacksonville City Directory, 1871–1872. Chicago: Western, 1871.

Holland's Ottawa City Directory for 1869–70. Chicago: Western, 1869.

Holland's Springfield City Directory for 1868–69. Chicago: Western, 1868.

J. S. Lothrop's Champaign County Directory, 1870–71. Chicago: Rand, McNally, 1871.

Nixon's Jacksonville Directory for 1868–1869. Reprinted by Jacksonville Area Genealogical Society, 1991.

Peoria City Directory. n.p., n.p.:1869.

Quincy City Directory and Reference Book—1871–1872. Quincy, IL: Addison Langdon and Edward Arntzer, 1871.

Root's Quincy City Directory for 1866. Quincy, IL: Quincy Whig and Republican, 1866.

Springfield City Directory and Business Mirror for 1866. Springfield, IL: Bronson and Nixon, 1865.

Contemporary Local Newspapers

Town	Paper name(s)
Alton	*Weekly Telegraph*
Amboy	*Lee County Journal*
Atlanta	*Argus*
Aurora	*Beacon*
Belleville	*Advocate, Democrat*
Belvidere	*Standard*
Bloomington	*Pantagraph, Leader*
Bunker Hill	*Union-Gazette*
Cairo	*Democrat, Times*
Carbondale	*New Era*
Carlinville	*Democrat*
Carlyle	*Constitution and Union, Union Banner*
Carrollton	*Gazette*
Carthage	*Gazette*
Centralia	*Democrat, Sentinel*

Champaign	*Champaign Union and Gazette, Gazette and Union, Champaign County Gazette*
Chebanse	*Herald*
Clinton	*Public and Central Transcript, Public, DeWitt Register,* 1868
Danville	*Commercial, Times*
Decatur	*Magnet, Weekly Republican, Herald, Review*
DeKalb	*County News*
Dixon	*Herald, Lee County Democrat, Republican and Telegraph, Weekly Telegraph*
Earlville	*Gazette*
East St. Louis	*Gazette, Herald*
Edwardsville	*Intelligencer*
Galena	*Gazette*
Galesburg	*Register, Times*
Greenville	*Advocate*
Harvard	*Independent*
Henry	*Marshall County Telegraph, Marshall County Republican*
Jacksonville	*Sentinel, Journal*
Jerseyville	*Jersey County Democrat*
Jonesboro	*Gazette*
Kankakee	*Gazette*
Lebanon	*Journal*
Lincoln	*Herald*
Litchfield	*Union Monitor*
Macomb	*Journal, Eagle*
Maroa	*Times*
Marshall	*Clark County Herald, Messenger*
Mendota	*Bulletin*
Metropolis	*Weekly Times*
Monmouth	*Weekly Review, Atlas*
Mound City	*Journal*
Mount Vernon	*Free Press*
Naperville	*Du Page County Press*
Nashville	*Journal*
Onarga	*Grand Prairie Review*
Oquawka	*Spectator*
Oregon	*Ogle County Reporter*
Ottawa	*Free Trader, Republican*
Pana	*Gazette*
Peoria	*Transcript, National Democrat*
Petersburg	*Democrat*
Pittsfield	*Pike County Democrat*
Princeton	*Bureau County Patriot, Bureau County Republican*

Quincy	*Weekly Herald, Daily Herald, Whig and Republican*
Rockford	*Democrat, Republic*
Rock Island	*Argus* (weekly), *Argus* (daily), *Union*
Springfield	*Illinois State Journal, Illinois State Register*
Sterling	*Gazette*
Streator	*Free Press*
Toulon	*Stark County News*
Urbana	*Illinois Democrat*
Warsaw	*Bulletin*
Watseka	*Iroquois Republican*
Waukegan	*Gazette*
Woodstock	*Sentinel*

Secondary Sources

Achorn, Edward. *Fifty-Nine in '84: Old Hoss Radbourn, Barehanded Baseball and the Greatest Season a Pitcher Ever Had.* New York: Harper-Collins, 2010.

Asinof, Eliot. *Eight Men Out and the 1919 World Series.* New York: Holt, 2000.

Banton, O. T. *History of Macon County.* Decatur, IL: Macon County Historical Society, 1976.

Bateman, Newton. *Historical Encyclopedia of Illinois and History of McLean County.* Chicago: Munsell, 1908.

Benson, Michael. *Ballparks of North America: A Comprehensive Historical Reference to Baseball Grounds, Yards, and Stadiums, 1845 to Present.* Jefferson, NC: McFarland, 1989.

Block, David. *Baseball before We Knew It: A Search for the Roots of the Game.* Lincoln: University of Nebraska Press, 2005.

Breslin, Jimmy. *Can't Anybody Here Play This Game? The Improbable Saga of the New York Mets' First Year.* New York: Ballantine, 1971.

Brinkerhoff, J. H. G. *Brinkerhoff's History of Marion County, Illinois.* Indianapolis: B. F. Bowen, 1909.

Brock, Darryl. *If I Never Get Back: A Novel.* Berkeley, CA: Frog Books, 2007.

Chadwick, Henry. *Haney's Base Ball Book of Reference.* Bedford, MA: 2004. First published 1867 by Haney (New York). A copy is in the collections of the Henry Ford Museum, Dearborn, Michigan.

De Tocqueville, Alexis. *Democracy in America.* Edited by J. P. Mayer. Translated by George Lawrence. New York: Harper and Row, 1988.

Dictionary of American Biography. s.v. "Pomeroy, Marcus Mills." Edited by Dumas Malone. New York: Charles Scribner's Sons, 1935.

Drennan, Dorothy D., and Helen B. Broverman. *Illinois Sesquicentennial Edition of Christian County History.* Jacksonville, IL: Production Press, 1968.

Eberle, Mark E. *Kansas Baseball, 1868–1941.* Lawrence, KS: University Press of Kansas, 2017.

Egan, James M. Jr. *Baseball on the Western Reserve: The Early Game in Cleveland and Northeast Ohio, Year by Year and Town by Town, 1865–1900*. Jefferson, NC: McFarland, 2008.

Freedman, Stephen. "The Baseball Fad in Chicago, 1865–1870: An Exploration of the Role of Sport in the Nineteenth-Century City." *Journal of Sports History* 5, no. 2 (Summer 1978): 42–64.

Gerlach, Harold. "Local Enthusiasm for Baseball Ran High in Those Early Days." *Centralia Evening Sentinel*, Golden Jubilee Edition, Centralia Area Historical Museum Archives.

Goldstein, Warren. *Playing for Keeps: A History of Early Baseball*. Anniversary ed. Ithaca, NY: Cornell University Press, 2009.

Hamill, Pete. *Downtown: My Manhattan*. New York: Back Bay, 2004.

Heaphy, Leslie A., ed. *Black Baseball and Chicago: Essays on the Players, Teams and Games*. Jefferson, NC: McFarland, 2006.

Hornbaker, Tim. *Turning the Black Sox White: The Misunderstood Legacy of Charles A. Comiskey*. New York: Sports Publishing, 2014.

Interstate Publishing Company. *History of LaSalle County, Illinois*. Chicago: Interstate, 1886.

Johns, Jane. *Personal Recollections of Early Decatur, Abraham Lincoln, Richard Oglesby and the Civil War*. Edited by Howard C. Schaub. Decatur, IL: Stephen Decatur Chapter, Daughters of the American Revolution, 1912.

Keiser, John H. *Building for the Centuries: Illinois 1865 to 1898*. Vol. 4, *The Sesquicentennial History of Illinois*. Urbana: University of Illinois Press, 1977.

Kirsch, George B. *Baseball and Cricket: The Creation of American Team Sports, 1838–72*. Paperback ed. Urbana: University of Illinois Press, 2007.

Landrum, Carl, ed., *Quincy: A Pictorial History*. St. Louis: G. Bradley, 1990.

Liepa, John. "Baseball Mania Strikes Iowa." *Iowa Heritage* 87, no. 1 (Spring 2006): 3–6.

Loomis, Steve. "Egyptian Summer." Unpublished ms. no. 21726. Centralia, IL: Centralia Area Historical Museum. Last revised, 2010.

McLean County, 1874 Atlas of. Chicago: Warner and Beers, 1874.

Morris, Peter. *Base Ball Fever: Early Baseball in Michigan*. Ann Arbor: University of Michigan Press, 2003.

———. *But Didn't We Have Fun? An Informal History of Baseball's Pioneer Era, 1843–1870*. Chicago: Ivan R. Dee, 2008.

———. *Catcher: How the Man behind the Plate Became an American Folk Hero*. Chicago: Ivan R. Dee, 2009.

———. *A Game of Inches: The Story behind the Innovations That Shaped Baseball*. One-volume edition. Chicago: Ivan R. Dee, 2010.

———. *Level Playing Fields: How the Groundskeeping Murphy Brothers Shaped Baseball*. Lincoln: University of Nebraska Press, 2007.

Morris, Peter, William J. Ryczek, Jan Finkel, Leonard Levin, and Richard Malatzky, eds. *Base Ball Founders: The Clubs, Players and Cities of the Northeast That Established the Game*. Jefferson, NC: McFarland, 2013.

———, eds. *Base Ball Pioneers, 1850–1870: The Clubs and Players Who Spread the Sport Nationwide.* Jefferson, NC: McFarland, 2012.

Nissenbaum, Stephen. *The Battle for Christmas: A Cultural History of America's Most Cherished Holiday.* New York: Vintage, 1996.

Prince, Ezra A., and John H. Burman, eds. *Historical Encyclopedia of Illinois and History of McLean County.* Chicago: Munsell, 1908.

Nosworthy, Brent. *The Bloody Crucible of Courage: Fighting Methods and Combat Experience of the Civil War.* New York: Carroll and Graf, 2003.

Ottawa Republican-Times. Ottawa: Old and New, A Complete History of Ottawa, Illinois, 1823–1914. Ottawa: Republican-Times, 1912.

Pierce, Bessie Louise. *A History of Chicago.* New York: Alfred A. Knopf, 1940.

Pruter, Robert. "Youth Baseball in Chicago, 1868–1890: Not Always Sandlot Ball." *Journal of Sports History* 26, no. 1 (Spring 1999): 1–28.

Ross, George E., *Centralia, Illinois: A Pictorial History.* St. Louis: G. Bradley, 1992.

Sampson, Robert D. "Fields of Battle: The Problem of Base Ball Playing Space in Post–Civil War Illinois." *Journal of the Illinois State Historical Society* 110, nos. 3–4 (Fall–Winter 2017): 283–304.

———. "'The Spirit of Discord Arose': The Birth Pangs of Base Ball in Central Illinois 1866–1868." *Journal of Illinois History* 15 (Winter 2012): 247–68.

Schiff, Andrew J. *"The Father of Baseball": A Biography of Henry Chadwick.* Jefferson, NC: McFarland, 2008.

Seymour, Harold, and Dorothy Zander. *Baseball: The Early Years.* New York: Oxford, 1960.

Shattuck, Debra A. *Bloomer Girls: Women Baseball Pioneers.* Urbana: University of Illinois Press, 2017.

Sullivan, Dean A., ed. and comp. *Early Innings: A Documentary History of Baseball, 1825–1908.* Lincoln: University of Nebraska Press, 1995.

Swanson, Ryan A. *When Baseball Went White: Reconstruction, Reconciliation, and Dreams of a National Pastime.* Lincoln: University of Nebraska Press, 2014.

Thorn, John. *Baseball in the Garden of Eden: The Secret History of the Early Game.* New York: Simon and Schuster, 2011.

———. *Past Time: Baseball as History.* New York: Oxford University Press, 2001.

Wallace, Joseph. *Past and Present of the City of Springfield and Sangamon County.* Chicago: S. J. Clarke, 1904.

INDEX

baseball (generally) *continued*
members, 75–79; humor and fun in, 71,
72–82 (*see also* "muffin" games/players);
injuries and fatalities (*see* baseball injuries and fatalities); key players in (*see*
batters and batting; fielders and fielding;
pitchers and pitching; umpires and umpiring); male vs. female clubs, 6, 96–98;
map of clubs in Illinois (1869), 5; "Massachusetts game," 7; mobility of players,
67–68; "muffin" games (*see* "muffin"
games/players); as the "national game"/
pastime, 12–13, 18, 40, 52, 54, 73–74, 80–
81, 86, 91, 97, 98, 113; "New York game,"
7, 15; notable individuals and teams,
119–40, 153–64; number of Illinois clubs
(1865–1870), 4, 5, 200n14; occupations
of players, 13–15, 17–19, 31–32, 67–70,
80, 86–89, 124, 126–27, 133, 143–45, 147,
149, 153–64; pioneers of, 13–19, 20–24,
153–64; playing fields (*see* baseball playing fields); practice and training for play,
2, 31–32, 117–18, 126, 127, 145; prizes,
102–3, 105–6, 118, 121–22; roster jumping
and loading, 101–2, 106, 107; rules of play
(*see* baseball rules); scandals, 54, 210n47;
"second nine" teams, 6, 34, 80, 107, 108,
134–35; as social activity, 4–6, 31–32,
34–37, 66; Sunday ball playing/Sabbath
restrictions, 40–41, 42, 44, 45; as symbol of civic pride and competition, 2,
4–9, 42, 50, 113–18, 129–31; unorganized
teams and games, 6, 17–18, 38–46, 56,
92, 97–98, 128, 141
"Base Ball" (poem), 57
baseball club organization, 20–37; club
constitutions and by-laws, 4, 8, 17–18,
22–24, 136; club member selection, 32,
66–71; customs and rituals (*see* baseball
customs and rituals); first Illinois clubs,
22–23; fundraising methods (*see* baseball funding/financial issues); playing
fields (*see* baseball playing fields); rules
of play (*see* baseball rules); training/con-
ditioning for players, 2, 31–32, 117–18,
126, 127, 145; transportation and (*see*
transportation/club travel); uniforms,
24–27, 34–35, 69, 94, 123, 124, 146
baseball customs and rituals: erosion of,
105–8; game ball presentation to winning club, 33, 35, 108; gentlemanly
behavior and, 8, 22, 32–37, 44, 105; hos-

pitality to visiting clubs, 3, 32–33, 107–8,
132, 133, 137; importance of, 6; newspaper accounts of games and, 34–37 (*see
also names of specific newspapers*)
baseball funding/financial issues: admis-
sions fees for games, 3, 40, 109, 123,
127, 143, 148; budgets of clubs, 123; club
members "chipping in" for tour expenses, 139; club sponsors, 74–75, 124, 126;
costs of intercity play, 139, 149–50; fund-
raising methods, 27–29; Grand Base Ball
Tournament of the Western States (Decatur, 1867) and, 89, 99; importance of,
2; inflation calculation method, 199n10;
lack of club account books, 27; touring
club charges to hosting clubs, 3
Baseball Hall of Fame, 3, 162, 164
baseball injuries and fatalities, 2, 54–58,
141; baseball-related deaths, 56–57;
humor and, 78–79; lack of gloves and
protective equipment, 8, 19, 55, 59–60,
64–66, 122; power hitting and, 3–4, 60,
70, 72, 75, 79, 104, 131, 135
Baseball Player's Chronicle, 124–25
baseball playing fields, 38–50; Alstyne's
Prairie (Quincy), 3, 40; basic features
and layout of, 13, 40, 59, 109; competition for space in Illinois, 38–40; on
county fairgrounds and racetracks,
39–40, 45, 99, 100, 124, 144, 148; disappearance of, 151, 164; Fairview Park
(Decatur), 40, 99, 100; Fifth Ward
School grounds (Bloomington), 42–46;
first regulation field in Decatur, 13,
40, 156; Fox River ball grounds (Ottawa), 55, 134, 135–37, 156–57, 220n47;
importance to club survival, 127–28;
local bans on baseball playing, 38–39,
40, 43; noise and profanity complaints,
38–39, 40, 42–43, 45, 51; political and
social standing of baseball clubs, 11,
44–45, 46–50; Polo Grounds (New
York), 48; pressure to locate, 31; Railway
Park (Springfield), 46–50, 68; safety
concerns, 38–44; Sportsman's Park
(St. Louis, MO), 48
baseball rules: "fly rule," 8, 20, 63, 65–66,
96, 97; foul balls caught on the fly or
first bound as outs, 8, 61; foul vs. fair ball
calls, 110; National Association of Base
Ball Players Rules of 1867, 21–24, 52, 101,
102; rule books and, 20–24, 32, 34, 66,

103, 111; scoring system, 20; senior players in junior clubs, 101, 162; umpires and, 108–13. *See also* umpires and umpiring

Bateman, Newton, 84

batters and batting: base stealing, 65–66; batting averages, 20; bunting, 144; "daisy cutters" (hard-hit ground balls), 81; early bats, 15; "humming birds," 70, 131; J. C. McQuigg as notable batter, 70, 131–33, 155; power hitting, 3–4, 60, 70, 72, 75, 79, 104, 131, 135

Beach, F. D., 112

Beadle's Dime Base Ball Player (Chadwick), 20–21

Beasley, Tom, 55

Bellán, Esteban Enrique "Steve," 146

Birdsall, David Solomon, 146

Black Crook theater troupe, 134, 220–21n49

Black Hawk Base Ball Club (Aurora), 61, 142

Black Hawk Base Ball Club (Camden Mills, later Milan), 35

Blaine, James G., 160

Blake, George W. W., 156–57

Bloomer Girls (Shattuck), 96, 97

Bloomington Base Ball Club, 50, 85, 149, 161–64; Atlantic Club (Chicago) and, 123–24; Excelsior Club (Chicago) and, 42, 44, 99–101, 123, 126, 163, 164; Fifth Ward School grounds and, 42–46; Forest City Club (Rockford) and, 42, 65, 143–45, 162; injuries of players, 55, 123; occupations of members, 44, 208n18; Olympic Club (Peoria) and, 62–63; origins of, 17–19, 109–10, 162–63; talent of players, 42, 70–71, 87, 88, 92–93, 143–46

Bloomington Junior Base Ball Club, 99, 100–101

Bloomington Pantagraph, 18, 38, 42, 45, 56, 65, 87, 88, 93, 99–100, 126, 141, 144–46, 149, 161

Blue Jacket Base Ball Club (Paxton), 129

Blue Stockings Base Ball Club (Chicago, African American), 93–96, 98

Bogan, Joseph L., 57–58

Bogan, J. S., 57

Bradford, E. F., 113

Bradly, Frank, 34

Brown, George, 93, 160

Brown, James, 49, 50

Bryan, William Jennings, 158

Bryant, William L., 137

Buckeye Base Ball Club (Cincinnati), 127, 145

Buker, Horace, 147

Bureau County Patriot (Princeton), 23, 72, 73

Bureau County Republican, 96

Byron Base Ball Club, 17

Cairo Democrat, 22, 52, 68, 80–82, 96, 102, 115–17, 141, 154

Cannon, Joseph, 128

Capital Base Ball Club (Springfield), 25–26, 32–33, 36–37, 46–48, 69, 75, 149

Capital Horse Railway Company, 46–50, 68–69, 84–85, 158

"cards," 106–8

Carrollton Gazette, 113

Carthage Gazette, 25

Cartwright, Alexander, 7

catchers and catching: baseball pioneers, 18–19; "gobbling the huckleberry," 81; injuries/lack of protective equipment, 55, 65–66, 122; positioning the catcher, 65–66; as specialist position, 65

Caterpillar Base Ball Club (Cairo, Muffin Club), 80–81

Celestial Base Ball Club (Pekin), 16

Central Base Ball Club (Decatur, Junior Club), 117–18, 132

Centralia Democrat, 104, 121

Centralia Sentinel, 97, 102–5, 121–22

Chadwick, Henry, 34, 52, 65; *Beadle's Dime Base Ball Player,* 20–21; catcher positioning and, 66; as "father" of baseball and baseball coverage, 18–24, 124–25; fielding and, 59–60; *Haney's Base Ball Book of Reference,* 20–22, 32, 59, 103; umpires and, 105, 108–9, 111

Champaign Gazette and Union, 86, 114

Cheney, Lee, 62–63, 71, 101, 146, 161–62

Chicago and Northwestern Railroad Company, 29–30

Chicago Cubs, 128, 149

Chicago Republican, 118

Chicago Times, 12, 63, 95, 97, 126–28, 139

Chicago Tribune, 11, 41–42, 53, 56, 73, 87, 88, 90, 93–95, 99, 125, 126, 128, 149, 153–54

cholera, 11, 16–17, 120

City Base Ball Club (Lacon), 26

Civil Rights Bill, 93

Fairview Park (Decatur), 40, 99, 100
Farmers Base Ball Club (Farm Ridge, today Grand Ridge), 136
Farmers Base Ball Club (Geneseo), 106
Faxson, Len, 81–82, 116
female players and clubs, 96–98
fielders and fielding, 59–64; base stealing and, 65–66; gloveless play and injuries, 8, 19, 55, 59–60, 64–66, 86, 97–98, 122; importance of, 65; playing off the bag, 144; power hitting and, 3–4, 60, 70, 72, 75, 79, 104, 131, 135; "skyscrapers" (high fly balls to the outfield), 41, 62, 63, 81
financial issues/funding. *See* baseball funding/financial issues
Finnan, Paul, 163
fly balls: "fly rule," 8, 20, 63, 65–66, 96, 97; foul balls caught on the fly or first bound as outs, 8, 61; "skyscrapers" (high fly balls to the outfield), 41, 62, 63, 81; "taking it on the fly," 81
Foley, Thomas J., 148
Forest City Base Ball Club (Rockford), 3, 24–25, 39, 66–67, 115, 123–27, 137–39, 143–48; Bloomington Club and, 42, 65, 143–45, 162; Blue Stockings Club (Chicago) and, 93–94, 95; Excelsior Club (Chicago) and, 42, 123, 124; talent of players, 7, 17, 21, 42, 53, 144, 147–48, 162; Washington (DC) National Club and, 17, 21, 53, 65, 125, 126, 147
Fort Clark Base Ball Club (Peoria), 30, 74–75, 118, 138
Franklin, William, 93, 160
Freeport Bulletin, 7–8, 119, 141

gambling/betting, 50–54, 84, 89, 103–4, 105, 109, 111, 125, 163
Garden City Base Ball Club (Chicago), 137
Geneseo Republic, 111–12
Gilbert, George, 24
Gillett, Sherry, 80, 81
Gleim, Edgar, 112
"gobbling the huckleberry," 81
Goldstein, Warren, 31, 33
Gondolf, Henry, 57
"Good Enough" Base Ball Club (Bloomington), 160
Gordon Base Ball Club (Chicago, African American), 94
Gorman, Arthur Poe, 91–92
Grand Base Ball Tournament of the West-

ern States (Decatur, 1867), 126, 132; financial returns and, 89, 99; "muffin" game, 150, 163; playing field (now Fairview Park), 99, 100; prizes, 121; tensions between clubs, 99–101, 102–3, 162; uniforms and, 24, 68, 69
Grand Prairie Review (Onarga), 27–28
Grant, U. S., 142, 154, 163
Grant and Coalblacks Base Ball Club (Quincy), 92
Grant Base Ball Club (Jacksonville, Junior Club), 25
Grasshopper Base Ball Club (Cairo, Muffin Club), 80–81
Gray Eagle Base Ball Club (Bloomington, African American), 93, 98
Greenhorn Base Ball Club (Toulon), 84
Greenville Advocate, 144–45
Grove City Base Ball Club (Kankakee), 35–36, 39

Haney's Base Ball Book of Reference (Chadwick), 20–22, 32, 59, 103
Hannibal and Naples Railway, 46
Hardin Base Ball Club (Jacksonville), 23, 25, 28, 32–33, 49, 60–61, 63, 73
Harrell, Mose, 82
Harris, C. G., 129
Harris, George, 93
Harrison, William Henry, 15
Harvard Base Ball Club, 35, 39, 117
Harvest Base Ball Club (Carlinville), 55
Hastings, Winfield "Scott," 148
Hatch, Ozias Mather, 11, 84
Hawkeye Base Ball Club (Keokuk, Junior Club), 31
Hay, Milton, 11
Heaphy, Leslie A., 95
Hercules Base Ball Club (Jacksonville), 25
Hickory Base Ball Club (New Rutland), 106
Holley, James, 93, 160–61
Holley, Marion, 93, 160–61
Hoosier Base Ball Club (Lafayette, IN), 129
Hoyt, James, 127
Hughes, E. M., 111–12
"humming birds," 70, 131

ice cream socials, in fund-raising, 29
Iles, Elijah, 50
Illinois Base Ball Club (Morris), 118, 134–35, 136

Montgomery, Samuel, 155
Morgan Base Ball Club (Jacksonville), 33,
  60–61
Morning Star Base Ball Club (Forrest), 109
Morris, Peter, 15, 17, 24, 28, 31, 33–34,
  38–39, 66–67, 71, 72, 79–80, 86–87, 89,
  122–24, 127, 143, 147
Mount Vernon Free Press, 102–3
Muffer Base Ball Club (Onarga), 27–28, 115
"muffin" games/players, 6, 59–60, 67, 72,
  78, 79–89, 115, 127; bachelors vs. married
  men, 85; Grand Base Ball Tournament
  of the Western States (Decatur, 1867)
  and, 150, 163; heavy vs. lean players, 80,
  82–83, 86, 138; occupation-based games,
  86–89; older vs. younger players and
  clubs, 1, 2–3, 7, 82, 83–85
"mumble peg," 73–74
Munn, Benjamin M., 68
Munn, Daniel W., 68, 154–55
Munn, James W., 55, 68
Mutual Base Ball Club (NY), 126
Mutual Base Ball Club (Warsaw), 25, 36,
  115
Mystic Base Ball Club (Springfield, Junior
  Club), 25

National Association of Base Ball Players
  (NABBP), 8, 18, 21–22, 75; convention of
  1864, 65; convention of 1867, 51, 90–92;
  convention of 1868, 52; racial discrimi-
  nation in baseball and, 90, 91; Rules of
  1867, 21–24, 52, 101, 102
National Association of Professional Base
  Ball Players (NAPBBP), 144, 147
National Base Ball Club (Springfield),
  36–37, 48, 50
National Base Ball Club (Taylorville),
  132–33
National Base Ball Club (Washington,
  DC). *See* Washington (DC) National
  Base Ball Club
National Baseball Hall of Fame, 3, 162, 164
Nattinger, E. A., 136
New York Clipper, 95, 104, 111–12, 211n12
Northwestern Female College (Evanston),
  "Diana Base Ball Club," 97

Oak Base Ball Club (Deer Park), 136–37
Oakland Base Ball Club (Chicago, African
  American), 94
Oberly, J. H., 81

Occidental Junior Base Ball Club (Quin-
  cy), 1, 3, 30, 31, 51, 53, 64, 109–11
Occidental Senior Base Ball Club (Quin-
  cy), 34, 40, 117, 118; Clipper Club (Mon-
  mouth) and, 30, 52–53; Red Stockings
  Club (Cincinnati) and, 1–4, 6–7, 56,
  148–49
O'Donnell, James, 56–57
Okaw Base Ball Club (Carlyle), 61, 121
O.K. Base Ball Club (Ottawa), 55, 134, 135,
  137
Old Fogy Base Ball Club (Toulon), 84
Olive Branch Base Ball Club (East St. Lou-
  is), 29
Olympic Base Ball Club (Peoria), 16, 24,
  62–63, 75–76, 118
Olympic Base Ball Club (Sheffield), 36
Olympic Base Ball Club (Springfield),
  47–48, 49
Olympic Base Ball Club (St. Louis, MO),
  2–3, 30
Onarga Senior Base Ball Club, 105–6
Oquawka Base Ball Club, 114
Ottawa Free Trader, 53, 75–76, 82, 88, 96,
  109, 135, 136–38
Ottawa Republican, 28, 51, 54, 88, 134–36,
  157
outfield. *See* fielders and fielding

Pabor, Charles H., 146
Paducah (KY) *Herald,* 81–82, 115–17
Pana Gazette, 12, 96–97, 131, 132–33
Pastime Base Ball Club (Amboy), 24
Pecatonica Base Ball Club/horn, 66–67,
  126–27, 219n25
Pennsylvania Base Ball Association, 91
Peoria National Democrat, 16
Peoria Transcript, 24, 54–55
picnics, in fund-raising, 28, 29
Pike County Democrat (Pittsfield), 11, 49
Pioneer Base Ball Club (Arcola, once
  known as Okaw), 129
Pioneer Base Ball Club (Geneseo), 36, 55,
  61–62, 111, 136
Pioneer Fire Company Base Ball Club
  (Springfield), 48
pitchers and pitching: baseball pioneers,
  13–15, 16; injuries, 55, 104; Patrick J.
  Keenan as notable pitcher, 71, 100–101,
  126, 127, 145, 163–64; Joe McGinnity as
  notable pitcher, 156; professional players, 71; Albert Goodwill Spalding as

Robert D. Sampson is the editor of the
Journal of the Illinois State Historical Society and
the author of *John L. O'Sullivan and His Times*.

The University of Illinois Press
is a founding member of the
Association of University Presses.

Composed in 10.5/13 Adobe Minion Pro
with Avenir and Rosewood display
by Jim Proefrock
at the University of Illinois Press
Manufactured by Sheridan Books, Inc.

University of Illinois Press
1325 South Oak Street
Champaign, IL 61820–6903
www.press.uillinois.edu